BEHAVIOUR MODIFICATION FOR
THE MENTALLY HANDICAPPED

# BEHAVIOUR MODIFICATION FOR THE MENTALLY HANDICAPPED

Edited by
WILLIAM YULE and JANET CARR

UNIVERSITY PARK PRESS BALTIMORE

Published in North America by
UNIVERSITY PARK PRESS
233 East Redwood Street
Baltimore, Maryland

ISBN 0-8391-4103-3

Library of Congress Catalogue Card Number: 79-92106

British Library Cataloguing in Publication Data
Behaviour modification for the mentally
handicapped.
1. Mentally handicapped children –
Rehabilitation 2. Behaviour modification
I. Yule, William II. Carr, Janet
362.7'8'3 RJ506.M4

Printed and bound in Great Britain

# CONTENTS

For Jack Tizard

# 1 INTRODUCTION AND OVERVIEW OF BEHAVIOUR MODIFICATION FOR THE MENTALLY HANDICAPPED

William Yule and Janet Carr

It is well recognised that the prevalence of mental handicap is 3.7 per 1000 in the age group below 20 years (Kushlick, 1966). What this stark statistic conceals is the large number of individuals who are severely handicapped in many ways – so handicapped as to pose considerable problems to their families and the community. According to recent estimates, there are 120,000 severely retarded people in England and Wales and, of these, some 50,000 are children. There are a great many more mildly retarded people. There are 7,400 beds for mentally handicapped children and 52,100 beds for mentally handicapped adults, although the latter figure could be reduced if there were better community services (Department of Health and Social Security, 1971).

1971 witnessed two important changes which have had far-reaching effects for all retarded individuals. The first of these changes was the implementation of the 1970 Education (Handicapped Children) Act. Until 1971, children who were found to be severely retarded were deemed to be ineducable, and they became the responsibility of the Health Departments. From April 1971, it was recognised that no child is ineducable, when education is interpreted in its broadest sense of preparation for living in the community. The impact of this change in legislation is still being felt.

In practice, what the change meant was that children who had hitherto not attended any schooling facilities or, at best, had attended a Junior Training Centre staffed by dedicated but often untrained personnel, now had the right to attend school. Moreover, this right can exist from the age of two years. Schools for the ESN (severe), as they became titled, suddenly found that they had come into the education system and had to provide education for many more children, many of whom were both more severely handicapped than their previous pupils and younger. In turn, this led to a need for much more appropriate teacher training, and in particular there was a demand for techniques of teaching new skills to severely retarded children.

The second major event of 1971 which affects retarded people was the publication of the White Paper, *Better Services for the Mentally Handicapped.* This document represents the culmination of a quarter of a century's thinking on how to change and humanise the care of the subnormal. In particular, the White Paper argues strongly for the need to care for most retarded people within the local community. As Bayley (1973) argues, care *in* the community is not synonymous with care *by* the community – all too often it means overburdened parents coping with a difficult situation without any real, practical help (Tizard & Grad, 1961). The White Paper recognises this danger and places strong emphasis on domiciliary help and advice on management of problems.

The converse of 'community care' is that, in time, the population of the long-stay subnormality hospitals and other such institutions will change. It is anticipated that, although the numbers of patients will be reduced, the patients who find their way into long term care in future will be more severely handicapped. The days have gone when it was thought that subnormality could be *cured.* The days are going where the function of subnormality hospitals is merely *custodial.* Current emphasis is on their role in *caring* for the subnormal – and caring is increasingly seen as an active, educative process.

But how are all these laudable goals to be achieved? More active care and education presupposes more appropriately trained personnel. Caring in the community implies an improvement in the domiciliary services, and in particular a shift from passive 'understanding' on the part of social services personnel to an active advice giving role. What techniques are available which can be used by so many varied professionals which can be of value in training the retarded?

## THE GROWTH OF BEHAVIOUR MODIFICATION

Simultaneously with the change in social attitudes towards the mentally handicapped in Britain, there was a revolution in intervention techniques developing primarily in the United States of America. Although there is a long tradition of experimental psychologists applying themselves to the problems of the mentally retarded, the bulk of the early work in this field was more related to diagnosis and the study of psychological process for their own sake, rather than to therapeutic endeavour. All this changed radically in the mid-1960s.

This is not the place to attempt a historical account of the growth of behaviour modification. Future psychology historians will probably point to the coming together of a number of different influences ranging from the emergence of applied psychology as a separate profession from its mainly medical beginnings to the arrival of experimental analysis of behaviour as a respectable subdiscipline having its roots in the animal-experimental laboratory but its new applications in individual human single-case studies (Kazdin, 1978).

Clinical studies and controlled experimental studies of single cases began to appear in the literature in the mid to late 1960s. Larsen and Bricker's *Manual for Parents and Teachers of Severely and Moderately Retarded Children* was published in Nashville, Tennessee in 1968, the same year that Patterson and Gullion's more general, semi-programmed text, *Living with Children: New Methods for Parents and Teachers*, appeared from Oregon. After this, the floodgates opened. Many manuals appeared from America. Gardner's *Behaviour Modification in Mental Retardation* appeared in 1971, and was followed two years later in 1973 by Watson's *Child Behaviour Modification: A Manual for Teachers, Nurses and Parents.*

The message from all of these sources was optimistic – retarded children can be taught a great deal more than most of us have hitherto accepted, provided we use appropriate techniques. The techniques of behaviour modification were presented in simple form, often in near-cookbook terms. The secondary message of these texts was that parents, nurses, teachers and other caretakers could be taught to carry out the 'therapy' with the child. There was no need for all treatment to be carried out by expensively trained (and thin-on-the-ground) psychologists.

As the promise held out by behaviour modification techniques became recognised, so individuals in Britain began to try out the techniques. Some workers visited centres in America to witness at first hand what such methods of treatment could achieve. Visitors from America held more and more symposia and workshops. By the early 1970s, one or two centres were well established in the application of behavioural techniques to the problems of the mentally handicapped. By 1975, a major symposium could examine both theoretical and practical problems in this new area (Kiernan & Woodford, 1975). Behaviour modification as a therapeutic tool in mental handicap was established.

## SERVICE NEEDS

It soon became evident that there were valuable treatment skills which could be taught to nurses, parents, teachers and others. A major problem facing those with responsibility for providing services for the mentally handicapped was how to ensure that these skills could be provided where they were most needed.

At an 'Action Workshop' organised by the Institute for Research into Mental and Multiple Handicap (Kiernan & Woodford, 1974) it was recognised that psychologists trained in applying behaviour modification techniques to the problems of the mentally handicapped were the key figures in expanding the services. There were, and still are, too few psychologists working in this area. Nonetheless, a few psychologists could train many other personnel. This had already been recognised by the Joint Board of Clinical Nursing Studies (1974) and their Scottish equivalent when they formulated their syllabuses for specialist nurse training in behaviour modification with the retarded.

To accelerate these developments, it was recognised by many people that short, intensive courses in the techniques of behaviour modification could serve a very useful function. This sort of thinking lay behind the writing of this text book.

## THE PRESENT BOOK

This book saw its beginnings in two one-week workshops run for psychologists and other professionals working with the mentally handicapped and held at the Institute of Psychiatry in May 1975 and November 1977. These intensive skill training workshops were planned by staff of the psychology department with the participation of two other colleagues.

As described in more detail in Chapter 13, the format of the workshop was that after a lecture and discussion on a particular topic (usually a set of related techniques and their theoretical underpinnings), the course members divided into small groups of about eight participants and two group leaders. During workshop sessions, the techniques discussed earlier were actively rehearsed – one staff member simulating a retarded child, the other acting as model, tutor and director. The main emphasis of the course was on skills training. This sort of format derives from the precision teaching methods of Keller

(1968) used to such good effect by Vance Hall in training teachers (Hall, 1971a, b) and by Montrose Wolf and his colleagues in training teaching-parents (along the Achievement Place lines) to work with young delinquents (Phillips *et al.*, 1971).

When preparing for these and related courses, it soon became evident that the material on which we wished to base the workshop was scattered throughout many related books and journal articles. We could find no suitable text which drew it all together in a manner relevant to this sort of skill training approach. One particular difficulty which all teachers face is that examples of good work in different social and cultural settings sometimes need elaborate explanations and interpretations before their value can be fully appreciated. The sorts of programmes found suitable in a hospital setting may need considerable alteration before being suited for a community setting. In any case, it is always more meaningful to trainees if their tutors incorporate examples from their own hard-won experience, and this is what we have tried to do in this text.

In compiling the book, we have tried to keep in mind the needs of all the various professionals who work with the mentally handicapped. We believe it is relevant to clinical and educational psychologists, teachers, nurses, social workers and occupational therapists working with retarded children. It will be of interest to specialist health visitors, paediatricians, child psychiatrists and other members of district handicap teams. We have not written this text specifically for parents, although many may find it helpful. A separate book has been prepared with parents in mind (Carr, 1980). We have used the material in this text in workshops that we have organised for psychologists, nurses, teachers and other professionals in Britain, Denmark and Sweden. The feedback we have received from such groups (see Chapter 13) encourages us to believe that the material contained herein is of real practical value.

The book opens with a discussion on selecting appropriate goals and targets when faced with a child with problems. This is followed by four chapters on a variety of ways of increasing desirable behaviours and one chapter on decreasing undesirable behaviour. Having discussed some of the basic behavioural techniques and some of the theoretical background on which they are based, there are three chapters which deal with applications to areas of particular importance in meeting the needs of the mentally handicapped – self-help skills such as feeding and dressing, toiletting and language development. The book ends with two chapters discussing ways of disseminating these skills to all those who work closely with the mentally handicapped, and includes a set of Appendices which give practical guidance for those who wish to set up their own workshop training.

We recognise that no amount of book learning can substitute for good skills training. However, we hope that, having read this book, the reader will be better prepared to benefit from opportunities to participate in future workshops. We have included a chapter describing the workshops that we ran. We hope that this will prove useful in guiding others who may wish to mount similar ventures.

We would welcome comments and constructive criticism from people who use this text. Feedback is important in learning skilled behaviours – even when it will be as delayed as such comments will necessarily be.

# 2 IDENTIFYING PROBLEMS – FUNCTIONAL ANALYSIS AND OBSERVATION AND RECORDING TECHNIQUES

William Yule

Mentally handicapped children, more than others, present their caretakers with a constant stream of problems. At times, the net result is overwhelming so that, by the time outside help is sought, it is difficult to know where to begin to help. Which problem should be tackled first? What should be the goals of intervention? There can be no single, fixed set of answers to such questions. Rather, what is needed is a problem-solving approach – and that is what behaviour modification offers.

As we see it, there are four main stages in implementing a behaviour modification programme:

(1) defining the problem objectively;
(2) setting up hypotheses to account for observations;
(3) testing these hypotheses;
(4) evaluating the outcome.

In other words, a behaviour modification approach is a self-correcting approach. Problems are clearly defined, data are gathered before, during, and after some treatment programme and success or failure is made self-evident. Where progress is made, the therapist can continue the programme with increased confidence; where little or no progress occurs, this will be evident at an early stage and so steps can be taken to alter the treatment strategy.

A whole technology has grown up around the practicalities of gathering data – clearly the key to good behaviour modification. On the whole, these technical treatises are valuable for the researcher, but overwhelming for the clinician. What we intend to do in this chapter is to present a brief overview of a strategy which should enable any clinician to analyse any problem at an appropriate level – that is, the analysis should be sufficiently complete to allow for efficient intervention, but neither so cumbersome nor so time consuming as to become an end in itself.

## IDENTIFYING PROBLEMS

Problems are problems for someone. It is the parent, the nurse or the teacher who will complain about a child's behaviour. It is one of the tasks of the therapist to help the caretaker to define the problem behaviour more exactly. Such complaints form the starting point of identifying problems which can be the subject of behaviour modification programmes.

Of course, the problems complained of may not be the most important behaviours from the child's point of view. Exasperated caretakers may seize on a florid difficulty such as temper tantrums which interferes with them rather than report that, for example, the child's lack of self-occupation and play skills results in temper tantrums when the staff cannot give him undivided attention. More careful questioning of what goes on around the time the problem manifests itself might prompt one to ask whether the child has skills of self-occupation and play. In other words, spontaneous complaints must be noted and fully investigated, but the pattern of the child's overall behaviour and adjustment must also be enquired into systematically.

In questioning the informant, one wants first of all to have a good, objective description of the child's behaviour.

## DEFINING BEHAVIOUR

The behaviour in which the therapist is interested must be defined in observable, objective and measurable terms. In everyday life, we are used to discussing behaviour at a fairly global, trait level. When a parent complains that her retarded eight-year-old boy gets jealous of his three-year-old sister, most of us would have a fair idea of what she meant – or would we? Does the boy hit his little sister? Does he sulk when his mother talks to his sister? Does he throw a tantrum when she snatches one of his toys? Some or all of these acts, together with countless others, could pinpoint what the mother means by 'jealous'. One of the tasks of the therapist is to help the complainant (parent, teacher, nurse or whoever is seeking help on behalf of the retarded individual) to translate their concerns into detailed observable behaviours (Mischel, 1968).

To emphasise the point, consider the question of what constitutes effectiveness of programmes. This can be complex and is discussed at length later. For the moment, let us consider the whole question of identifying appropriate therapeutic goals.

## SELECTING TARGETS

Just as we want parents to be clear what it is that they are complaining of, we also want to make the goals of treatment explicit. This helps to let us see whether the goals are being reached. But how are these goals decided upon?

These questions are considered in detail in Chapters 8-10. For the present, we should note that goals are selected on the basis of what is in the best interests of both the child and his social setting. There is little disagreement that language handicapped children should be encouraged to develop as much language as possible. There might be some disagreement as to whether it is right to encourage a child to sit quietly if such a goal is more to meet the needs of staff than the child himself. In other words, goal setting is value-laden, and this needs to be acknowledged.

Initially, many parents may set goals which are too far removed from their child's present level to be attainable within a relatively short time. For example, parents may wish their child to talk, and can be helped to achieve this aim by working initially on, say, simple motor imitation. In other words, one task of the therapist is to help break down complex behaviours into component skills. One way of helping people to select appropriate goals is to use developmental charts such as those published by Gunzburg (1965). By asking parents to report in detail on what their child *can* do, this often has the helpful effect of focusing their attention on hitherto unnoticed positive achievements. It also makes clear what, in terms of normal development, the next milestones are and, in the absence of evidence to the contrary, these become the next goals. Of course, some developmental charts are too gross, and the next goal may have to be analysed into many sub-goals, but the principle remains – mentally handicapped children should be regarded as very slow developers who achieve the same milestones as normal children in the same sequence.

Mager & Pipe (1970) present a scheme for analysing problems which is particularly relevant to devising programmes of treatment for the mentally handicapped. One of the basic questions which they pose is whether, when presented with a problem, the problem is one of skill deficiency or of motivation. If the patient's life depended on it, could he do it? Where the answer to that question is, 'Yes', then one is faced with a problem of motivating the patient to put his existing skills to better use. Techniques of positive reinforcement (see Chapter 3) are particularly relevant here. If, however, the answer is, 'No', then the therapist has to devise ways of training the patient in a new skill. The techniques discussed in Chapters 3 and 5 are particularly relevant here.

Thus the sequence of a behavioural analysis is as follows:

(1) Gather data from interviews on both problem and adaptive behaviour.
(2) Conduct preliminary observations to clarify hypotheses.
(3) If necessary, conduct more formalised observations as described below.
(4) Select target behaviours and begin treatment.
(5) Continue recording to monitor progress.

It is not possible to give hard and fast guidelines about which level of problem analysis is most appropriate in any given circumstances. At times, it will be clear from a parent's initial account what the problem is, and a solution will be suggested. It may be sufficient to accept the parents' assurance that the problem disappears.

At other times, expected solutions will not work. Then, one needs to be able to conduct a much fuller, more formal analysis of the problem, and this is where more detailed, direct observational techniques will be necessary (Sackett, 1978).

## MEASUREMENT TECHNIQUES

According to Hall (1971), there are three major groups of recording techniques used in behaviour modification. These are:

(1) automatic recording;
(2) measurement of permanent product;
(3) observational recording.

As will be seen, the third group is the most relevant to behaviour modification with the retarded, and so it will be considered in a separate section.

### (1) AUTOMATIC RECORDING

In laboratory studies of animal behaviour, a sophisticated array of automatic recording devices has been developed. Sensitive microswitches can record the areas of a cage entered by a rat. The relationship between a pigeon's pecking at a target and the delivery of grain are both recorded automatically and, as is well known, such sensitive recording procedures have yielded rich results in understanding the nature of reinforcement.

Similar automatic recording devices have been used in studying the behaviour of human subjects, but almost always in a laboratory setting. Hyperactivity in retarded children has been studied by recording their fidgety movements on a special seat (Sprague & Toppe, 1966). However, such devices are expensive and are not suited for recording behaviour in the more natural environment. Whilst there may be occasions, particularly in institution settings, where such equipment will be installed to help deal with specific problems, in the main, automatic recording is not recommended.

### (2) MEASUREMENT OF PERMANENT PRODUCT

One method of gathering data which is often overlooked is the direct measurement of any permanent product produced by the child or adult in whom we are interested. In workshop situations, the number of completed units can be easily counted. In a school setting, the number of words written or copied can be counted. The beauty of this type of measure is that it can be obtained simply and reliably, often at one's leisure.

Fewtrell (1973) used a permanent product ingeniously to monitor treatment of enuresis in an institutional setting. Since there is a high relationship between wetting and soiled linen sent to the laundry, they weighed the amount of linen sent for laundry one day each week. As their treatment programme proceeded, and as their patients improved, so the amount of soiled linen fell from 80 pounds at the beginning of treatment to 15 pounds after about 20 weeks.

## OBSERVATIONAL RECORDING

In most cases when setting up a behaviour modification programme for a retarded individual, the therapist will have to rely on observational recording. Someone will have to observe the patient and record relevant aspects of his behaviour. The type of observational recording selected will depend in large part on the type of behaviour being worked on. Practical constraints such as the availability of observers and the environment in which the problem occurs will also partially determine the recording procedure. In what follows, practical considerations will be emphasised.

### (1) CONTINUOUS RECORDING

It is impossible to record continuously everything that is happening in a given situation. Many beginners, or at least those who have never tried it, believe that they can write down all that a child does. Whilst rich, anecdotal records emerge, it can be quickly established that no two people will record the same events. This is a useful exercise to carry out in order to convince people of the need for some structured method of observing.

Even with the greater availability of videotape recording, continuous recording is not a practical venture, mainly because it is too time-consuming to extract data from the tape at a later time. For example, in studying the effects of training the parents of autistic children to use behaviour modification techniques, it was found that every one hour of audiotaped mother-child conversation took no fewer than three hours to transcribe later on (Howlin *et al.*, 1973). After that, it took untold man-hours to reduce the transcriptions to manageable data.

This is not to say that unstructured observation or videotape is not of value in behavioural treatments. Unstructured observations approximating to continuous recordings can be very useful at the beginning of a programme when trying to pin-point the problem. Likewise, one can study a videotape over and over again in an attempt to isolate particular difficulties. However, for most people working in the cinderella of services, such equipment will not be readily available. Eyes, hands, stopwatches and paper have to suffice.

### (2) EVENT RECORDING

Once the behaviour of concern (the 'target behaviour') has been defined, if it is a relatively discrete act such as hitting, waving, raising a cup to the mouth or whatever, then it may be decided to count each occasion that the behaviour occurs. When the number of events is divided by the time during which the patient was observed, the result is a measure of the *frequency of occurrence* of that behaviour.

Event recording is a relatively simple procedure. Tally marks can be made on a piece of paper, or a simple wrist counter (of the sort used by golfers) or even a knitting needle counter can be used. Anything more elaborate can intrude too much into the situation.

Despite the ease of gathering data, it can be too time-consuming to record occurrences over a whole day. It is necessary to reduce the time spent observing to practical limits. As soon as one samples the whole day by choosing a portion of it, the question of validity, or rather representativeness, is raised. Unless one is reasonably certain that the target behaviour occurs (or does not occur, if one wants to increase it) more or less equally frequently throughout the day, then it is too easy to be careless and bias one's results. To take a glaring example, let us say that a ten-year-old retarded girl is reported to have temper tantrums in class. If these were counted only during craft lessons, one might miss the fact that she has more tantrums when called to read during English lessons. Worse still, if pre-treatment measures are taken at times when the target behaviour occurs most frequently, and post-treatment measures are taken at other times (either because of the availability of observers, or because the school timetable is altered) then the apparent change in behaviour will not be a valid indicator of the change in the girl's tantrums.

In summary, event recording is easily made when the class of behaviour of interest has been clearly defined. It is usual to observe for only short periods of the day. Unless there are times of greatest interest – e.g., mealtimes; bedtimes; free-play – then it is necessary to ensure that the selected time is truly representative of the longer period. Unless the patient is observed for the same length of time each day, the results are usually expressed as a frequency count per unit of time (i.e., a rate measure).

### (3) DURATION RECORDING

With some behaviours, one is more interested in *how long* they last for. For example, parents frequently complain that their children are slow in getting ready in the morning. Assuming that the child has all the necessary skills for getting himself ready, then it would be reasonable to target the length of time between his being called to get out of bed and his arriving washed and dressed at the breakfast table. The time taken is best recorded by stop-watch, although any clock or watch will serve.

It is worth noting that duration can be a more sensitive measure than merely noting occurrence. For example, during the early stages of a re-training programme, a child may still have the same number of temper tantrums in a day, but their intensity and duration might be less. Since it is always desirable to use the index which is most sensitive to change, duration recording is frequently employed.

(4) INTERVAL RECORDING

As with other forms of psychological measurement, ways have to be found to sample the behaviour of interest. One method is to divide the total length of observation into equal intervals, and then to note whether the target behaviour occurred at all during each interval. By recording in this manner, for the first time, the sequence of events is noted. This extra information can be made use of, particularly if more than one behaviour is monitored simultaneously.

Hall (1971a) comments that 'the chief advantage of the interval recording method is that it gives an indication of both the frequency and the duration of the behaviour observed. . .A disadvantage of the interval recording method is that it usually requires the individual attention of the observer.'

Many workers have developed elaborate observation systems using variations on the interval recording technique. Patterson *et al.* (1969) used a 29-item coding system to record interactions between family members in their own homes. Hemsley *et al.* (1978) have developed a reliable method for studying mother-child interactions using 17 categories to classify the child's behaviour and 19 to describe the mother's behaviour. It should be noted that the more complex the coding system, the more training is needed by the observers, and the more difficult it is to obtain reliable measures.

Continuous monitoring is very tiring. In any case, no matter how skilled the observer becomes, he is likely to miss occasional target behaviours while recording. It is usual to allow some time for recording, for example, 10 seconds of observing, followed by 5 or 10 seconds for recording. The disadvantage of this is that sequences of behaviour cannot be so readily recorded.

The precise meaning of the recorded data should be understood. Although, as Hall (1971a) notes, the data *indicate* both frequency and duration, they reflect neither accurately. Take a child who is self-injuring by scratching his face. If he does it once, a check mark is placed in the appropriate interval. If, however, he has a sudden burst of many scratches, still only one check mark is placed in the one time interval. If he is indulging in a slow, deliberate scratch it may stretch across two time intervals – will it be counted in both, or only in the interval in which it starts? Obviously, coding rules have to be worked out, and these will further distort the data collected.

It is in the nature of coding rules that they are hierarchical. To stick with the self-injury example, it would usually be the case that this behaviour would occur less than four times per minute. Even so, when it does occur, it is vital that it is noted. Thus, when the patient survives nine seconds of a recording interval without scratching, but commences scratching in the last second, scratching is recorded.

For other purposes, other hierarchical rules of coding may be more appropriate. If the target behaviour is 'co-operative play' then that might take precedence over 'fighting'. If, as is more likely, one is operating a multiple treatment programme to reduce fighting and increase co-operative play, then both behaviours would be recorded separately, but simultaneously.

Recently, the validity of interval sampling has been called into question. Powell *et al.* (1977) carried out a series of empirical investigations to test whether different forms of observing introduced different biases. They concluded that interval sampling contains so much error as to have little to recommend it. Instead, they find that momentary time sampling (see below) is both more accurate and more easily accomplished.

In summary, interval sampling can be used to sample a stream of behaviour. It has the advantage that it records the sequence of occurrence of behaviour, but it loses out on precise measurement of frequency and duration. What is recorded is the number of intervals in which the target behaviour occurred, however momentarily. The coding rules adopted by the observer can distort the observations made. Moreover, recent evidence suggests that the method yields unreliable data.

### (5) TIME SAMPLING

A different way of sampling is to observe the patient or client only at the end of a particular predetermined interval. The length of the interval will, as always, depend on the frequency of the target behaviour as well as the time at the disposal of the observer. This method has the advantage that it does not require continuous observation.

One disadvantage of the method is that it requires precise timing to avoid biasing the results. For example, take the case of a nurse on a busy ward who is observing a patient every five minutes to record whether the patient is rocking or participating in some other self-stimulatory activity or is sitting, usefully occupied. Unless the nurse does look at exactly the end of the five-minute interval, then she may find herself remembering to record only when she sees the patient engaging in the undesirable activity. Again, the recording can be interrupted if another patient demands immediate attention.

Despite the potential biasing factors, time sampling is often the most acceptable and least time-consuming method of observation that is practicable when the observer has other things to do. Whilst an ordinary wall clock can serve as a sufficient cue for timing, a kitchen timer or automatic timer that emits a tone every few minutes is to be preferred. Patients usually habituate quickly to such tones, as can observers if they are not careful.

## RELIABILITY AND VALIDITY

During the preceding description of the basic observational techniques, it has been repeatedly stressed that the observer must ensure that his observations are truly representative of the broader class or classes of behaviour in which he is interested. To readers familiar with the concepts of traditional psychometric measurement, this will appear self-evident. At all times, one must be concerned with the reliability and validity of the measures being made.

For reasons which are not altogether clear, but which appear to be related to a general movement to get away from psychometric *tests* as the sole measures in intervention studies, many behaviour modifiers have shown a great concern to establish the inter-rater reliability of observations almost to the exclusion of establishing the validity of the observations. As will be shown in the next section, even the calculation of inter-rater agreement is full of difficulties, many of which have been overlooked in early studies.

An interesting methodological study by Wahler & Leske (1973) underlines the point being made here. They made fifteen videotapes of six-year-old children who were apparently engaged in silent reading. There was no sound on the tapes because what the children were actually reading was a 'script' of how to behave. Every 20 seconds each child had to act through one of five responses for the remainder of the interval. The responses included 'reading' and four distractible activities such as talking to a neighbour. One child was programmed by her script so that she was distractible for 75 per cent of the time in the first tape. With each successive fifteen-minute tape, her percentage of distractible behaviour was reduced by 5 per cent until in the fifteenth tape it was reduced to only 15 per cent. All the other children were scheduled to be distractible around 40 to 60 per cent of the time.

These tapes were then viewed by teachers, one at a time. The teachers thought they were helping to devise a scale of distractibility.

One group of teachers viewed the tape and then rated distractibility for each child on a seven-point scale. This was the 'subjective' group. The 'objective' group of teachers had first to count behaviours and then make summary ratings.

There were interesting differences in the ratings made by the different groups of teachers. The 'subjective' observers agreed very well among themselves – they agreed that the target child was extremely distractible, but they continued to agree that she was extremely distractible until the thirteenth tape, by which time she was significantly less distractible than her classmates. By contrast, the 'objective' observer did not have such good inter-rater agreement, but as a group their ratings of the target's distractibility dropped consistently. This study clearly demonstrates to behaviour modifiers what testers have known for a long time, namely that high reliability does not necessarily guarantee high validity. As Wahler & Leske (1971) conclude, 'while our untrained observers demonstrated good agreement on the target subject's behavior, they were not responding to reality; their beliefs were consistent, but erroneous. . .One cannot glibly assume that a reliable observer is also an accurate observer.'

Put another way, observers are human, and human beings process their observations before reporting them. Observers will behave differently during occasions when they are participating in reliability studies than when they are on their own. This has been well demonstrated in a series of studies by Reid and his colleagues in Oregon (Reid, 1970; Taplin & Reid, 1973). Reid has shown that inter-observer agreement is higher when observers are aware that they are being checked up on but that, afterwards, there is a gradual drift away from satisfactory levels of agreement. His solution is to employ professional observers who are re-trained weekly – not a solution that can be translated into the everyday situation. Perhaps one should bear the problem in mind, and demand spot checks on the reliability of observations throughout a study rather than, as is typical, merely at the beginning. This is one remedy suggested by Johnson & Bolstad (1973) in their methodological critique.

Clearly, if simple observational measures of behaviour can become unreliable, and if they can be readily biased by factors both in the observer and in the situation, then it is unwise to rely on single measures as outcome criteria in any investigation. The results of treatment will be more convincing if a number of independent measures all point to change occurring. This is what investigators such as Patterson (1973) and Johnson & Bolstad (1973) call convergent validity.

## COMPUTING RELIABILITY

Whilst avoiding the term 'reliability' in preference for 'index of observer agreement', Johnson & Bolstad (1973) discuss a number of pitfalls to avoid when calculating observer agreement. Firstly, it is important to be clear about which ratings are being compared. If there is a complex coding system in operation, such that an 'X' is scored if either A or B or C or not D is observed, then two observers could apparently agree by recording 'X' whereas one sees A and the other sees C.

Secondly, comparing overall percentage agreement even on a single-item scale is pretty meaningless. Let us say that in the course of an hour, employing a 15-second interval recording technique, two observers each agree that the subject engaged in co-operative play during 27 intervals. If on inspection of the record forms it is discovered that the first observer recorded all 27 play intervals within the first 10 minutes, and the second observer only noted play during the last 10 minutes, should one then conclude that the observers agree? Only a point-to-point or interval-to-interval check can indicate agreement, and this is a very stringent criterion.

Thirdly, it is no good reporting some composite measure of over-all-categories agreement and then using data from only one category to illustrate change in behaviour. It is necessary to quote separately the percentage agreement for each category that is used in any data presentation. Apart from being an obvious move once it is drawn to the attention, there is another good reason for insisting on this – and that has to do with the base rate frequency of the behaviour of interest.

Consider a simple two-choice observational situation, where the patient's behaviour at meal-time is rated acceptable or unacceptable. Let us assume that acceptable behaviour generally occurs only 20 per cent of the time. In ten consecutive intervals, the following may be recorded by two observers.

| | | | | | | | | | | |
|---|---|---|---|---|---|---|---|---|---|---|
| I | U | A | U | U | U | A | A | U | U | U |
| II | U | A | U | U | U | A | U | U | U | U |
| Intervals | 1 | 2 | 3 | 4 | 5 | 6 | 7 | 8 | 9 | 10 |

U = unacceptable

A = acceptable

Classically, for both time and interval sampling, reliability is calculated by the formula:

$$\frac{\text{Number of agreements}}{\text{Number of agreements + number of disagreements}} \times 100\%$$

In the above example, there are nine intervals in which the two observers, I and II, agree in what they recorded. Thus the percentage agreement is

$$\frac{9}{10} \times 100\% = 90\%$$

However, now consider the reliability of the less frequently noted category of acceptable meal-time behaviour. Here, observer I recorded three As, while observer II recorded two As, which agreed with two of observer I's recordings. Thus their percentage agreement for acceptable behaviour is

$$\frac{2}{3} \times 100\% = 67\%$$

Obviously, no reader of this volume would ever express percentages on such a low number of observations, but the moral is clear. The reliability of low base rate behaviours may be masked by the agreement obtained on high base rate behaviours. Where one is interested in low rate behaviours – as one always will be when shaping up a new skill in a retarded client – then the agreement on the class of behaviour must be computed separately.

It is always problematical to decide what level of agreement should be obtained before using the observation schedule. Johnson & Bolstad (1973) suggest that it is possible, knowing the frequency of occurrence of the behaviours, to calculate the level of agreement which should be obtained by chance. It is clearly desirable that the actual level of agreement should be substantially greater. In practice, levels in excess of 80 per cent can be considered usable.

Before leaving the issue of translating observations into numerical data, two other sets of issues should be raised. The first of these has already been touched upon, and that is the question of observer bias. The second issue concerns the mathematical properties of observational data.

A number of recent reviews have indicated some of the biasing factors which may affect the behaviour of both the observers and the observed (Hemsley *et al.*, in preparation; Johnson & Bolstad, 1973). Up until this point, observer error has been concentrated on. These reviews also note the effects of the observer on the behaviour of the people being observed.

Whilst few observers can become 'flies on the wall', it is generally agreed that it is desirable for non-participant observers to avoid interacting with their subjects. In particular, a good tip is to avoid eye contact. Then, it is generally found that the effects of the presence of the observer are minimised.

It should be borne in mind that the presence of the therapist to undertake observation may become a discriminant stimulus for any caretaker to alter their interaction with their charges. In a way, this relates to the point on the representativeness of the observation, and no easy solution to the problem is forthcoming. All one can say is that therapists should at all times remember that the presence of observers may have uncontrolled effects on the behaviour of the client.

This is not the occasion to go too deeply into the mathematical properties of observational data, except to draw attention to the writings of Jones (1973, 1974) on this subject. Basically, Jones presents the case for observational data being different (in mathematical terms) from the sort of psychological test data which are more familiar to most of us. As he says, 'The measurement characteristics of behavioral observation scores may differ from psychometric test scores for at least three reasons: (a) temporal dependencies among observation raw scores, (b) comparability of assessment conditions under which observations are collected for different individuals, and (c) ipsatising features of observation scoring procedures' (Jones, 1973).

In elegant examples, Jones demonstrates that the operations performed on raw observations to reduce the data to manageable proportions can unintentionally render the data unusable within conventional mathematical procedures. In essence, the problem is that, whilst frequency counts and rates of occurrence yield numbers which are cardinal in nature and have a fixed zero point, the proportion scores which are yielded by interval and time sampling procedures yield scores which are 'ipsatised' or interdependent within the boundaries of the coding system employed. The figures so derived cannot be added or correlated in the usual way without yielding meaningless results.

Thus, it can be concluded that, by following the earlier guidelines, behaviour can be sampled and recorded. However, even when all the practical difficulties involved in gathering the observations have been overcome, the resulting data must be handled with care. Data processing, data reduction and data analyses are all sophisticated procedures, each having its own internal logic and requirements. Applied behavioural analysis is not a task for the innumerate.

## PRESENTING DATA

It has become customary to present data from behaviour modification studies in graph form. Although traditional operant work with animals was often displayed as cumulative records, few people are trained to read these. Since one of the functions of the visual display of data is to provide feedback to both the therapist and the client, the method of data presentation should be kept as simple as possible.

One of the simplest methods of presentation is to graph the data. The vertical axis is usually marked off in percentages – so that data are transformed into the percentage of intervals in which a target behaviour occurred, or the percentage of time samples at which the behaviour was recorded. Alternatively, the vertical axis is calibrated in terms of the absolute number of events recorded in a fixed time period (permanent product or event recording), rate of occurrence of behaviour (frequency per time unit) or duration.

The horizontal axis is marked off into units of intervention, be they treatment sessions or days of treatment. It is conventional to record the level of occurrence of behaviour prior to the start of intervention – i.e., to obtain a basal level or *baseline.* This is then separated from the treatment phase by a vertical line so that, at a glance, one can see whether any change occurred when treatment began (see Figure 2.1).

More will be said about appropriate single-case general designs in Chapter 10. At this point, it is as well to deal with the question of how long a baseline to obtain before starting treatment.

Often it is argued that one wants a stable baseline, and therefore that recording should be continued until a stable baseline is obtained. This is an oversimplification. The purpose of a baseline is to obtain a valid index of the patient's behaviour before treatment. The behaviour may already be improving, getting worse, remaining steady or even fluctuating in a regular or irregular manner. Ideally, then, the baseline observations should be continued until the patient's behaviour is reliably represented.

Reality is far removed from this ideal picture. The time which staff

Figure 2.1: Graph of Treatment

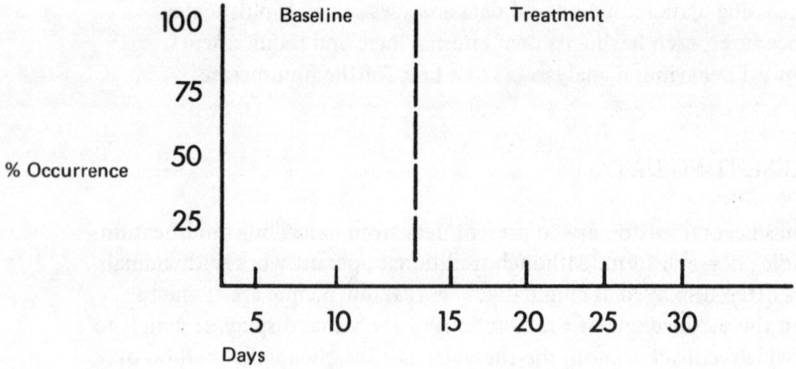


and patients will tolerate observations without treatment will vary a great deal and, in part, will depend on the presenting problem. Thus, it would be unethical to continue observing self-injurious behaviour merely to get a 'stable' baseline. Considerations such as these have to be accommodated in selecting the most appropriate research design which will both monitor change and allow the therapist to infer whether his intervention has been successful.

## CONCLUSIONS

In the technology of behaviour modification, there are powerful techniques for improving the self-reliance and the general quality of life of retarded individuals. Broadly based methods of functional analysis can assist in pin-pointing problem areas. Once identified, problems can be objectively defined, observed and recorded. Although the observational techniques are, in concept, quite simple, in practice observation is a skilled activity. The data yielded by observational techniques have certain properties which make them tricky to handle by conventional data reduction techniques. Even so, with adequate precautions, good data collection is the key to good behavioural intervention. The data should quickly reflect change, allowing for alterations in the treatment programme. The following chapters will describe the principles and practices of good behavioural treatment.

# 3 WAYS OF INCREASING BEHAVIOUR – REINFORCEMENT

Rosemary Hemsley and Janet Carr

It is a commonplace to point out that reinforcement, like others of the methods used, is not peculiar to behaviour modification but is widely used in everyday life. Few of us, apart from the affluent or altruistic, would go regularly to work if we were not paid to do so. Teachers and parents expect to help children learn by encouragement, praise and prizes. What distinguishes reinforcement in behaviour modification is the systematically careful way in which it is analysed and applied so as to make it maximally effective.

## DEFINITION

Reinforcement may be defined as any event which, when it follows a behaviour, strengthens the probability or the frequency of that behaviour's occurrence. Or as Baumeister (1967) puts it, 'the frequency of a response is subject to the consequences of that response.' We can then bring the frequency of the response under control by identifying and arranging the consequences. If a certain consequence is found to strengthen a behaviour that consequence is described as a reinforcer. This way of describing a reinforcer makes no assumptions as to its qualities: it does not describe a reinforcer as 'something nice' or 'pleasant'; it would come nearer the mark to describe it as 'something the individual child likes very much' but that too may be mistaken. We have often tried to teach a child using as a 'reinforcer' something that he liked very much only to find that he didn't like it enough to work for it (Moore & Carr, 1976). Only if the consequence, when it follows the behaviour, results in an increase in the frequency of the behaviour can the consequence be described as a reinforcer. This is an important principle, and one sometimes overlooked by those drawing up behaviour modification programmes.

This definition of reinforcement is often found to be confusing to people new to the area. Some critics object that the definition is 'circular' – i.e., if a behaviour is *not* strengthened then the stimulus which was applied contingently was not reinforcing. Within the logic of operant conditioning, this very 'circularity' is seen as a strength, not a weakness. It means that the therapist should never make any assumptions about what the child will find reinforcing. All assumptions have to be put to the harshest of all tests – they have to be shown to work by producing an effect on the child's behaviour in the desired direction.

Another source of confusion is that frequently the adjectives, 'positive' and 'negative', are used as alternatives for 'pleasant' and 'unpleasant' when describing the stimuli which are applied contingently. This can lead one into the semantically strange situation of stating that applying a negative stimulus such as shouting at a child can act as a positive reinforcer when, as happens not infrequently, the child's naughty behaviour is strengthened. The point is that *reinforcement* is always defined retrospectively in terms of its actual effect on the child's behaviour. Having said that, then it must be noted that there are two types of reinforcement: positive reinforcement and negative reinforcement. Both have the effect of strengthening behaviour and can best be understood diagrammatically (Table 3.1). Punishment is discussed in detail in Chapter 7.

Table 3.1: The Relationship between Applying or Removing Stimuli and Strengthening or Weakening Behaviour

| Stimulus | Applied | Removed |
|---|---|---|
| Positive or pleasant | Positive Reinforcement – behaviour strengthened | Punishment by Removal – behaviour weakened |
| Negative or unpleasant | Punishment by Application – behaviour weakened | Negative Reinforcement – behaviour strengthened |

## TYPES OF REINFORCERS

Reinforcers may be divided into three categories: primary, secondary and social. Primary reinforcers are those which are essential for life – food, drink, warmth, sleep. In work with human subjects, our use of foods as primary reinforcers is not quite as simple as it sounds, in that these subjects are seldom so deprived as to be reinforced by *any* food or drink (although this may occur in animal studies). Instead we have to discover which are the preferred foods that are reinforcing. Secondary reinforcers are those events or things which although not intrinsically of value have acquired reinforcing properties through pairing with primary reinforcers. Money is highly reinforcing to most adults not because of the metal, paper and print it is made up of but because the money represents a vast range of back-up reinforcers for which it may be exchanged. Tokens, stars, points and so on may similarly acquire reinforcing properties. Social reinforcers – attention, praise, smiles, hugs and so on – have often been included among the secondary reinforcers, the assumption being that they only become reinforcing for the young child through being paired with primary reinforcers, especially food. This hypothesis may seem improbable but for ethical reasons has never been tested with human infants, and it has continued in vogue (Jordan & Saunders, 1975). Other work with young infants, however, has shown that social stimuli may be responded to in the absence of any previous pairing with primary reinforcers (Schaffer & Emerson, 1964). It seems uncertain as to whether social reinforcers are a class of primary reinforcers, but equally they do not appear to be secondary, and should perhaps be in a class of their own.

Most reinforcers used in the natural environment are secondary or social. They have many advantages over primary reinforcers, especially to those delivering them; they are more convenient, less bulky and messy, easily available, acceptable to the general public, and probably less subject to satiation than are most primary reinforcers. Social reinforcers in particular may be favourably regarded in contrast with primary reinforcers (Kiernan, 1974) and may be thought of as preferable in being less like bribes. The crucial point, with these as with all other reinforcers, is: do they have the effect of increasing the frequency of the behaviour they follow? If they do not, then, regardless of how convenient and acceptable they are, they are not reinforcers in this case, and it may be profitable to return to using primary reinforcers. When children do not respond to social reinforcers we usually attempt to increase their influence by pairing them consistently with effective primary reinforcers. This may well be successful with normal and mildly handicapped children, but more difficult to achieve with severely handicapped children. Lovaas *et al.* (1966) found that autistic children were not reinforced by the comment, 'Good', after numerous pairings with food. When the children were required to attend to the social reinforcers, by approaching the therapist for the food when he said, 'Good', it then became a reinforcer for new behaviours.

## SELECTING THE REINFORCER

It is obvious, from the preceding discussion, that what is a reinforcer can only be defined *post hoc*, when its effect on the behaviour is apparent. However, in order to arrive at that position we have to select a probable reinforcer for trial, using a variety of approaches to make an intelligent guess at what is likely to be effective.

(1) Ask the individual directly. This is the most straightforward way of determining a child's preferences (Clements & McKee, 1968) but may not be possible with severely retarded non-verbal children.

(2) Ask the people most familiar with the child – parents, sibs, nurses and so on. We stress that we are looking for things that the child likes *very much* as otherwise we may be given a catalogue of things the child is mildly interested in or even of things that he barely tolerates.

(3) Use the indirect preference technique. If other methods have not elicited an effective reinforcer, a variety of possible reinforcers – foods, drinks, toys, etc. – may be offered to the child on a number of occasions to see which one he selects most often. This method was used with severely handicapped children, and repeated testing over 10 days showed a high stability of choices (Kiernan, 1974).

(4) Use the Premack principle. There are some children who appear to have no particular preferences, are uninterested in toys, unaffected by cuddles, attention or scolding and are so uninterested in food that they may be difficult to feed. In this case it can be useful to observe the child to see what he does when he is left to himself. According to the Premack principle (Premack, 1959) this preferred, high-frequency activity, whatever it is, may be used to reinforce a less preferred, low-frequency one. For example, some severely retarded children spend much of their time in stereotyped behaviour, flapping their hands, rocking, twisting scraps of paper or string and so on. These stereotyped behaviours may then be used as reinforcers, by allowing the child access to them only after he has shown another more desirable behaviour. For example, one boy would usually sit twiddling a plastic cup on his thumb. When we wanted him to do a more constructive task – threading a wooden ring over a curved wire – he learned to do this when he was allowed his 'twiddler' only when he had performed the task.

A dilemma is reached when the child's preferred activity is in itself undesirable, such as overactive running about, or masturbation or head banging. Whether or not we make use of these sorts of activities as reinforcers depends first of all on whether other reinforcers are available for that child, in which case it may be preferable to use them. If no other reinforcer is available, the decision will depend on whether the need to teach the new behaviour outweighs the undesirability of the child's preferred activity. For example, it might well be worth allowing the child to run about or rock repetitively if this helped him to learn some constructive play; it would be unlikely to be worth letting him bang his head.

## VARIETIES OF REINFORCERS

For children, probably the most commonly used kinds of reinforcers are foods and social approaches such as attention, hugs and praise. For a child for whom neither of these is effective or desirable, it may be necessary to be both imaginative and ingenious in seeking other reinforcers. Clapping may be an effective social reinforcer, as may gentle stroking and tickling. Music is reinforcing to some children: an 18-year-old severely retarded girl was taught to obey simple commands using as a reinforcer snatches of her favourite record. Another child liked to look at a mirror for a few seconds while he was wearing sunglasses; another to sing nursery rhymes and carols at the top of his voice; another, with a passion for bizarre-tasting foods, liked to lick an ice-cube, bite raw potato or lick at a bar of soap. Other sensory stimuli should be explored: bright or flashing lights may be particularly reinforcing to partially sighted children; one autistic boy would work for the reinforcement of short periods of an electric toothbrush in his mouth. A systematic study of a wide range of sensory stimuli and their effect on retarded children is under way (Campbell, 1972) in an attempt to provide novel reinforcers for children who are difficult to reinforce.

The methods described in considering the selection and varieties of reinforcers have suggested ways to attempt to discover what children like. The next essential step is to use the chosen reinforcer in a treatment programme to find out whether it is powerful enough to change the child's behaviour. Only if it is, can it be described as a reinforcer.

It is important to remember that, if a powerful reinforcer exists, it may function to increase or maintain any type of behaviour, desirable or undesirable. For example, a child who enjoys adult attention may find that the quickest way to get adults to attend to him is to tip over furniture or pull the hair of the child next to him. It is our job to ensure that, once reinforcers have been identified, they are as far as possible made contingent on desirable behaviours only.

## NEGATIVE REINFORCEMENT

Negative reinforcement, like its positive cousin, *increases* behaviour. Therefore the term is not synonymous with punishment, which aims at *decreasing* behaviours (see Chapter 7). In negative reinforcement the desired behaviour is followed immediately by the removal of an unpleasant stimulus. The use of negative reinforcement is seen most simply in the example of a person's behaviour on a freezing cold day. Experiencing the cold is aversive to most people. As soon as he puts on a warm coat, the aversive circumstances are avoided. Thus, the act of putting on the coat is (negatively) reinforced by the removal of the sensation of cold (Craighead *et al.*, 1976). Negative reinforcement is seldom used in work with children, but it can sometimes be seen having an effect on adults. For instance, a mother taking her child to the supermarket may be assailed from the minute she sets foot in it by a non-stop barrage of whining: 'Wanna sweetie! Wanna sweetie! Mum give us a sweetie.' When the mother can stand it no longer she seizes a packet of sweets and thrusts them into the child's hands. Instantly the whining stops, the *mother* is negatively reinforced by escaping from its unpleasantness, and she may be likely to buy the bag of sweets more promptly next time. Simultaneously, of course, the child is being positively reinforced for his undesirable behaviour, and the situation for the mother may actually get worse. The effect of negative reinforcement on the trainer may help to explain why some ineffective programmes are continued. Some mothers who smack their children for bad behaviour do so because the smack has the effect of stopping the behaviour at the time, so relieving the mother of the immediate unpleasantness, although they may realise it does not have any more permanent effect: 'It works, but it doesn't really alter his behaviour' (Carr, 1975).

## HOW TO PRESENT REINFORCEMENT

There are four important rules as to how reinforcement should be presented if it is to be maximally effective. Mnemonically, we may say that reinforcement should be delivered with a CICC.

CONTINGENCY

Reinforcement should be given when the desired behaviour occurs, and not at other times in the session. When tangible rewards are being used for teaching they should, if possible, be limited in their availability at other times of the day to ensure their continued motivating properties.

IMMEDIACY

Reinforcement should be given as soon as the desired behaviour is shown, with the smallest possible time lag. This means that the trainer must be alert to what the child is doing, so that he will notice the appropriate response as soon as it occurs. He must also be ready with the reinforcer; if it is a tangible one, it should be already in his hand before the response occurs, so that he can deliver it at once and not have to search or fumble for it.

If reinforcement is not given immediately following the desired behaviour, there is the possibility that another, less desired, behaviour may take place in the intervening period and it may be this that is reinforced. For instance, a child who has just correctly imitated a sound may then resort to rocking or hand-flapping. If the reinforcement is delayed until this ritual has begun it may be the ritual and not the imitation that is reinforced. Delay in reinforcement may also delay learning; Schoelkopf & Orlando (1965) found that delay of as little as five seconds between the behaviour and the reinforcement was sufficient to slow down learning.

CONSISTENCY

A new behaviour will be most rapidly established if it is reinforced every time it occurs. Therefore at the beginning of a training programme best results are achieved if responses are reinforced consistently. Once a behaviour has been firmly established, different reinforcement patterns are more effective for maintaining the behaviour (see the section on schedules of reinforcement).

CLARITY

It is essential for the child to be clearly aware that reinforcement has been given. This applies especially to social reinforcement. Praise should be enthusiastic, smiles broad and hugs and kisses given warmly. The restrained British mumble of 'Good boy' may be indistinguishable to a severely retarded child from other verbal communication, whereas the more frenetic approach described above, besides being more pleasurable to the child, gives him a clearer indication of his success. It is also important to state clearly which behaviour is being reinforced. It is better to say, 'Good. I like the way you did up that button', rather than merely to say 'Good boy' mechanically.

## SCHEDULES OF REINFORCEMENT

Reinforcement may be given on either a *continuous* schedule (following every appropriate response) or on an *intermittent* schedule (following certain responses only). We have already discussed briefly a continuous reinforcement schedule, or CRF (see the section on consistency p.39). The advantages of this type of schedule are, first, that it is effective for establishing a new behaviour and, secondly, that it is relatively easy to administer within a structured session. An intermittent reinforcement schedule has the advantage of being much nearer to the kind of reinforcement pattern likely to be met with in the natural environment; in the everyday world, people are likely to notice and enthuse about only a minority of our commendable actions. Busy parents or ward staff with other demands on them cannot reward the child for every correct response throughout the day. Second, and more importantly, behaviour that has been maintained by intermittent reinforcement is very much more resistant to extinction than is behaviour maintained by continuous reinforcement (Bandura, 1969; Baumeister, 1967). Some researchers have attempted to discover whether behaviours which have been maintained on an intermittent schedule will become more subject to extinction if they are transferred to a continuous schedule (Spradlin & Girardeau, 1966). This, if it were established, would be extremely important in cases where undesirable behaviours, maintained by intermittent reinforcement, are strongly resistant to extinction. Unfortunately, the studies have not shown that moving from an intermittent to a continuous schedule makes the behaviour more subject to extinction, though the authors point out that the experiments may have been too brief for such an effect to be shown. The disadvantages of an intermittent schedule are that it is, first, less effective for establishing a new behaviour and, second, rather more difficult to administer systematically (see below).

## TYPES OF SCHEDULES

Reinforcement may be given on either a *ratio* or an *interval* schedule. On a ratio schedule, reinforcement depends on the frequency of appropriate responses; on an interval schedule, reinforcement depends on a response following a specified lapse of time. So a child on a ratio schedule might receive reinforcement for every second or third piece that he placed correctly in a puzzle; while on an interval schedule the child might be reinforced after every 15 or 30 seconds that he is working on the jigsaw.

Reinforcement schedules of either kind may be further categorised as *fixed* or *variable*. On a fixed schedule, reinforcement is given regularly, following a certain number of responses or after a certain length of time. So on fixed ratio schedules reinforcement may be given following, say, every third, tenth or twentieth response: these schedules are designated as FR 3, FR 10 and FR 20. Similarly, fixed interval schedules, where reinforcement is given following the response occurring after say, 5 seconds, 15 seconds and 20 minutes, are described as FI 5 seconds, FI 15 seconds and FI 20 minutes. On a variable schedule, reinforcement follows after numbers of responses or periods of time that can vary considerably but which *average* out at certain specified numbers or times. For example, on a variable ratio schedule with reinforcement given for every third response on average (VR 3), the reinforcement pattern might be as follows (reinforced responses are indicated by an asterisk):

| | | | | | | | | | | | | | | |
|---|---|---|---|---|---|---|---|---|---|---|---|---|---|---|
| Responses | ı ı ı ı ı ı ı ı ı ı ı ı ı ı ı ı ı ı ı ı ı ı ı ı ı ı ı ı ı ı ı ı ı ı ı ı ı ı ı ı ı ı | | | | | | | | | | | | | |
| Reinforcements | * | * | * | * | * | * | * | * | * | * | * | * | * | * |
| Response No: | 1 | 4 | 6 | 10 | 13 | 18 | 20 | 24 | 27 | 28 | 32 | 35 | 40 | 42 |
| No. of responses intervening | 1 | 3 | 2 | 4 | 3 | 5 | 2 | 4 | 3 | 1 | 4 | 3 | 5 | 2 |

With reinforcement given 14 times for a total of 42 responses, the average number of responses per reinforcement is 3, though the actual number varies considerably. A similar programme may be worked out for any variable ratio schedule (VR 5, 20, 45, etc.) or for variable interval schedules (VI 10 seconds, 60 seconds, 30 minutes), in which case it is the length of time rather than the number of responses that is varied.

Work with institutionalised retarded children has shown that the use of different reinforcement schedules results in different patterns of responding (Orlando & Bijou, 1960). On a fixed ratio schedule there were high stable rates of responding with pauses following the delivery of the reinforcer. Variable ratio and variable interval schedules produced almost identical patterns of responding, high stable rates with short infrequent pauses not related to the time of reinforcement. Fixed interval schedules led to the greatest diversity in response patterns in these children. To those working with the retarded the most significant finding associated with reinforcement schedules is that variable schedules produce greater resistance to extinction (that is, the behaviour is maintained for longer after the discontinuation of reinforcement) than do fixed schedules (Spradlin & Girardeau, 1966). Since our aim is usually to establish a behaviour which will function independently of extrinsic reinforcement in the natural environment, we should aim to 'thin out' reinforcement once the response pattern has been learned and the adoption of a ratio or interval schedule largely depends on the nature of the task being taught (see below).

It must be said that variable schedules are more difficult to deliver systematically and accurately than fixed schedules. The reinforcement programme must be planned in advance (similar to that on page 41) whereas on a fixed schedule it is simple enough to determine that reinforcement will be given for every correct response, or every third or fourth correct response. If a variable schedule is to be applied strictly then the programme must be strictly adhered to or the average rate decided upon will become distorted. It is of course quite possible to use a haphazard 'variable schedule', with reinforcement given at random, from time to time, and in real life, in the natural environment, this is what normally happens. The danger in moving from a fixed to a haphazard schedule is that reinforcement may rapidly become so infrequent that the behaviour is extinguished.

## SOME PROBLEMS ASSOCIATED WITH REINFORCERS

### SATIATION

Once a powerful reinforcer has been identified for a child our troubles are not necessarily over. If it is repeatedly and invaryingly used the child may get tired of it and cease to work for it. Satiation seems to take place most quickly with foods and least with social reinforcers. Two possible strategies to minimise the effects of satiation are, first, deprivation and, second, the use of multiple reinforcers. Most reinforcers are found to be more effective if the child is allowed access to them after a period of mild deprivation; this applies particularly to consumables – a child is more likely to work for these before rather than after a meal. An autistic boy who was said by his mother to be very fond of toast and honey was not making progress on the task she was teaching him. It transpired that she was working with him, using toast and honey as the reinforcer, after he came home from school and had had his tea – for which he had unlimited amounts of toast and honey. Satiation seems to occur particularly readily in the case of sweets, though these too may be subject to the effects of deprivation; extended experiments have been carried out with institutionalised retarded children using a lever-pressing task and candy reinforcement which was evidently so continuously effective that the authors concluded, 'Motivation is seldom a problem for the retarded' (Orlando & Bijou, 1960).

The use of multiple reinforcers avoids most of the problems of satiation. Either a variety of different reinforcers may be given in a session, so that at one time a food, at another a toy and at another a cuddle is given for each appropriate response; or a number of different reinforcers may be given in series for each response (Kiernan, 1974); for example, the behaviour could be followed immediately by praise, by a sweet 3 seconds later and by stroking 5 seconds after that. Children who have learned not to grab handfuls of any reinforcer in sight may be presented with several reinforcers at once from which they may choose the particular one that appeals at the moment. This last approach has been found especially useful for the presentation of back-up reinforcers for children working on token programmes.

No research exists to show that any one method is particularly effective in avoiding satiation. The important thing is for the trainer to be alert to the possibility that satiation may result in reduced effectiveness of the reinforcer and to be prepared to do something about it.

### EDIBLE REINFORCERS AND OBESITY AND DENTAL DECAY

Many of the early studies relied heavily on 'candy' as a reinforcer (indeed 'reinforcement' became almost synonymous with M and Ms, translated on this side of the Atlantic into Smarties) and sweet things are preferred by many children. This raises problems with children who are over-weight or who have bad teeth. Our practice is always to explore first the effectiveness of non-edible reinforcers, and then that of other, less damaging, foods such as fruit, drinks, crisps, cheese, etc. Finally, if only sweets are effective reinforcers, we break them up into very small pieces (a Smartie is normally divided into four), thus also minimising satiation problems.

### REINFORCERS FOR PARTICULAR BEHAVIOURS

The behaviour to be changed may also to some extent affect the choice of reinforcers. If the child responds to a number of reinforcers it may be possible to choose the most suitable one for the occasion. For example, when teaching a child to sit quietly it may be disruptive to use frolicking as a reinforcer. Similarly it may be thought inappropriate to use sweets as a reinforcer for eating meals; in fact in two cases known to the writers this has proved highly effective and has even, on one occasion, resulted in the child learning to eat foods that he previously would not tolerate. Edible reinforcers have been found to be inconvenient also in speech training programmes (Howlin, 1976) since the child spends several seconds in chewing and swallowing, which reduces the time available for training. In the writers' experience even quartered grapes took too long for one child to consume, since the child kept the grape skin almost indefinitely in his mouth – peeling the grapes got over that difficulty. Drinks are more quickly consumed than foods. The problems of spilling and of the amount of liquid taken can be overcome if the drink is given in a squeezy (well-washed-out) liquid detergent bottle.

Clearly where a choice of reinforcers is available it is sensible to choose the most appropriate one for the task in hand. If only one, less than ideal, reinforcer is available then the decision has to be made whether to make use of it or to give up the idea of teaching the child.

## OBJECTIONS BY PARENTS AND OTHERS

Occasionally parents, nurses, teachers and others are found who object to the whole idea of using reinforcement to teach children. This is discussed more fully in Chapter 11. On the whole, it is found that *a priori* objections disappear when the child can be shown to be making reliable progress.

## IMPLEMENTING A REINFORCEMENT PROGRAMME

The following example, illustrating all the stages involved in setting up a behaviour programme, might help to clarify some of the principles of reinforcement and the sequence of events involved.

1. SPECIFY THE GOAL

Let us assume that we have been asked to devise a programme for a hyperkinetic retarded boy, John, and that everyone concerned with his care and teaching – parents, nurses and teachers – have decided that getting him to sit for a few minutes and attend to some constructive activity would open the door to many possibilities for him. John is a very active child who is rarely still for even a few seconds. He will not sit still for meals, or to be taught any activities like puzzles or picture matching, nor will he stay on the toilet long enough for toilet training to begin. He has very little understanding of speech, responding only occasionally to his name. The initial goal is to have John sitting for 1 minute and attending to the therapist's instructions. We now have a clearly defined goal which we can reasonably expect John to achieve (asking him to sit still for 5 minutes would probably be too difficult at this stage).

2. IDENTIFY THE REINFORCER

The next stage is to identify the reinforcement for which John will be prepared to sit down for a second or two. Since John is such a hyperactive child, we expect that we will need quite a powerful reinforcer to teach sitting, since running about is itself so motivating for him. There are many possible reinforcers for John. He enjoys running and jumping, he loves orange juice, crisps and ice cream, and he also likes to be cuddled. All of these reinforcers could be used in teaching John to sit. The orange juice would be better in a squeezy bottle than in a cup, as this will save spilling if John knocks it over. The crisps should be put out on a plate, ready to hand, and broken up into smaller pieces. Ice-cream is not an easy reinforcer to use as it is difficult to get it at the right consistency, neither rock hard nor melted; an insulated butter box helps to keep it from going liquid, and we should certainly keep the ice-cream in mind in case John becomes bored with the other foods. Cuddles are easy to give and a few moments of running about could appropriately be interspersed with the sitting. We plan then to use as reinforcement a cuddle plus a food or drink together with praise, followed by a few moments of running.

3. TEACHING THE BEHAVIOUR

We begin to teach sitting using a plain bare room with as few distractions in it as possible. A chair for John is placed in the middle, preferably with arms to help prevent him squirming off it. John is called by his name to get his attention, told gently but firmly, 'Sit down', and then held and seated on the chair. Immediately we praise him – 'That's good, John' – and give him a crisp and a cuddle. With a very active and resistant or a large child it might be necessary to have a second trainer to hold the child while the reward is given, otherwise he may slip off the chair before receiving his crisp and inadvertently be rewarded for being off his seat. If this should happen (and accidents occur in the best-run treatment programmes even if they are not always written up in the journals), we withhold the reinforcer, repeat the command and the physical prompt and this time get the reinforcer in fast. Then John is released and allowed to get up and run around. After a few seconds we carry out a further trial, calling John, leading him to the chair and seating him, then praising and rewarding him for sitting on the chair.

How many trials should be given per session and how long each session should last will depend on the individual child. On the whole, we prefer short sessions of 5-10 minutes with 10-20 trials per session, and several short sessions a day seem preferable to one long one. As the programme progresses, we may give more trials but usually 10 minutes intensive training is enough for both therapist and child. When we train ward staff or parents to do the sessions themselves it is often difficult, especially at the beginning of a programme, to convince them of the need to keep the sessions short. Sometimes a parent will go on with a language session for 45 minutes and then wonder why the child is reluctant to co-operate the next time.

4. FADE OUT REINFORCEMENT SCHEDULE

Let us say that John has now had a week of training in sitting. He has rather lost interest in crisps and orange juice, so ice-cream is now being used as reinforcement. He will now come to the chair when told to sit and will wait there to receive his spoonful of ice-cream and then get up and run around the room until the request is repeated. John probably does not yet understand the actual meaning of the command, 'Sit down', but has learnt that, each time he is given an instruction in this situation and he sits down, he receives ice-cream; he is reacting to the cues of the environment. At this stage, when he is sitting each time he is told to do so and is anticipating the reinforcement, we can begin to fade out the reinforcement, moving on to an intermittent schedule. Now John receives edible reinforcement every second time he sits to command, then every third time, after which we may, if we are sufficiently well-organised, move on to a variable ratio schedule

(VR 3 perhaps). At the same time we may move on to training John in a slightly different task, that of remaining seated. For this we may begin with a fixed interval schedule – FI 5 seconds for example, so that John is now reinforced every 5 seconds that he is sitting down. Gradually we extend this to FI 10 seconds, 30 seconds, 1 minute and so on, eventually going on to a VI schedule when John is reasonably good at sitting still in order that this behaviour may be the better maintained. In addition, once John will sit for 30 seconds to a minute we may insist that meals are only eaten when he is seated, or introduce constructional material such as simple form boards, colour matching and so on. Providing that we ensure that the constructional material is interesting and at a level appropriate for the child, we may be able to use these activities as reinforcement: the child is allowed to put the pieces of puzzle in the board if he is seated. Now we may be able to dispense with edibles and use interest in the task plus praise as reinforcement. If, however, under these conditions the child's learning slows down, we should always be prepared to go back to edible or other tangible reinforcers.

## CONCLUSIONS

Reinforcement is not, as is sometimes implied by the critics, the whole of behaviour modification, but it is an important aspect of it. Some retarded children receive little reinforcement in their everyday lives, and may have little expectation of success. They may on the contrary have well-founded expectations of failure or of the probability of aversive consequences. If we can identify, arrange and deliver reinforcers so that a child's appropriate behaviours are strengthened, we shall increase his learning, his social acceptability and his own enjoyment of his life.

# 4 THE USE OF TOKENS WITH INDIVIDUALS AND GROUPS

Chris Gathercole and Janet Carr

At times it is not convenient, practicable or possible to deliver tangible reinforcers immediately after a behaviour has been performed. For example, if you are teaching a child the components of good road sense it may not be possible to reinforce his stopping at the kerb by giving him a sweet if, in turn, that means you have to wait for him to eat the sweet and thereby miss the gap in the traffic. Equally, many parents despair of reducing temper tantrums during shopping trips. Threats of what will happen when the child returns home are ineffective: immediate corporal punishment brings the wrath of passers-by to bear on the harrassed mother. How can a child's behaviour be influenced in these settings?

As was discussed earlier, one aims to bring the child's behaviour under the influence of social attention from parents and others. Where social attention is not yet a powerful reinforcer, some other way must be found of bridging the gap between the appearance of the behaviour and the later awarding of reinforcers. One way of bridging this gap and of delivering a form of reinforcement which need not unduly interfere with the ongoing behaviour is to use token reinforcement.

Tokens are one form of generalised reinforcer; others include points, stars, plastic money or indeed real money, which later serves as an effective generalised reinforcer for most people. In each case the token, star, point or coin has no intrinsic value for the individual, but it has come to be valued because it represents the possibility of obtaining that which is of value. The tokens themselves then become of value; since the exchange of tokens leads consistently to reinforcement, the tokens acquire reinforcing properties. When we use tokens our aims are the same as when we use other reinforcers – to teach skills, to maintain established skills and to reduce undesirable behaviours.

The following examples illustrate the use of tokens with individuals:

(1) Roderick is receiving individual training in speech and language development. Whenever he gives an appropriate, well-articulated verbal response to pictures shown him in a scrap book, the trainer gives him one penny in plastic money, which he puts

into a plastic jar beside him on the table. At the end of the 10-minute training session he takes his jar, with a screw-on lid, back to the ward, where he exchanges his plastic tokens for real money, which he can then spend in a real shop. This is a very simple token system, which is only used in his speech and language training sessions.

(2) A more complex programme has been worked out for Stephen who works in an Adult Training Centre, where he is extremely difficult to control. Each member of the training staff carries a number of coins, with impressions of footballers. These coins were used in a sales campaign by one of the petrol companies some time ago. Whenever Stephen follows an instruction and does what he is told he is given a token by the trainer. He is also given a token if he enters the dining area for a midday meal or a drink during the tea break, as well as for participating in the work of the Centre. Stephen may therefore be given tokens by any member of staff at any time of the working day. He can exchange his tokens for drinks during the tea break, and coloured stars, which he sticks on to a chart kept in the Manager's office. The token economy is in operation at all times when Stephen is at the Centre.

## ADVANTAGES OF USING TOKENS

Tokens have a number of advantages over conventional reinforcers. First, they allow for the use as reinforcers of a wide variety of events and items that could not be used in the conventional way – that is, delivered immediately and contingently on the desired behaviour. For example, if a child is very fond of swimming, it may be desirable to use swimming to reinforce, say, bed-making. However, it may not be possible for the child to go swimming immediately after he has made his bed. If then he is given a token when he has made his bed, and if he has to give a token to be allowed to swim, then he is more likely to make his bed. Here the token bridges the time-gap between the required behaviour and the back-up reinforcer. Furthermore, the use of tokens enables a large reinforcer to be used by requiring a number of tokens to be exchanged for it. Since each token is given for relatively minor behaviours the reinforcer follows after a series of desirable behaviours. So it might be that the child would be given the chance of going swimming only once a week and would have to earn seven tokens – make his bed every day – for the privilege. This aspect of tokens is particularly valuable with the brighter child who has little interest in foods or drinks but is keen to have, and willing to work for, a particular toy, record, article of clothing and so on.

Tokens also have the advantage that they allow sequences of responses to be reinforced without interruption of the teaching. Sweets and cigarettes, for example, take time to be consumed, which can hold up teaching and cause particular problems in, say, speech training. If consumption of the back-up reinforcer can wait until the end of the training, then time is not wasted. Again, tokens maintain their reinforcing properties because they are independent of deprivation states, whereas other reinforcers are more likely to be affected by satiation (Gewirtz & Baer, 1958; Winkler, 1971). For example, after a meal, the effectiveness of food as a reinforcer is greatly diminished. A trainee, although not hungry, may still be willing to earn tokens, which he may be able to spend on food or sweets later. Tokens allow trainees to exercise some choice in their selection of back-up reinforcers. They will use their tokens for the reinforcers they want most. This allows trainees with different preferences to select what is most rewarding for them at that particular time. The trainer then does not have to worry too much about the possible loss of interest of a trainee in one particular reinforcer, so long as a range of reinforcers is made available.

Tokens also have a number of advantages for staff. When he dispenses reinforcers a trainer also gives praise and attention. This allows the trainer to increase his personal social reinforcement value to the trainee, since he becomes a discriminative stimulus for the occasion of reinforcement. Since tokens are reinforcers, and since many tokens may have to be earned before exchange can take place, there are many opportunities for the trainer to increase his reinforcement value. Tokens may also be useful in situations where real money cannot be used. For example, it may not be appropriate for staff to require a trainee to pay cash for the opportunity to go for a walk or a ride on a roundabout. There are also situations where staff may not wish to have a lot of transactions with real money which might require an elaborate accounting procedure. For the trainee, of course, tokens can provide a valuable preparation for the use of real money. A token system may involve the trainee in counting, saving, checking of change, looking after tokens and possibly even a banking system. Again the use of tokens may help to shape staff training skills, while staff are often found to be particularly enthusiastic and positive when they are working in a token economy (Fernandez, 1978; Kazdin, 1977). Lastly tokens may be used flexibly, from an individual programme to a full-scale token economy. A start may be made with a simple small-scale system for one trainee, and this may be gradually extended and increased in complexity as staff feel confident to cope with a more sophisticated system.

## FORMS OF TOKENS AND STORAGE

There are many different kinds of token which can be used. Tiddley-winks are suitable, as they are robust and come in several different colours; plastic money as used in schools can lead on to the use of real money; coloured stars can be stuck onto a wall chart or onto cards which the trainee carries with him; ticks or crosses in a book or on a card, or points written as numerical values can be used for the trainee who is able to recognise numbers; tickets can be used which can be punched like a bus ticket.

Which form of token is to be used depends partly on the ability of the trainees to keep and store them. If a points card gets torn up by other trainees it may have to be covered with plastic or stuck onto more rigid material, to prevent its being destroyed. Tiddley-winks may be kept in a purse, and if the purse is attached to a belt they will be even more secure. A token in the form of a washer or plastic disc with a hole in the middle can be threaded on to string around the trainee's neck or hanging from his belt, or stored in a jar for safe keeping. For a group it might be useful to make a token bank out of transparent perspex, so that each trainee has a section with a hole at the top into which he can drop his tokens. If the bank is screwed to a wall, he can then see his tokens mounting up. If the bank is locked, tokens can only be taken out in the presence of the trainer who has the key.

## TEACHING TOKEN USE

Although token systems were originally developed for use with groups of people, as in ward management and subsequently classroom management, tokens can be very helpful in individual cases, whether in hospital, classroom, hostel or in the home.

Even quite severely handicapped people can learn to use tokens if they are given individual tuition. The first step is to assess the trainee's ability to use tokens. This is simply done by freely giving the trainee a token and requiring him to present his token in exchange for a back-up reinforcer, such as a drink of milk. It quickly becomes apparent whether he can look after the token and hand it over in exchange at the appropriate time. If he is not able to do this, then he is taught to do so. A task analysis of all the skills required in token use indicates that the trainee should be able first of all to hold out his hand to receive the token. Then he should be able to look after it safely in his hand or his pocket, a purse, or in some form of piggy bank. Then he must be able to present the token when he wishes to exchange it for a back-up reinforcer. Reinforcement, shaping, prompting, modelling and fading are all used in teaching these skills.

So if the trainee does not understand the purpose of the tokens he should first be given one and then, almost immediately, prompted to hand it back in exchange for his back-up reinforcer. When he has learnt, by repeated trials and fading of the prompts, to do this readily he should be given a token and prompted to retain it for a short time, 10-15 seconds, before exchanging it. Later he must learn to retain two tokens, and later still he can be taught to keep the tokens for a longer period and to store them, for instance in a purse. Once these skills have been established and the trainee is exchanging them appropriately for the back-up reinforcer, they can begin to be given contingently on the performance of some skilled or required behaviour.

With less severely handicapped people, it is often possible to explain the contingencies of reinforcement and even write down a list of the behaviours being reinforced, together with token payments, and a price list of back-up reinforcers for which tokens can be exchanged. The written statement is a useful reminder to the trainer of what the prices and wages are at any particular time. It can also be considered as a form of contract between the trainer and trainee when the list has been agreed by both parties. It may even be signed by both parties to give it a more official status. Having a written contract helps to avoid disputes about what has or has not been agreed in the past. A contract is not essential, however, and for more severely handicapped people it is only necessary that they are exposed to the contingencies of reinforcement. It is essential, however, that once a token economy has been worked out, it should be adhered to consistently. If arbitrary changes are made or the trainer forgets to make token payments or he omits to provide the back-up reinforcers, then the system would certainly break down, and become ineffective.

## SCHEDULING REINFORCEMENT

When the tokens can be used appropriately and the trainee is not losing them, throwing them away, chewing them, allowing them to be stolen or giving them away, but is looking after them carefully, then we can begin to use them in actual training of other skills. To begin with, they would be used as reinforcers after every successful performance. As the behaviour becomes established, intermittent reinforcement can be introduced. Every other correct performance is reinforced, then every third, every fourth and so on, gradually increasing the number of correct performances before token reinforcement is presented. Eventually the ratio may change to one in a hundred, so that he is working very hard for very little token reinforcement. If the number of correct performances before token reinforcement is now varied, the behaviour will become even more strongly established, and it will be easier for other reinforcements in the natural environment to take over the reinforcing functions of the tokens, so that eventually the tokens can be eliminated altogether. The benefits of intermittent reinforcement are discussed more fully in Chapter 3. The important point is that behaviour is more resistent to extinction when reinforced intermittently than when reinforced every time it occurs.

In the early stages of training, it is necessary to allow the trainee to exchange his tokens for back-up reinforcers fairly frequently. Eventually it will be possible for the trainee to work for 10 minutes, or 20 minutes, or longer, during which time he may accumulate fifty or one hundred tokens before he makes his token exchange. At an even higher level of functioning, it will be possible for the token exchange to be delayed for half a day, or a day, or even longer.

## SOME RULES FOR TOKEN ECONOMIES

Ayllon & Azrin (1968) describe a number of rules, very carefully worked out on the basis of both theory and practice, which provide essential ingredients for the success of a token economy.

We need to describe the current behaviour which we wish to change in specific terms that require a minimum of interpretation. For example, it is more helpful to record that

Paula bit Brenda on the arm

than to say that

Paula was aggressive to Brenda

The first description is specific, whereas the second includes interpretation. On reading the second we would still have to ask, 'What exactly did Paula do to Brenda?'

We should also describe the objectives of training in behavioural terms. A good behavioural objective (Mager & Pipe, 1970) will state WHO – WILL DO WHAT – UNDER WHAT CONDITIONS – TO WHAT CRITERION; e.g., 'Paula will clap hands un-assisted when you say, "Paula, clap your hands", and demonstrate, 4 out of 5 times.' Such an explicit statement of the required behaviour will enable the trainer to know when the desired behaviour has been achieved.

We should aim to select as behavioural objectives or targets for training as far as possible only those behaviours which will continue to be reinforced after training, so that time and effort are not wasted in teaching skills which are unlikely to be maintained after the training period. This means that we need to look at the reinforcers available in the trainee's natural environment and to judge how effective these will be and for which behaviours they are likely to be delivered; and thus which behaviours stand a good chance of being maintained. This is especially important with token programmes as the trainer will wish to wean the trainee from the arbitrary token reinforcement used during the training period.

## SELECTION AND USE OF REINFORCERS

The basic principles governing the selection and delivery of reinforcers generally (contingency, immediacy, consistency, etc.) also apply to tokens. In addition, however, a token programme offers the opportunity to make use of a wide range of potential back-up reinforcers for which the trainee can exchange his tokens. Moreover, there is less danger of the trainee becoming satiated and losing interest in particular reinforcers, and the tokens are more likely to retain their reinforcing value, when there is a wide variety of back-up reinforcers to choose from. Since multiple reinforcers are valuable in token programmes it is also important that the different reinforcers are equally available, and that choosing one does not automatically exclude another. For example, if TV and swimming were scheduled to occur at the same time, the trainee could not choose to exchange his tokens for both, even if he had sufficient tokens for both. If these events were scheduled at different times he could exchange his tokens for both activities and enjoy a wider range of back-up reinforcers.

Before using events as reinforcers we may have to provide opportunities for the trainee to try them, without having to pay tokens for them, to see whether or not he likes them. In a hospital, for example, it may be possible to offer as a reinforcer the opportunity to have a single room; but if a resident has been sleeping in a dormitory for many years he may not know whether he is likely to enjoy having a single room until he has tried it. When he has sampled the single room for a week or two he will be able to decide whether he wishes to spend tokens in order to gain access to that single room. In effect, we are teaching the trainee to make use of many potential reinforcers and to enjoy a wide range of activities. The more he wants to exchange his tokens, the more effective they will be in training, so we have to do all that we can to interest him in the reinforcers that are available. If possible the trainee should be able to see, touch, smell or hear the reinforcer – supermarkets and salesmen have long recognised the importance of exposure to reinforcers. It may help to have him watch someone else actively enjoying it (Doty *et al.*, 1974; McInnis *et al.*, 1974).

## ADMINISTERING REINFORCEMENT

Ayllon & Azrin (1968) suggest several ways for ensuring that the token reinforcement is carried out as planned. First, we should specify for trainers the time and place of the response occurrence and the reinforcement delivery. For example, if the trainee has the job of laying the meal table for dinner, the staff member whose job it is to observe this behaviour must be prepared to visit the dining area at the appropriate time.

Then we should assign one and only one person to act as the reinforcing agent for a given occasion. If each trainer knows his responsibilities clearly, he is more likely to be in the right place at the right time to carry out the training. If responsibilities are not specified clearly then one trainer may assume that another is doing the training, with the result that possibly the training does not get done at all.

We should provide systematic and direct observation of the reinforcement procedure. It is not necessary that this should be done continuously – occasional spot checks should provide sufficient feedback on whether training is being carried out as planned. If the feedback indicates that the system is beginning to break down, and training is not being carried out consistently, then steps can be taken to remedy the situation. It may be that staff have been insufficiently trained, that there are not enough staff, that decisions have not been communicated adequately. The trainee's report of the reinforcement he has received can be used as an additional check on the reinforcement transaction.

Different people should deliver the reinforcement at different times. If only one person provides the reinforcement during training, the behaviour required may come to be produced only in the presence of that trainer. Generalisation is assisted by arranging for different people to provide the reinforcement on different occasions.

## RECORD KEEPING

A decision will have to be made as to whether every token payment and exchange is to be recorded. If this is done it will provide data to check on how the economy is functioning. The records will show whether hoarding or stealing is taking place, whether wages are too high or too low and whether prices need to be increased or reduced. Records will provide a check on whether staff are implementing the token economy as the team has agreed. Staff can record transactions on forms suitably prepared, or the tokens could be accumulated in a jar or locked perspex token bank attached to the wall. If the trainee carries a card which is marked, or a ticket which is punched, he carries with him a record of the tokens he has earned, which can be handed in and analysed at the end of each day.

It is important that the recording system should interfere as little as possible with the carrying out of training. Instead of having complete recording of all token transactions it may be feasible to have occasional spot checks to ensure that the system is running smoothly. The supervisor can make sample observations, as is done by quality inspectors, to see whether trainees are receiving their agreed wages and prices are being adhered to.

Whatever records of token transactions are kept, there should certainly be records of the behaviour being trained. It is only by looking into records of behaviour change that one will be able to determine whether a token economy is having the desired effect.

## FIXING WAGES AND PRICES

Fixing the level of wages is often a fairly arbitrary matter. There are no rules to say exactly how many tokens should be paid. Token payment will partly depend on their value to the trainee, that is, what it will buy for him. A bag of crisps may cost 1000 tokens, which could be earned by the trainee making his bed each day. It would be just as effective to arrange the payment for making his bed to be 1 token if the price of the crisps is 1 token. Wages and prices therefore have to be considered together. Payment should not be too low in relation to prices, otherwise the tokens will be ineffective. If the level at which they are set is such that the reinforcer is effectively unavailable to him, the trainee will simply not work for them. If they are too high the trainer may have difficulty in providing enough back-up reinforcers and the trainee will be able to get all the reinforcers he wants with very little work.

The number of tokens required for the purchase of a back-up reinforcer has to be specified. The trainee may be required, for example, to pay twenty tokens in exchange for one toffee. Or he may have to pay three tokens for thirty minutes of television viewing time. One telephone call home, lasting not more than five minutes, might cost one hundred tokens. Price fixing will be determined by the availability of reinforcers, how many tokens a trainee can earn, how keen the trainee is to purchase the particular reinforcer and prices of other available reinforcers. It is possible to increase or decrease the prices to be paid for the reinforcers or the token payments made to the trainee. Inflation and deflation occur in a token economy, just as they do in a wider monetary economy.

It may become apparent, after the scheme has started, that wages and prices are not sufficiently in balance and that one or other is too high or too low. Some change will be needed to achieve a better balance. The trainer may fix prices as he sees fit, or he may negotiate them in discussion with the trainee. Obviously in changing prices and wages, care has to be taken that changes are introduced in such a way as to maintain the desired behaviour. If wages are lowered too quickly or prices increased too much, the trainee may go on strike. To avoid resentment, then, changes should be introduced slowly. The ratio of reinforcement to performance can be altered as was described in the section on scheduling reinforcement in such a way as to maintain the behaviour. The effect of this is that during a training session the number of tokens earned may stay the same but the trainee is gradually working faster or longer or harder.

Another way of avoiding difficulty is for trainees to select tasks each day or each week. The wage for each task is set for the period but at the end of the period the wage may be reset. The trainee could opt for the same task he had the previous week or for another. In this way he would get used to changes in wage levels and, should he object to the wage for a particular task, he can vote with his feet by choosing to do something else.

A decision has to be made on whether to introduce a standard scheme in which all trainees are paid at the same rates for the required levels of behaviour and the prices of back-up reinforcers are all standardised, or whether each trainee will have an individually tailored programme. It is probably easier for staff to run a standard scheme, because if wages and prices vary for each individual then the whole token economy can become very complicated. However, a standard scheme may not cater for the individual needs of the trainees in sufficient detail and therefore may be less effective than having individualised programmes for each trainee. It may be possible to combine the two approaches, so that a standard scheme forms the basic economy but some individual variations are used for particular trainees for limited periods of time.

## WEANING FROM TOKENS

The aim of training with tokens is to help the trainee improve his skills to the point where they become so useful to him that he does not require tokens to maintain them. The token system therefore should have built-in procedures for weaning trainees off tokens at the earliest opportunity. If this is not done they may become dependent on the token economy.

As a first step, reinforcement may be changed from a continuous to an intermittent schedule. This has been discussed already in the section on scheduling reinforcement (p.53). Then opportunities should be sought for moving from tangible to social reinforcers. Praise should always be given when tokens are being given, so that, in time, praise should acquire reinforcement value and, as the token reinforcement is reduced, the behaviour can be maintained by social reinforcement. The significant people in the trainee's natural environment should be taught to maintain the desired behaviour using reinforcers other than tokens, especially praise and attention where these can be shown to have reinforcing value for the trainee. This means that other members of the family, teachers or nurses,should be able to recognise and reinforce the behaviour acquired during the training when tokens were used.

When the trainee is behaving in the desired way and his behaviour is being maintained by the tokens, he can move into a special privilege phase. At this stage he is not required to earn or pay tokens. Instead, he may have a credit card to enable him to gain access to all the reinforcers he previously had to purchase with tokens. Checks are still made on his behaviour, and as long as the desired behaviour continues he is allowed to retain his credit card. If his behaviour falls below an acceptable level he has to return to earning and paying tokens.

## PUNISHMENT

Fines can be used as punishment but should not be used excessively, or the trainee may get to a stage where he is never able to exchange tokens for back-up reinforcers. Indeed, he may be constantly in debt. When fined for some undesirable behaviour, he could be given a chance immediately to earn back, say, half his fine by practising the desired behaviour. This provides an opportunity for positive teaching rather than merely suppressing unwanted behaviour. However, the teacher has to be creative in thinking up a task on the spur of the moment, and in fixing appropriate payment for it; this might be set at roughly half or a quarter of the fine previously imposed, or it might be more satisfactory to have no fixed payment for practising the desired behaviour.

This illustrates the need for flexibility in running a token economy but, if such flexibility is to be successful, staff have to be highly trained and experienced. It is only possible to achieve such flexibility where the scheme is small because if many staff are involved the problem of communication – say, between shifts – becomes very great. Adapting the scheme is easiest in a classroom or family style setting, because there are fewer people concerned in decision making.

## STARTING A TOKEN ECONOMY

Token economies have been found useful in many situations where more than one person is being taught or trained: classrooms, adult training centres, hospital wards, hostels, group homes.

It is essential for the person introducing a token economy to have had prior experience of working with tokens. This could be with individuals, when lessons learned with a small-scale scheme can be extended to a group scheme. Supervised experience in running a token economy for a group would be a good alternative form of preparatory experience.

The support of all relevant personnel must be sought before the scheme is introduced. In a hospital, for example, the nursing administrators, who can make or break any training scheme, should be involved in planning discussions from the very start.

The planning team should identify early on the person who will be the main source of expertise and knowledge about token economies, normally a psychologist. It is essential that his responsibilities, as well as those of the other members of the team, be agreed and made explicit before the scheme is started.

Although it may be possible to work with the staff already in post in the area selected for the token economy, it may be better to select staff and train them for the job. This approach will ensure that the staff are interested in the approach. If they are 'press-ganged' into a scheme they would rather not be involved with, then they may not be successful in working in it.

As decisions are made about the running of the economy, they should be noted, and every effort must be made to ensure that all members of the team are aware of any changes. Changes should only be introduced when the team is coping with the system as it has developed. It is better to introduce small changes one at a time rather than introduce big upheavals in the system which can seriously affect morale and effectiveness.

A recording system should be introduced, so that behaviour change can be monitored carefully. This will allow the team to evaluate particular procedures used in the scheme, as well as the effectiveness of the overall scheme.

## GROUP-ORIENTATED CONTINGENCIES

Token reinforcement may be arranged for all members of a group in several ways. In a workshop, where several people contribute to the output of the team, payment can be made contingent on the productivity of the group. Another form of group-orientated contingency is demonstrated when an isolated child's peers are given tokens to give to him when he approaches them, and they too receive tokens at the same time. The more usual procedure would be for a trainer to reinforce the child's approach. In getting the other children to present the reinforcement, not only are they being trained to shape his behaviour but also their social reinforcement value is being enhanced. The focus of interest in this situation is on the behaviour of one particular member of the group.

Yet another form of group-orientated contingency operates when all group members have to achieve a criterion before tokens are dispensed to everybody. An example might be the requirement for all children in a family to have tidied their rooms before pocket money is given.

The aim of using group-orientated contingencies is to make use of the peer group. The members of a group can arrange contingencies which may be more powerful and more effective than those arranged by the trainer. There is the danger, however, that peers could arrange unacceptable punishing consequences for group members who hold the group back.

## STAFF TRAINING

Staff need some training in what is required of them. Before using tokens they should have been trained in straightforward behaviour modification skills using forms of reinforcement other than tokens. They will then appreciate that tokens are merely adjuncts in training.

The basis of training should be the demonstration of practical procedures which the psychologist can show to be effective in practice. Staff can then be supervised as they attempt to copy those procedures, during which time they receive feedback and have their skills shaped up. Films, video television, tape and slides and case discussions are very helpful at this stage in providing demonstration and feedback.

When tokens are to be introduced in the training it is often useful if the psychologist can introduce an individual token scheme for one trainee so that teaching examples are available daily in staff training.

Principles should emerge in practice and as staff gain experience they can be given lectures and selected books and articles to improve their knowledge of the principles. It is generally a mistake to start staff training with theory before moving on to practice, although most staff training has been based on the assumption that theory is a prerequisite of practice.

## THE EFFECTIVENESS OF TOKEN ECONOMIES

Reviews of the extensive research on token economies (Fernandez, 1978; Gripp & Magaro, 1974; Kazdin, 1977; Kazdin & Bootzin, 1972) show that token schemes can effectively change behaviour. Many client groups have been helped in many kinds of situations, including not only retarded and autistic children and adults but also delinquents in foster homes and institutions, psychiatric in-patients, especially chronic schizophrenics in long-stay wards, children in classrooms and at home.

A wide variety of token programmes have been used with the mentally handicapped, and many different behaviour deficits targeted. Several programmes, run in hospitals, have been concerned with general behaviours and skills on the wards, including self-help and social behaviours and the decrease of inappropriate behaviours (Bath & Smith, 1974; Brierton *et al.*, 1969; Girardeau & Spradlin, 1964; Musick & Luckey, 1970; Sewell *et al.*, 1973; Spradlin & Girardeau, 1966). Lent *et al.* (1970) reported improvement in the behaviours of retarded adolescent girls in hospital; at follow-up a year later, significant improvements were being maintained in self-care, personal appearance and deportment but not in social and verbal skills. Two programmes (Horner & Keilitz, 1975; Wehman, 1974) have concentrated on tooth-brushing and oral hygiene; in the former, tokens were exchangeable for sugarless gum and, using a multiple baseline, the effectiveness of the use of tokens in teaching correct tooth-brushing was demonstrated.

Hunt *et al.* (1968) used tokens to improve the personal appearance of 12 mildly retarded men who were being prepared for discharge from the institution. Tokens were awarded for such things as being clean, shaved and laundered, having keys in pocket not dangling from the belt, and wearing not more than one pair of trousers. Tokens delivered on either a continuous or an intermittent schedule produced high levels – 80-90 per cent – of appropriate appearance in the group as a whole, which declined to 62 per cent at the end of a 10-day period in which no reinforcement was given. However, there were considerable differences in response to the programme; three men appeared unaffected by the tokens, showing relatively high levels of appearance through all three phases of the study.

The effects of tokens has been more extensively studied in classrooms than in any other setting (Kazdin, 1977). Birnbrauer *et al.* (1965), in one of the earlier studies, looked at a group of 15 mildly retarded children working in class in a token system. When the tokens were withdrawn for 21 days, the achievement and behaviour of ten of the children deteriorated, and returned to normal when the tokens were reinstated. For five children no changes were observed, suggesting that their behaviour was not controlled by the tokens; while another child's behaviour may have been more influenced by the reinforcement from other children for his disruptive behaviours, which was discontinued when the tokens were in force ('Leave me alone, I've got work to do'). Other classroom programmes are reviewed in Kazdin (1977), as are also programmes focusing on language and social behaviours.

Zimmerman *et al.* (1969) and Hunt & Zimmerman (1969) used tokens in a sheltered workshop for retarded clients and found that productivity increased, although the latter study found productivity also increased in periods of the day when tokens were not in operation. Goldberg *et al.* (1978) used an ABAB design to study the effect of tokens on the productivity of seven mildly retarded young people. Group mean production rates rose when tokens were in operation and fell when they were discontinued, but again there was considerable individual variation, with two subjects showing no extinction effect in Phase 2 and one actually increasing production in Phase 1 when tokens were discontinued.

The programmes discussed above have looked at the effects of token programmes in changing behaviours. A few studies have compared the effectiveness of tokens with other forms of treatment (Baker *et al.*, 1974; Stoffelmayr *et al.*, 1973) but very few of these have been concerned with the mentally handicapped. A few studies have compared the effect of tokens with that of various drugs on the behaviour of mentally handicapped people. Christensen (1975) and McConahey (1972) found tokens to be more effective than the drugs in increasing attention, working, self-care, etc., and in decreasing undesirable behaviours such as aggressiveness, and this was supported in a subsequent study (McConahey *et al.*, 1977).

Apart from the comparison with drugs, comparisons with other forms of treatment reviewed by Kazdin (1977) do not in any case refer to mentally handicapped populations. Perhaps this should not be seen as surprising as, apart from behavioural methods and drugs, treatments in mental handicap are thin on the ground. One approach which has become important in recent years has been that of normalisation, and the attempt to provide optimal living conditions for the mentally handicapped (Gunzburg, 1976; Nirje, 1970). In view of the findings of

Baker *et al.* (1974) that changes of ward and of routine had effects on the behaviour of chronic schizophrenic patients that were not subsequently surpassed by the addition of tokens to the regime, a comparative study of the effect of a normalised environment with that of a token economy for mentally handicapped people is surely overdue.

## SOME PROBLEMS INVOLVED IN TOKEN PROGRAMMES

### 1. NON-RESPONSIVENESS

Many studies have found that, although the use of tokens has a favourable effect on the behaviour of the majority of clients, a minority do not alter their behaviour as a consequence of the use of tokens (Birnbrauer *et al.*, 1965; Goldberg *et al.*, 1973; Hunt *et al.*, 1968). In some cases clients working under conditions of tokens delivered contingently are not adversely affected by the withdrawal of tokens (Birnbrauer *et al.*, 1965) while in others clients do not respond positively when a token system is instituted (Goldberg *et al.*, 1973). Explanations for the latter (failure to respond positively to tokens) have received the most attention. Kazdin (1977) suggests that the explanation may lie in the ineffectiveness for individuals in the back-up reinforcers; or in the possibility that the required responses are not in the clients' repertoire; or that the clients may not understand the relationship between performance and reinforcement. Kazdin suggests strategies to deal with these problems and says that the variability of response patterns in different subjects 'should come as no surprise' (p.154).

The second kind of non-responsiveness is shown by the client whose performance does not extinguish when tokens or other extrinsic reinforcement is discontinued. This event seems to dismay many behaviour modifiers, who appear to regard it as undermining the proven effectiveness of their intervention. However, in some cases at least, such an event may point to a highly successful intervention in that the client, having been persuaded by the use of extrinsic reinforcers to undertake an activity, later finds reinforcement within the activity itself. Far from being ineffective, the intervention allows the client to sample, and to discover reinforcement in, an activity he would not otherwise have attempted (cf., Carr, 1980). Other explanations for the failure of a behaviour to extinguish include the possibility that those administering the programme (teachers, parents, etc.) have changed in their behaviour towards the client and may continue to provide more effective reinforcement than they had done previously, even in the absence of a systematic programme (Kazdin, 1977, p. 176). Such an effect has certainly been observed where parents are taught to use behaviour modification methods, and constitutes one of the most hopeful aspects of such teaching (Callias *et al.*, in preparation; Carr, 1980).

### 2. ADVERSE EFFECTS OF TOKEN PROGRAMMES

More serious than the possibility that some clients may not respond to token programmes is the finding that some are made worse by the programme (Hemsley, 1978). In some cases this may have been due to distress caused by disturbance of routine. In others, Hemsley suggests that cognitive factors in the client may be important and that these should be taken into account when selecting patients for this type of treatment. The clients considered here were chronic schizophrenics; how far similar effects may be found in the mentally handicapped is unknown, but their possibility should obviously be borne in mind.

### 3. DIFFICULTIES IN THE MAINTENANCE OF BENIGN EFFECTS

Token programmes, like others undertaken to change behaviour, are intended to produce changes which are permanent, and which will eventually be maintained by reinforcers, especially social reinforcers, that are readily available in the natural environment (Kiernan, 1974). Thus the tokens should gradually be faded out, and generalisation to normal –ideally, community-based – living conditions should be the goal from the start. Fernandez (1978), visiting ten institutions in the United States where token programmes were in operation, found that all attempted to programme generalisation, though this tended to be unstructured and to rely on gradually substituting social for token and other reinforcers. Kazdin (1977, p. 175) states that 'behaviours *usually* extinguish when a programme is withdrawn', and goes on to suggest ways of counteracting this, including the selection of behaviours likely to be maintained by the natural consequences of the environment, the use of intermittent token reinforcement contingencies and the gradual fading of these, and also the gradual expansion of stimulus control.

Although it is generally agreed that tokens should not last for ever but should eventually give place to other, less artificial, forms of reinforcement, it may not always be possible to achieve this. Lindsley (1964) has distinguished between a therapeutic environment, designed to teach new skills, and a prosthetic environment, designed to maintain behaviours already established. A token economy is usually established with therapeutic aims in mind, but it may in some cases be impossible to wean all clients off it, if only because the 'natural' reinforcers, especially the social reinforcers, may continue to be ineffective for these clients. In this case the token economy may have value as a prosthesis, if this allows for higher-level behaviour to continue in these clients; but opportunities to supersede it should be constantly sought.

## ETHICAL ISSUES

The use of tokens and of token programmes has come under attack for their potential in violating human rights, freedom and dignity. Concern has centred round the external control and manipulation of human behaviour; the possibility that this control may be exerted for undesirable ends, or ends not related to the client's welfare; that methods of control may be used which interfere with the client's basic human rights; and that treatment methods may be employed which have not been agreed to by the client or his relatives.

Clearly these concerns do not relate only to behaviour modification programmes. Human beings have made determined and variably successful attempts to control and to influence the behaviour of other human beings, whether as parents, teachers, police, judiciary or government, since the beginnings of social organisation. Similarly, society has always made use of rewards and punishments, and especially of the latter, in order to control or eliminate what is seen as socially undesirable behaviour. Nevertheless, perhaps because behavioural methods are seen as constituting a powerful technology whereby one group may be able to control the actions of others, particular ethical issues have been raised.

These issues are well discussed by Kazdin (1977, pp. 255-77), and it is not possible to cover them all here. However, two that particularly affect the operation of token, and other, programmes with the mentally handicapped are, first, the question of human rights and the restrictions thereby placed on the availability of back-up reinforcers; and, second, the question of consent to treatment. Early token economies made use of a variety of 'privileges' which were not freely available to the clients but had to be earned and paid for in tokens (Ayllon & Azrin, 1968). These 'privileges' included such things as a comfortable bed, recreational activities, particular items of food, etc., which may now be regarded as due to the client as of right, and not to be withheld (Wyatt *v.* Stickney, 1972). Consequently these 'privileges' may not be used as back-up reinforcers. The solution may be to provide additional privileges over and above the conditions available to all clients but, as the requirement for these conditions becomes higher, it will become increasingly difficult to surpass them in the 'privileges'. A particular problem posed by some severely or profoundly handicapped people is the paucity of reinforcers that are effective for them. For example, a boy for whom other reinforcers were not effective learnt to dress himself only when his breakfast was used as the reinforcer (Moore & Carr, 1976) – a practice that might now be thought inadmissible. In some cases the effective reinforcers are so limited that unless one which may constitute a basic right is used it may become impossible to devise treatment for some clients. It may be that for these clients permission may have to be sought for certain events, which in the normal way would be regarded as theirs by right, to be restricted and used as reinforcers, following full discussion with the client's parents or guardian. This permission would be sought only if it could be shown that without the use of these events adequate and beneficial treatment of the client would not be feasible.

There is a potentially damaging side effect to the current climate of concern with the rights and protection of clients in token and other programmes; that is, that the strictures on those attempting to provide this treatment may become so severe that few will be willing to undertake it, with the result that clients who might have benefited from this treatment will not have the opportunity to do so. This position has not yet been reached in this country; it is to be hoped that therapists will be sufficiently alert to the needs of their clients and for adequate ethical safeguards in their treatment that such a position will never be reached.

The restrictions now placed on treatment programmes pose considerable problems for psychologists. Nevertheless, that psychological, as well as other, treatments are now explicitly required to be humane and to inflict as little discomfort as possible, especially where these treatments are directed to relatively vulnerable groups of people such as the mentally ill and the mentally handicapped, must be taken as a welcome sign of the greater sensitivity of society to its less fortunate members.

## CONCLUSIONS

Token programmes have an important part to play in the teaching and training of the mentally handicapped. This applies particularly to the moderately and mildly handicapped, for whom tokens provide the opportunity to make use of effective reinforcers in a way which is closely similar, and may lead on, to the earning and purchasing conditions that operate for normal people. Among the many advantages of token programmes is their flexibility, which makes it possible to devise programmes for individuals or for groups, or indeed to allow for particular contingencies for individuals within groups. Hitherto, the published reports have been predominantly concerned with the results obtained from programmes on whole groups but, in view of some reports of variable response by individuals and even, in some cases, of adverse effects, it seems important that future reports should pay particular attention to these and to reporting what attempts were made to overcome the problems.

It has not yet been made clear what is the effective ingredient in token programmes. One that may well play a part in programmes run in institutional settings is staff enthusiasm; this is generally found to be high (Kazdin, 1977, p. 151; Fernandez, 1978), although this has been questioned by Tizard (1975), who sees the token economy as operating primarily for the convenience of staff and offering little positive to the clients. There may be particular dangers in large-scale, long-term programmes running in institutions that the behavioural principles on which the programmes were based will be forgotten and the token system will become an end in itself. Clearly, it is essential that all concerned with token programmes, and especially the managers and those responsible for the inception and development of the programmes, should keep ever before them the aims on which they must be based: of teaching skills and developing behaviours that will allow the mentally handicapped person to realise his maximum potential, and allow him and his family to enjoy their lives to the full.

# 5 BUILDING UP NEW BEHAVIOURS – SHAPING, PROMPTING AND FADING

Mona Tsoi and William Yule

Many parents, teachers and nurses would claim that they already know about the importance of positive reinforcement. As the last chapter showed, 'knowing about' and 'knowing how to' are not synonymous. Even so, if one accepts that the adult knows how to reinforce a child, one is immediately faced with a problem – how do you get the child into a situation where reinforcement can be delivered appropriately? This chapter will focus on three groups of techniques which are used in building up new behaviours – a frequent problem when considering children who are severely retarded.

## SHAPING

Shaping is an art. It is the art of the therapist, using all the skills and ingenuity at his or her disposal, in getting the child to produce a novel response. Fortunately, it is an art-form which has some ground rules.

Having carefully analysed the problem the child presents with, and having decided that there is really a skill deficiency (Mager & Pipe, 1970), then one has a clear picture of the difference between what the child can do now and what we want him to do. We could wait around until he does what we want by chance, and immediately reinforce that chance occurrence, but that is obviously an inefficient strategy. (That is not to say that one should not constantly be on the look-out for improvements in behaviour and reinforce them when they occur. It is just that skill teaching is too important to be left to chance.)

A more active way of intervening is to analyse the components of the skill behaviour you want to teach. Having done so, then decide roughly on the steps needed between where the child is now and where you want him to be at the end of the programme. This means that you have to work on one aspect of the skill *which is already in the child's repertoire.* The child has to develop this skill in the desired direction under the therapist's guidance.

The therapist begins by reinforcing the existing behaviour. Once it is firmly established and can be reliably elicited, then the therapist begins to use differential reinforcement – concentrating reinforcement on those responses which approximate more closely to the desired goal, and ignoring (and hence extinguishing) those responses which are less like the required behaviour. Thus, the therapist reinforces successive *approximations* to a desired behaviour. An example will help to clarify this.

Let us say that the task is to teach a child to have good eye-to-eye contact. The child will sit on a chair, but will not look at the therapist's face. Having identified a powerful and convenient stimulus which is reinforcing, the therapist could sit opposite the child and wait. He would wait until the child happened to move his upper body towards the therapist. Immediately, the reinforcer would be delivered. Movement of the upper body would continue to be reinforced in this manner until it was reasonably established. Next, the therapist might wait until not only was the upper body oriented towards the therapist, but the child's head was also in the same direction. Then, he might withhold reinforcement until the child's face was showing opposite the therapist's. Finally, he would deliver reinforcement contingent upon their eyes meeting, however fleetingly. Having established that behaviour, it would be a simple matter then to withhold reinforcement until eye-to-eye gaze had been maintained for longer and longer periods.

Notice what is happening in this training sequence. The therapist selects a response which is already in the child's repertoire, which he can see is related topographically to the desired response. Reinforcement is made contingent upon successive alterations in the topography of that initial behaviour until the end point is reached. But how does the therapist know what speed to go at? What pitfalls lie in this approach?

Gelfand & Hartmann (1975) have some excellent advice on these issues, although they admit that their advice owes more to intuition and clinical experience than to experimental findings. They recommend that, when the desired approximation occurs, a powerful reinforcer should be delivered immediately. Otherwise, there is a danger that with rapidly changing behaviour, the therapist might reinforce an incorrect response. Such reinforcement should be delivered at almost 100 per cent frequency.

There are no hard and fast rules for deciding when to move on to the next step. It makes sense to ensure that one step is reasonably mastered before moving on, but one can only know that one's judgement is right or wrong if the child duly masters the next step. If, when the requirements of correct performance are made more stringent, the child's performance breaks down, then one of two major errors may have been made. (1) The previous step was not sufficiently well established. This means that you should repeat the steps so that the child overlearns the previous one. (2) The therapist has demanded too big a jump. In this case, can the skill be further analysed into component steps? As Gelfand and Hartmann (1975) put it, the art of shaping is to *think small*!

A further practical tip to facilitate such shaping sessions concerns the way of ending a session. By their very nature, such sessions are proceeding from easy items to making successively greater demands on the child. But the training sessions should not become aversive for the child. Therefore, always ensure that the session finishes on a high note. If the child is beginning to fret and to fail, back down to a lower level of performance and ask the child to do something that is well within his capabilities. As soon as he responds correctly, give an extra big reinforcer and finish the session.

Risley & Baer (1973) argue that shaping or response differentiation 'is so consistently successful that it suggests that some sequence of shaping can *always* be found which will produce the behavior change planned, if effective reinforcement is available'. This is a very strong claim and, as will be seen below, the availability of an effective reinforcer is probably necessary but not sufficient.

Even so, the technique has been put to good effect. For example, Wolf *et al.* (1964) used shaping techniques to teach a 3½-year-old autistic boy to wear glasses which were essential to preserve his vision following an operation for the removal of both lenses. The child had refused normal entreaties to put on the spectacles, and threw tantrums, banged his head, slapped his face and pulled his hair when asked to wear them. The therapist decided on new tactics. Just before lunch-time, the boy was offered empty spectacle frames. He was reinforced with food for holding the frames for longer and longer periods. Then, reinforcement was only delivered if he held them closer to his face, and in the correct orientation. Once he was reliably placing them on his face and tolerating them for lengthy periods, the lenses were inserted. Then, reinforcers other than food were used so that the new behaviour would be maintained by a variety of reinforcers in a variety of settings.

As can be appreciated from this example, shaping can be a very lengthy business. It depends on the child emitting the responses and the therapist sensitively perceiving minute changes and reinforcing them. Somehow, life would be a great deal easier and progress a great deal faster if the approximations to the desired response could be 'forced' out of the child. The next sections deal with techniques whereby this can be facilitated. Basically, there are two approaches: the therapist can manipulate the child so that he produces the desired response, or he can alter the environment in such a way that the restructuring facilitates the appearance of the new behaviour.

## PROMPTING, CUEING AND FADING

Let us return to the example of shaping up eye contact. Whilst the technique as described should eventually be successful, the therapist would probably be ready to close his own eyes with exhaustion! To speed the process up considerably, the therapist could do the following: Sitting opposite but close to the child, he says, 'Johnny, look at me!' Then, he reaches over and physically turns Johnny's head until it is facing him. Again, fleeting eye contact is reinforced. If an edible reinforcer is being used, the process can be further accelerated by holding this at eye level. As the child looks at the reinforcer, he automatically looks at the therapist. Thus, a judicious use of physical prompting and placement of the reinforcer will maximise the likelihood of eye contact being made.

Prompting has been used to great effect in training in self-help skills such as feeding (Berkowitz *et al.*, 1971), as well as areas such as instruction following (Whitman *et al.*, 1971) and learning generalised imitation skills (Baer *et al.*, 1967). Again, an example will help to give a flavour of the versatility of this technique.

Zeiler & Jervey (1968) report on the case of a retarded girl who was taught to feed herself. Initially, the therapist prompted (i.e., manually guided) her through the whole sequence from picking up the spoon, scooping the food, raising it to her mouth, to placing it in her mouth. After a few trials, the therapist gradually released the child's hand when it was near her lips, and the girl completed the sequence of feeding on her own. In subsequent trials, the therapist gradually reduced the amount of guidance (or faded out the prompts) so that the girl took the food to her mouth from a progressively greater distance, until eventually she could bring it the whole way from the plate. Notice that, in this instance, the prompts were first faded from those aspects of the sequence of behaviours closest to the final link in the chain of responses. More will be said about such use of 'backward chaining' of responses later in this chapter.

Clearly, using prompts can speed up the acquisition of new

behaviours. But again, this process is slightly problematical in that it demands that the therapist must be very close physically to the child throughout the training session. There is a danger that the child may only go through the sequence when the therapist is seated next to him. In any case, where the therapist is a busy mother, teacher or nurse, they will want more 'remote control' methods which will allow them to get on with other things simultaneously. This is where other cues or discriminant stimuli become important.

For example, when the therapist is prompting a child through a spoon-feeding sequence, instead of merely making encouraging noises, he could clearly label each action – 'Pick up the spoon', 'Scoop the food', 'Lift it up', 'Put it in your mouth', and so on. Then, later, if the child gets in a muddle during feeding, the therapist can get him back on track by calling the appropriate cue.

When children have learned to imitate the therapist, then gestural and other visual cues may be used. In fact, children can be taught to imitate by the judicious use of gestural cues and physical prompts (see Metz, 1965; and Chapter 6).

The different quality of prompts and cues can best be seen in language training. Nelson & Evans (1968) paired arbitrary signs – e.g., tapping the teeth or touching the lips – with particular sounds. They hoped that these visual cues would serve as extra discriminative stimuli, thereby facilitating the learning of the different sounds. Notice, however, that the arbitrary cues in no way force out the correct sounds, and therefore they cannot be considered prompts in the restricted sense that the term is used here.

Sometimes such extra cues can be more confusing than helpful. This seems to be particularly true of autistic children. Schreibman (1975) found that, if cues were added which bore no intrinsic relationship to the critical dimension in a discriminative learning task, autistic children were not helped. However, when the cue was an exaggeration of the relevant component of the training stimulus, then the children were greatly helped. In other words, just because extra cues serve as useful mnemonics for normal adults, this does not mean that retarded children will be able to utilise them in the same way.

Risley *et al.* (1971) describe an ingenious use of cues and fading to teach expressive language. Briefly, once the child is reliably imitating what the therapist says, they shift the stimulus control of the child's expressive language from imitating the total utterance to answering questions. Thus, the therapist holds up a ball and says, 'What is this?' Then, before the child has time to imitate the question, the therapist continues with the answer, 'It's a ball.' If the therapist gets his timing and emphasis correct, the child will answer (i.e., echo), 'It's a ball.' In subsequent trials, the therapist will gradually *reduce* or *fade* the verbal cues he provides, until the child's answer is reliably produced when the question is asked.

The use of prompting, cues and fading is very much an art-form. The therapist must judge how quickly to remove the extra supports dependent on the child's performance. If the performance begins to fall off, extra cues are needed. This is an active process and, as Risley & Baer (1973) point out, by these methods the therapist actually produces behaviour change rather than merely waiting to reinforce it if and when it occurs spontaneously.

## ALTERING THE ENVIRONMENT – THE USE OF GRADED CHANGE

Another way of forcing a response out of a child is to alter the environment in which the child finds himself. Physical aspects of the environment may assist the appearance of the required behaviour. Let us look at a few examples.

Wickings *et al.* (1974) were faced with a 10-year-old retarded child who would not drink from a cup. He appeared to be phobic of all cups, and would only drink from a spoon – a slow and inefficient method. The problem here was not to teach him how to drink, but rather to shift the stimulus control of drinking from the spoon to the cup.

If Mahomet won't come to the mountain, then. . . In this case, if the boy won't approach the cup, the cup must approach the boy. Over a period of several weeks, the spoon the boy used for drinking was deepened (see Figure 5.1). Later, the handle was shortened, and finally bent over to become the cup handle.

The whole process took eight months, partly because of the need to make the spoon-cups. Care was taken to ensure that the boy's new skill was generalised to other settings, and six months after returning to his own school, his progress had been maintained. Follow-up four years later showed that he continued to drink from a cup.

A similar technique was used by Marchant *et al.* (1974) in the treatment of attachment to unusual objects in young autistic children. In one case, a 4-year-old boy was carrying a blanket to such an extent that it grossly interfered with his learning normal hand-eye co-ordinative skills. His mother was asked to cut bits off the blanket in gradual stages.

Figure 5.1

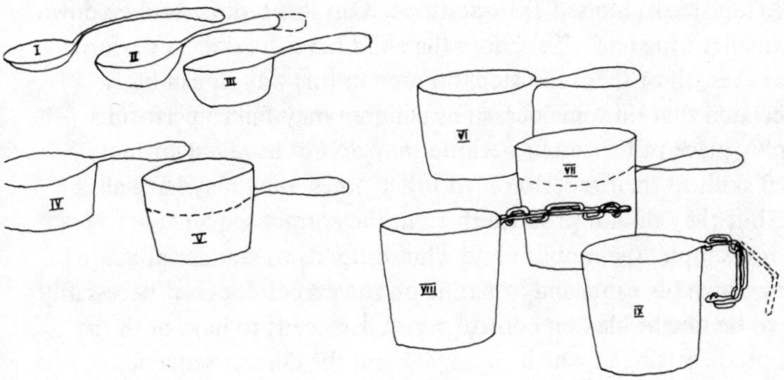


Source: Wickings *et al.* (1974) p.6. Reprinted with the permission of the authors and editor.

After one week it was down to 2 X 8 inches without provoking any reactions from the child. Some three weeks later he had given up carrying the small bundle of threads and began to make strides in learning new tasks. The critical aspect of this approach appears to be the gradualness of the change, thus having a certain similarity with desensitisation approaches.

There are other ways of restructuring the environment to assist learning. Probably the most effective restructuring of recent years has been the introduction of feeder cups. Many toddlers can skilfully drink unassisted from training beakers – thereby upsetting many developmental check lists! Spoons can have their handles enlarged to make them easier for spastic hands to grip; plates can be placed on non-slip surfaces, thereby greatly facilitating feeding. Walking frames can aid walking. In many ways, these are prosthetic devices – without them, the skill disappears. The aim of therapy will be to fade out these aids, but if that proves impossible then at least the patient's quality of life can be improved through their use.

## CHAINING RESPONSES

So far, we have been discussing the different techniques whereby a therapist can help a child learn new behaviours as if each behaviour was a discrete entity. In reality, the task is often to teach the child a complex *sequence* of behaviours which will occur in the appropriate environmental setting. When a child fails to perform a complex task, the therapist asks himself the questions, 'Can this task be broken down into smaller sub-steps? If so, does the child have the skill to perform any or even all of these sub-steps?' Posed in this way, it can be appreciated that on some occasions children may fail to perform a complex piece of behaviour because they do not have one or more crucial skills in their repertoire. At other times, they may have all the skills, but they do not produce them in the correct sequence.

For example, the mobile child who responds to bladder pressure by pulling down his pants and urinating on the carpet does not necessarily need to be taught bladder control *per se.* He needs to have both the appropriate setting in which to urinate and the correct sequence of movements which will take him from wherever he is to the toilet. The task of the therapist in such an instance is to train the child to go to the toilet (initially on command), perform all the necessary undressing actions, urinate, dress, pull the chain, wash his hands and return to the class. Mahoney *et al.* (1971) describe such a programme in some detail.

What one is aiming for in these circumstances is a complex form of stimulus control whereby the completion of one act in a sequence is both reinforced by the commencement of the next act and also acts as a cue to begin the next act. Arriving at the toilet is the signal for pulling down the pants, which is the signal for urinating in the pot, which, in turn, is the signal for flushing the toilet and so on. Each behaviour forms part of an orderly chain which leads smoothly from the initiating step to the final action.

In training a child to master a chain of behaviours, there are logically two ways of going about it. Either you start with the first step, master it, go on to the second step, and so on: this is *forward chaining.* Or, alternatively, you can start with the final step, then move to the penultimate step, and so on in reverse order: this is *backward chaining.*

By and large, there is a consensus among therapists (although there are not many hard data) that backward chaining is the more efficient method for teaching skills, particularly skills such as feeding, dressing and other motor skills. The argument given is as follows: By teaching the child to complete the chain, he can be given a large reinforcer for this. By association, the last step takes on the characteristics of a secondary reinforcer. Therefore, whatever is done immediately prior to the last action is itself reinforced. A judicious use (at early points of the chain) of extrinsic reinforcers, which can thus be quickly faded, can establish the earlier actions in the chain.

Put in the jargon, the technique may sound formidable. In practice, what it means is that a careful analysis of the sequence coupled with good, sensitive data collection should quickly identify difficult stages. The therapist then decides whether the child is sticking because the step was too large, because a component skill was missing, because motivation (i.e., reinforcement) was not strong enough or because of some other problem. It is a matter of clinical judgement to decide how long to persevere in a training scheme before altering it.

Both forward and backward chaining have been used in programmes to teach dressing. For example, backward chaining was used by Moore & Carr (1976) in teaching a 15-year-old severely retarded boy to put on his vest, pants and socks. A similar procedure was used by Minge & Ball (1967), while Martin *et al.* (1971) successfully applied forward chaining to teaching dressing skills.

As noted earlier, there is an absence of comparative data which would allow one to select between the two methods of chaining. In our current state of knowledge, therapists would be well advised to try backward chaining first.

It is as well to remember that where the problem is one of having to put old skills in a new order, then modelling (which is discussed in more detail in Chapter 6) is an extremely powerful therapeutic tool.

## CONCLUSIONS

Although they have been presented separately for ease of exposition, the techniques described in this chapter are usually used in combination to establish new behaviours. For example, prompting and fading are often used together with backward or forward chaining. The decision to use particular techniques depends on the nature of the problem and the level at which the learner is performing. Thus, at the initial stages of teaching a child to use speech sounds, greater reliance may be placed on simple shaping techniques, whereas later, when the child has learned to imitate, more emphasis will be placed on his imitating in the presence of the correct cue.

What all these techniques have in common is a rigorous behavioural and task analysis. Shaping, prompting, fading and chaining all require that the large responses be broken down into small steps. Continuous evaluation of progress is important for isolating unexpected difficulties. Further task analysis then points the way to remedial action.

As is by now obvious, the application of these techniques in behaviour modification is an art, but it is an art-form which is increasingly susceptible to rigorous scientific analysis. Even so, the therapist must always be sensitive to the child's progress and needs. The therapist must respond to the behaviour changes in the handicapped child, and alter the training techniques in a flexible manner to ensure the most effective progress. Undoubtedly, many of the spectacular successes in helping handicapped children stem from the sensitive and imaginative application of the techniques which have been described in this chapter.

# 6 IMITATION, GENERALISATION AND DISCRIMINATION

Janet Carr

This chapter follows on directly from the last in considering ways in which behaviours may be acquired and developed in retarded people. The first topic, imitation, concerns a process by which skills may be acquired; generalisation (as used in this book) concerns the extension of an acquired skill from a restricted to a wider area of application; discrimination concerns the refinement of a skill so that increasingly specific responses become possible.

## IMITATION

In Chapter 5, we saw that new skills can be taught to the child by shaping – that is, by successively reinforcing aspects of his behaviour that approximate gradually more and more closely to the specified behaviour. We saw too that the shaping method, though effective, is a slow and laborious way for the child to acquire skills. In some cases other teaching methods may be more appropriate. 'No parent would take his teenage son into the car for the first time and then shape up his car-driving repertoire in a step-wise fashion, praising the skilled aspects and ignoring the bumps. Rather, the father will instruct his son, and in particular he will *show him what to do*' (our italics) (Yule, 1977). In other words, the son will learn what to do by imitating what he first sees his father do. In this case, as in many others, imitation is an effective and economical way for the child to learn a skill.

Imitation is a basic means by which new behaviours may be learnt, and occurs readily in young normal children. Infants normally begin to imitate a variety of simple movements at around 9 to 10 months, while the two-year-old toddler may spend much of his time following his mother around and imitating her activities. 'He wants to do everything I do' is a frequent comment, mixing exasperation with acknowledgement of the child's need to learn in this way. Imitation in these normal children may appear unprompted or require very little prompting, and may be continued without overt reinforcement such as reward or praise (although other factors to be discussed later may be instrumental in initiating or maintaining the behaviour). Through imitation a child may acquire many behaviours, such as speech or social behaviours, which because of their complexity or inaccessibility to prompting might be slow or difficult to teach by other methods.

The capacity to imitate is, then, a valuable aid to learning, and one which retarded children often lack – a deficit which may be related to another, that of spontaneous learning (Clarke & Cookson, 1962). For these children it may be helpful, in the interests of speeding up their learning generally, to teach them imitation skills, using the methods described in Chapters 3 and 5: *modelling* the required response, *prompting* the response from the child (subsequently *fading* the prompts) and *reinforcing* the resulting response. Initially it seems best to train only one response. The trainer should give the command, 'Do this', and make the response himself: if the child does not respond and needs to be prompted it is helpful to have an assistant to do this, so that the trainer can continue to model the response while the child is being prompted. The assistant should prompt the response and then gradually withdraw his own hands so that the child shall receive the reinforcement when he is holding the position without help (Bricker & Bricker, 1970). Two points may be noted here. First, it seems preferable that the trainer, and not the prompter, should deliver the reinforcement, so that the child's full attention shall remain on the trainer-model. Second, since the child is being trained not in specific actions but in imitation, the trainer should always use the command, 'Do this', for whatever action he models, and not, 'Stretch out your arms', or 'Touch your nose' (or whatever the action is to be). What actions the trainer chooses are then unimportant in themselves: what is important is that the child shall develop an imitative set to reproduce the actions whatever they may be. That this set to imitate can be developed in retarded children has been shown by Baer *et al.* (1967). At the start of their training the children never imitated an action at its first presentation, but they did so increasingly later in the programme. While imitation is being trained, reinforcement is given only if the child produces an action in response to a demonstration by the trainer: if the child produces the action spontaneously he does not receive reinforcement.

Large simple movements are often trained before finer ones, as they are easy to prompt, though whether there is any major advantage in this training sequence is open to queston. Garcia *et al.* (1971) and Bricker (1972) found that imitation of responses trained in one topographical class – either of large movements or of hand movements –

did not easily generalise to responses in the other topographical class. This finding, however, was not replicated by Kiernan & Saunders (1972), who found no evidence that particular types of training resulted in a greater tendency to imitate a similar rather than a dissimilar probe task. In view of this conflict of evidence, and of the small number of subjects involved in these studies, the question of the best sequence of motor imitation training has not yet been satisfactorily resolved.

Another important factor to be taken into account in selecting early items for training should be the relative ease or difficulty for the children themselves. Garcia and his colleagues report that object-oriented actions (ring bell) are more easily imitated than are body-oriented actions (clap hands), and this is supported by Bricker & Bricker (1970), who found that, of 20 actions imitatively learnt by severely handicapped children, the first (easiest) six items were object-oriented and the last fourteen body-oriented. Kiernan & Saunders (1972), however, found considerable variation in this difficulty among individual children; their data suggest that if a child is having great difficulty with imitation of one type of action it may be helpful to switch to another.

Where large movements are selected for initial training, for example of the arms, it is simpler to train movements of both arms rather than one-arm movements as this avoids the question of laterality or mirroring as the basis of the imitation. This question may have to be faced when finer, single-handed movements are trained, but the difficulties it involves will be more easily overcome when the child has developed some degree of imitativeness.

Training should continue on the one action until the child can produce it in response to only the verbal command and the modelled gesture, physical prompts having been gradually faded until they disappear. How often the child shall be required to respond appropriately before a second gesture is introduced is a decision for the trainer: the criterion set by Paloutzian *et al.* (1971) was 90 per cent accuracy over two sessions of 25 trials each. This seems heroic, and retarded children can become bored with lack of variety. Kiernan & Saunders (1972) were unable to reach a 90 per cent criterion with any but one of their subjects, and finally accepted 65-70 per cent accuracy.

Once the child has reached criterion on the first movement, a second may be introduced and trained to the same criterion level. After this, the two movements may be mixed and given in random order, after which a third movement may be introduced, and so on. When several (8 to 10) large movements have been trained, smaller hand movements may be introduced, leading on to finger movements and then to movements of the hand, face and mouth. It is likely that as the child's repertoire of imitated responses increases he will need less physical prompting, while at the same time the proportion of responses given at the first demonstration of the action is likely to increase. For these reasons it should be easier to teach verbal imitation once motor imitation is firmly established; but there is as yet no research to show whether this approach is either quicker or more effective in training verbal imitation than an approach which focuses on verbal imitation from the start (Yule *et al.*, 1974).

## REINFORCEMENT IN IMITATION TRAINING

It has been suggested that the *model* should be reinforced for producing the appropriate response, both so as to facilitate the learning of complete chains of behaviour (Bandura, 1969, p.145) and to indicate to the subject that reinforcement occurs. In this case it may be necessary to have a third person (besides the trainer and subject) as the model, and for the reinforcement to be something highly valued by the subject. Another technique used by Paloutzian *et al.* (1971) to demonstrate the availability of reinforcement was to give non-contingent reinforcement in the first session. It seems likely, however, that reinforcing the subject in the actions he is prompted (and not allowed to fail) to do, would be equally effective.

Once the child has learnt some imitative responses, reinforcement is not necessary for all subsequent responses. Baer *et al.* (1967) found that so long as some responses were reinforced, others, which were never reinforced, would be reliably produced. Obviously the subject would have to reach this level of responsiveness before he would imitate a new action on its first presentation. It seems likely that in some subjects some other factor than the presented reinforcer may become effective in maintaining the imitative behaviour; one of the subjects in the study by Baer *et al.* continued to respond when the reinforcer was delayed for up to 60 seconds after the subject's response, and only extinguished when the response was prevented. One might hypothesise that the subject 'enjoyed' the imitation activity, and indeed subjectively this often seems the case.

## CHARACTERISTICS OF THE MODEL

A subject may be more willing to imitate the actions of one model than another. Gardner (1971) points out that behaviours modelled by a 'neutral or aversive' teacher may be less closely attended to and imitated than those modelled by a high-prestige peer. Subjects may be influenced by the competence of the model (Strichart, 1974; Strichart & Gottlieb, 1975) and by his age, sex, social and ethnic status (Bandura, 1969). Since these studies on model characteristics were done on mildly retarded and normal people it is uncertain how far the findings may be applied to the severely retarded; nevertheless the commonplace observation of the ease with which some severely retarded children 'pick up' the behaviours of other children suggests that the use of peer models might be worth trying with these subjects. Indeed, Gardner (1971) suggests that modelling of new behaviours and their reinforcement may have particular importance for the retarded since new situations and new behaviours have often resulted for them in unpleasant consequences. They may need evidence that the behaviours will result in reinforcement before they are willing to attempt them at all.

## EFFECTS OF ADULT IMITATION OF THE CHILD

Another aspect of imitation training concerns the effect of imitation by the adult of the child's response. In some cases imitation by the adult of the child's response results in a subsequent increase in the child's imitativeness of the adult's actions (Hallahan *et al.*, 1977). Here it appears that the child experiences the adult's imitation as reinforcing (Miller & Morris, 1974), while Hallahan also refers to 'the social norm of reciprocity (which) demands that the person imitate after having been imitated'. In other cases, however, imitation of the child's response by an adult results in a *decrease* in the child's imitated actions (see Case 1, in Kauffman *et al.*, 1975; Kauffman *et al.*, 1977), suggesting a possible mechanism whereby imitation could be used to reduce undesirable behaviours as well as its more conventional use in facilitating behaviours. It remains unclear what are the different factors involved which result in imitation having diametrically opposed effects on the imitated behaviour. Kauffman *et al.* (1975) suggest age and I.Q., as well as other characteristics of both imitator and subject, as possible differentiating factors; others might be the type of action imitated, the previous consequences of the action and other concomitants of the imitative process. Here is an area in which it is impossible to avoid the hackneyed conclusion that further research is needed.

Imitation, then, is a valuable means by which children may learn desirable behaviours and, perhaps, unlearn some undesirable ones. Where a child lacks all imitative skills these have usually been trained through motor imitation (as described on pp. 80 and 83). Once motor imitation has been established, imitation may be used to teach other useful skills such as self-grooming (Bry, 1969), social interaction (Paloutzian *et al.*, 1971) and speech (Baer *et al.*, 1967), while many others are obviously possible.

## GENERALISATION

When behaviour which has been reinforced in certain situations occurs also in other situations we say that generalisation has taken place. For example, a child who has learnt to drink from a cup will also drink from a glass, and another who has learnt to take off his coat at home will also take it off when he gets to school. Generalisation is a time and effort saver: through it we are able to learn from experience, finding that behaviour that is reinforced in one situation is likely to be reinforced in another, similar, situation. We learn that when we approach a front door and ring the bell the door is likely to be opened, and that this is likely to happen with all doors. Thus we are saved from having to relearn appropriate behaviour in every new situation.

Generalisation occurs readily in most spontaneously learnt behaviours of normal children. The child who will drink from one cup is willing to drink from another: the child who labels the kitchen stove 'hot' has no difficulty in applying the same label to her porridge plate. When this normal readiness to generalise breaks down, consternation ensues, as when the child will sleep only in her own cot and flatly refuses to go to sleep when away from home. Generalisation may also need to be worked for, even with normal children, where the behaviours have been artificially rather than naturally acquired (Patterson *et al.*, 1973). Where retarded children are concerned, generalisation cannot be taken for granted.

A retarded child may learn a piece of behaviour and become skilful in its performance, but the behaviour may be confined to one place, with one object and one person. For example a child with toiletting problems became reliably trained to use clinic toilets in the presence of clinic staff; he continued to refuse to use the toilet appropriately at his home in the presence of his mother. If it is necessary for a child to exhibit a skill in a setting other than that in which it was trained then this must be included as part of the programme: the trainer must be prepared to re-teach the skill in another setting or in the presence of other people, and to continue to extend this re-teaching until the behaviour is regularly exhibited in all the settings in which it is required. In the toileting example already referred to, the child's mother began by visiting the clinic and supervising his toiletting there; later, clinic staff took him to his home, where first staff and later his mother supervised his toiletting; later again, since he was also very difficult to take to unfamiliar toilets, the programme was repeated in many different places (Levick *et al.*, in preparation).

One way to minimise generalisation problems is to teach the activity in as natural a setting as possible. If a child needs to use a behaviour primarily at home or at school then, other things being equal, it will be best to teach him in those settings rather than in a laboratory. In this way the discriminative stimuli ($S^D$s) that control and elicit the behaviour will be those that will normally have that function. In some cases however the setting and the $S^D$s associated with the normal environment may have become cues for inappropriate behaviour. Kiernan (1974) points out that it may be necessary to remove the child from the natural setting in order to control discriminative stimuli, develop new ones which are associated with reinforcement and then gradually to generalise back to the natural environment. Once the behaviour has been learnt in more than one situation it is usual to find that generalisation to other situations occurs increasingly rapidly.

## DISCRIMINATION

Whereas when we teach generalisation we are trying to show the child that behaviour which is appropriate in one situation is equally appropriate in another, in teaching discrimination we are trying to teach him the specific conditions in which a particular behaviour is appropriate and will lead to reinforcement. A child may learn to offer a kiss to members of his family when he meets them; he may then have to learn that this behaviour is not appropriate when he meets strangers. He needs to learn the cues that indicate that a behaviour is acceptable (i.e., likely to be reinforced) and which indicate that it is not, and he must learn to discriminate between these. These cues may be subtle ones which are not easily perceived by retarded children. Wing (1975a) believes that the embarrassing behaviour of many autistic children is due to their inability to discriminate the appropriate cues for behaviour in various situations.

Discrimination may be established through differential reinforcement of responses: correct responses are reinforced, while incorrect ones fail to elicit reinforcement, or are punished. To go back to the example of the child drinking from a cup: if the child always found that cups contained pleasant fluids and glasses unpleasant ones or no fluids at all the behaviour of drinking from a glass would extinguish and the child would learn to drink only from a cup. That handicapped children may be able to make discriminations (in this case between different adults) and that this is related to the reinforcement history of the child is shown by the studies of Redd & Birnbrauer (1969) and by Kiernan & Saunders (1972). In each study, children who had been reinforced for certain behaviours (play and imitation, respectively) by certain adults performed these behaviours readily in the presence of these adults. When adults who had not reinforced these behaviours were present the children displayed very little of the behaviours until these adults too reinforced the children contingent upon the production of the behaviours, thus generating generalisation of the behaviours.

However, some retarded children may need to learn discrimination, to learn that certain responses will be reinforced in certain situations and not reinforced in others: undressing in the bedroom or bathroom at bed time is welcomed, undressing at mid-day in the supermarket is not. The child needs to learn what cues will indicate that reinforcement is or is not likely to follow his action: a discriminative stimulus ($S^D$) signals that reinforcement is likely, whereas an $S^\Delta$ does not have this function. $S^D$s may consist of a variety of stimuli – people, places, events, words. A headmaster may be an $S^D$ to children to behave themselves; an open field an $S^D$ for them to run about and kick footballs; the words, 'Lunch is ready', an $S^D$ for them to come to the table. Similarly $S^\Delta$s for these behaviours might be a permissive teacher, a highly cultivated garden, and the words, 'Lunch isn't ready'. The child must learn to discriminate between these $S^D$s and $S^\Delta$s, and, especially for the retarded child, the fineness of the discrimination required of him may be too difficult for him and lead him into errors. Gardner (1971) puts forward the idea that the retarded child receives, through his failure to respond discriminatingly, unpredictable positive and negative consequences and so goes on to produce a variety of 'neurotic' behaviours. It is necessary then to teach the child to discriminate between the $S^D$s and the $S^\Delta$s in his environment, essentially by increasing the distinctiveness of the stimuli. Multidimensional cues are attended to better than unidimensional ones, so that a cue that employs size and shape is learnt better than one that employs shape alone (Gardner, 1971; Baumeister, 1967), and depth, pattern and colour are other cues that may be used. Although the principle of the greater efficacy of multidimensional cues is almost axiomatic, it should be applied with some caution in view of the finding that extra cues could be confusing rather than helpful (Schreibman, 1975; see Chapter 5). How far these findings are applicable specifically to autistic and not to other groups of retarded children is unknown. The cues that the child is expected to use should also be clearly distinguishable from other stimuli occurring in his environment: so, for example, when a child is being taught to discriminate certain words, these should be spoken especially clearly.

Verbal learning can provide an example of the ways in which discrimination may also be learnt. Suppose the child is to learn the words 'car' and 'doll'. These two objects might well be selected for early verbal training since they are clearly distinguishable both visually and auditorily: it would be inadvisable to start with objects with rather similar names, such as 'ball' and 'doll'. The child is seated at a table and a doll put in front of him. The trainer says, 'Give me the *doll.*' If the child does not respond the trainer puts the doll into the child's hand and guides it towards him (the trainer). The trainer takes the doll and reinforces the child. This continues until the child will give the doll to the trainer without prompting. Next the process is repeated using the car and the instruction, 'Give me the *car.*' At this point, although the child is obeying the instruction, there is no evidence that it means anything more to him than, 'Give me the object on the table.' He must now learn to discriminate between *car* and *doll*. Now the trainer puts both objects on the table and asks for (say) the doll. If the child does not at once respond, the trainer guides his hand to the doll and when the child gives it to him reinforces him. The trainer uses the least amount of prompting that is effective, and later this will be reduced to a gesture and later still perhaps to a glance. The trainer should, however, be fully aware of the potency of the latter and be careful not to credit the child with knowing the word until he is able to select the object in response to the word only, and without a vestige of eye-pointing from the trainer (or anyone else).

The trainer may now continue to ask for the doll, always varying its position on the table and relative to the car: otherwise the child might begin to rely, not on the word as related to the *doll* but on such $S^D$s as 'object on the left' or 'object farthest from me'. When the child reliably responds to this request the trainer may go on to ask for the car, and then to mix the requests in a random order. When the child is consistently successful at this task it is possible to say that he is able in this situation to discriminate between car and doll. The trainer may wish to move on to other words – for instance, bringing in a new object such as a book to pair with either the doll or the car and finally mixing all three; or he may wish to teach finer discriminations such as between the *red* car and the *blue* car; or he may wish to teach generalisation of the words already learnt, so that the child learns that the words car and doll do not refer only to *that* car and *that* doll but to a whole range of similar objects. The opportunities for further learning along these lines are, almost literally, endless.

## CONCLUSIONS

The capacity to imitate provides a short cut to learning, especially of complex skills and those which, like speech, are difficult to prompt. Those children who do not spontaneously imitate may well benefit from being specifically taught to do so – one perhaps unexpected bonus is that some retarded children appear to get pleasure out of the imitative skill itself, quite apart from any other benefits that may accrue to them from it. The first steps in teaching a child to imitate are usually slow and laborious but, as he acquires a number of actions that he is able to copy, so his ability to imitate increases and new actions are learnt more quickly.

Generalisation is a process not related to imitation but is of crucial importance. The skills which the child learns will be of no benefit to him unless he is able to make use of them in a wide variety of situations. There must be many retarded people who have once learnt, and then lost, important skills because nobody thought of ensuring that they would be maintained outside the laboratory. The importance of programming generalisation is now clearly recognised (Patterson & Brodsky, 1966), and that generalisation involves programming reinforcement for appropriate behaviours in new environments. In teaching discrimination, as in teaching generalisation, reinforcement has an important part to play, as have prompting and fading. Here, as in other areas of work with behaviour modification methods, the different aspects of it are inseparable from and interdependent on each other.

# 7 DECREASING UNDESIRABLE BEHAVIOURS

Glynis Murphy

## INTRODUCTION

People in contact with handicapped children, whether they be parents, teachers, nurses or others, are usually aware that, although lacking numerous desirable skills (which is certainly an important feature of the retardate's repertoire of behaviour; see Bijou, 1963), many handicapped individuals do manage to learn undesirable behaviours. Frequently these 'undesirable' behaviours appear to demonstrate the existence of a malicious, plotting, internal being who shows a tremendous facility for devising irritating or objectionable schemes and a remarkably reduced facility for developing new and useful skills. There is, however, mounting evidence that these undesirable behaviours can be brought under control using behaviour modification techniques; conversely, this suggests that many of these behaviours *may* have resulted from unfortunate environmental contingencies which have combined to 'teach' the individual the inappropriate behaviours.

So far, previous chapters concerned with training have concentrated on methods for increasing behaviours (i.e., on acceleration targets). This chapter is devoted to the methods available for decreasing undesirable behaviours, i.e., it concerns itself with deceleration targets, or behaviours to be reduced in frequency. Such behaviours include: tantrums (of excessive frequency and/or duration), self-injury, stereotypies, aggression, meal-time misbehaviours, toileting misbehaviours (urinating on the carpet, smearing faeces and so on). Many of these behaviours are not incorrect or undesirable *per se* but may merely be undesirable in a particular context or if occurring with undesirable frequency. For instance, banging a drum-stick on a drum is generally not considered to be inappropriate, but banging a spoon on the table at meal-times is. Similarly, many 3-year-olds have tantrums, but few have as many as 10 a day or for as long as an hour. Thus, in the case of tantrums, the decision as to the level from which a behaviour should be reduced is influenced not only by the context of tantrums, but also by the frequency and duration of the tantrums in relation to the child's developmental level. Decisions about whether a particular child's behaviour is undesirable and in need of treatment can, therefore, be somewhat arbitrary. Clearly, care must be taken not to expect too much of an individual (no one would expect a 2-year-old to sit down quietly with a book for half an hour) nor, of course, too little (even profoundly handicapped individuals can be taught not to indulge in undesirable behaviour).

Deceleration targets may sometimes need to take priority over acceleration targets. Specifically, if a child's undesirable behaviours interfere with his learning of appropriate behaviours, the deceleration targets may need to be tackled first. Such interference may take various forms: for instance, a child's stereotypies may occur at such a high rate as to interfere with play skills (Koegel *et al*., 1974) or a child's tantrums whenever he is placed on the potty may prevent him from being taught to use the potty. On occasions, an individual's undesirable behaviours may make him so objectionable, particularly if the behaviours tend to occur when staff or parents or peers approach, that others may avoid him (such a person could be said to have others on an avoidance schedule). An example of this would be the child who kicks out at or pulls the hair of any approaching person. In this kind of case undesirable behaviours need to be tackled urgently in order to allow adults to approach and teach new skills and children to approach and interact socially, without receiving aversive consequences for their behaviour.

The techniques which have been found to be useful in decreasing undesirable behaviours can be classified as follows:

(A) restructuring the environment;
(B) extinction;
(C) punishment (of various types, such as time-out, response cost, restitution);
(D) reinforcement of other behaviours (DRO schedules) and reinforcement of low rates of undesirable behaviour (DRL schedules).

Generally, these techniques are used in combinations, for instance: restructuring the environment and DRO schedules; extinction and DRO schedules; punishment and DRO schedules. There can of course be no hard and fast rules determining which specific technique to use for which inappropriate behaviour. A thorough functional analysis of the individual case is the only way to decide upon an appropriate technique for teaching a handicapped child either to do something more or to do something less. A 'cook-book' approach of selecting a particular technique, such as restitution, for a particular misbehaviour, such as throwing furniture, is liable to produce poor results. By chance, the technique may be appropriate, but effective treatment is more reliably produced by a treatment programme designed for an individual person using the facts gained from observation of the person's behaviour, its antecedents and its consequences. An event may be punishing for one child and not for another, just as other events may be reinforcing for one child and not for another. Thus it is not possible to designate certain techniques (like restraint, restitution, isolation) as appropriate for certain undesirable behaviours; it is only possible to suggest general procedures (such as non-presentation of reinforcers, time-out from positive reinforcement, contingent punishment) which may be effective once the reinforcers and punishments for the individual have been identified.

## A. RESTRUCTURING THE SITUATION

The operant view of behaviour is that not only is the future probability of a behaviour a function of its present and previous consequences, but also its occurrence is in part a function of its present and past antecedents. This is the concept of stimulus control (see Terrace, 1966) and it can provide a powerful treatment tool in the decreasing of undesirable behaviours. Thus if, during the preliminary functional analysis, it becomes clear that the undesirable (target) behaviour occurs only in one situation and not in others, then one possible method for reducing the frequency of the target behaviour is to prevent the presentation of the discriminative stimuli which precede the inappropriate behaviour. For instance, suppose a child is exceptionally distractible in a classroom situation, in that he frequently turns round and interacts with adults or peers, spending little time 'on task'. Suppose also that he turns round far less if his view of the classroom is blocked, and then spends more time 'on task'. One way of reducing his off-task behaviour might be to place a screen around him, to block off his view of the room. Clearly, as a long-term solution here this technique would be inadequate, and so in practice other methods may need to be combined with the restructuring of a situation. In other cases (e.g., Sajwaj and Hedges, 1973) it may be sufficient merely to omit the discriminative stimuli altogether.

A 9-year-old child, verbal mental age approximately 4 years, presented a distinct behaviour problem at meal-times, when not at home. In the hospital situation he would throw his plate onto the floor (and eat off the floor if allowed to do so), steal food from other children, throw food, spit food and so on. If prompted to eat appropriately (by physical prompts) he would struggle, stiffen his arms, sweep food onto the table with his spoon, spit food out, and turn his head away. When eating meals at home he ate like a normal boy.

The possibility was, therefore, that appropriate eating behaviour had come under the stimulus control of his parents sitting down at the table in his home dining room, while inappropriate eating behaviour had come under the control of the hospital unit stimuli and procedures. Experimentation revealed that the essential aspects of the stimuli controlling appropriate eating behaviour were not his parents *per se*, nor his home dining room *per se*, but the presence of adults sitting down at the table with him. Once this procedure was used in the unit the boy ate as well as at home, this effect being immediate and not a function of further training in the unit.

Typically, stimulus control is exerted as a function of differential reinforcement of behaviour in the presence of different stimuli. If stimulus control is not complete (i.e., if generalisation occurs to other stimuli) then, even after the removal of a particular discriminative stimulus for an undesirable behaviour, it is likely that the behaviour will at some time occur in the new situation. If the deceleration target behaviour elicits reinforcement in this new situation then, effectively, the subject is being *taught* to generalise, and the undesirable behaviour can become an equal problem in the new situation. Consequently it is essential to combine a programme involving the removal of discriminative stimuli with one or both of the following:

(a) non-presentation of reinforcement if the undesirable behaviour appears in the new situation;
(b) reinforcement of appropriate behaviours in the new situation.

In the example given above, neither of these two procedures was included on the programme and, predictably, the child gradually learnt to behave in the previously undesirable ways even when adults also sat down at the table with him in the unit. Unfortunately, this inappropriate meal-time behaviour did generalise to some extent to the home situation, as might be expected.

The method of restructuring the situation can be an extremely effective and rapid way of eradicating or reducing an undesirable behaviour or at the very least, with extremely frequent target behaviours, it can reduce the undesirable behaviour sufficiently to allow the occurrence of some appropriate behaviours which may then be reinforced in preference to the inappropriate ones. It will not always be possible to discover a situation in which the undesirable behaviour does not occur and in such cases it will be necessary to turn to alternative methods (see below). Occasionally, however, it may be felt that the new situation, while preventing the undesirable target behaviour from occurring, is not in itself desirable. For instance, to use an earlier example, if a child is sat behind a screen to reduce off-task classroom behaviour it will at some stage be necessary to remove the screen and integrate him back into his peer group. The success of reintegration will depend in part on the adequate reinforcement of the 'new' appropriate behaviour and the non-presentation of reinforcement of the undesirable behaviour when it occurs again. The preferable method to use for such a return to the original situation is probably a gradual fading from the new situation back to the old one, with the aim of gradually establishing stimuli from the old situation as $S^D$s for appropriate behaviours, by contingent reinforcement.

## B. EXTINCTION

An essential feature in any technique for teaching a new skill is contingent reinforcement of the target behaviour. Conversely, it is possible to reduce the frequency of a behaviour by not presenting contingent reinforcement. This process is termed extinction, and may be used in the reduction of undesirable behaviours.

Evidence from the animal literature (see for example, Ferster & Skinner, 1959; Morse, 1966) gives two important characteristics of extinction: first, once extinction is begun, a temporary rise in the frequency of the target behaviour occurs before it drops off and, second, the rate at which the behaviour reduces in frequency is, in part, a function of the previous reinforcement schedule (intermittent schedules providing some 'protection' from extinction). It seems likely that these two characteristics also hold true for extinction in humans at least on some occasions (head-banging in Figure 1b, self-biting in Figures 1a and 2a in Duker, 1975; jabbing in Jones *et al.*, 1974; self-injurious behaviour, Figure 6, in Romanczyk and Goren, 1975). These two characteristics may explain the rare use of extinction by untrained staff and parents: for instance, if a child's misbehaviours are reinforced occasionally by the attention he receives, then although staff or parents may try ignoring the behaviour they will be discouraged firstly by the rise in the rate of the behaviour when they start ignoring it, and second (if they continue) by its slow rate of fall afterwards due to the previous intermittent schedule of reinforcement.

Extinction was used for two severely retarded boys, one aged 4 and one aged 8, the latter presenting a problem because of persistent tantrums (consisting largely of loud screaming) and the former showing 'naughtiness' of various kinds. The older boy's tantrums usually occurred when he was being asked to do something he disliked (for example, to do a jig-saw or look at a book) and generally resulted in his teacher abandoning the task with him. The tentative functional analysis suggested that the boy's tantrums were being reinforced by being allowed to escape from tasks he disliked, contingent on screaming. The extinction programme entailed non-presentation of the reinforcement contingent on screaming, i.e., continuation of the task despite the tantrum. The reduction in the number of tantrums that followed was evidence of a correct functional analysis, and a favourable outcome ensued.

The 4-year-old boy's 'naughtiness' was mainly displayed when his mother's attention was directed towards others, particularly when visitors came to the house. At such times he would turn on the television or radio to full volume, swing on the curtains, hit the dog, go into the kitchen and pull things off the table. His mother's response was, of course, to interrupt her conversation at very frequent intervals to tell her son to turn the volume down or not to swing on the curtains. His undesirable behaviour seemed to be reinforced by contingent attention. During the extinction programme his mother ignored the 'naughty' behaviour and, although the undesirable behaviour increased at first, it soon reduced to mere verbal interruptions, which were felt to be acceptable for a 4-year-old.

Extinction may not always be an appropriate way of reducing undesirable behaviour, for the following reasons:

(1) It may be impossible to prevent the contingent presentation of the reinforcer. For example, when a child's aggressive behaviour to his peers is reinforced by their cries and screams, or where a child's continual masturbation is reinforced by the contingent sensory stimulation, non-presentation of reinforcers is difficult. Such cases usually involve peer reinforcement that cannot be controlled, or sensory reinforcement. An extinction programme then cannot be set up, and other methods (restructuring the environment, punishment,

reinforcement of other behaviour) will need to be used.

(2) It may be undesirable to withhold the contingent reinforcer for practical reasons. This generally becomes a problem only when the reinforcer in question is adult attention and the target behaviour is part of a chain of behaviour normally interrupted by the adult. For instance, if the undesirable behaviour is stuffing towels and toilet rolls down the toilet until the toilet becomes blocked and/or overflows and the reinforcer is the adult attention involved in intervening before disaster ensues, then an extinction schedule requiring non-intervention would be rather impractical, as the damage done would be temporarily irreversible. Again, restructuring the environment, punishment and/or reinforcement of other behaviour will be necessary.

(3) The expected increase in the rate of the undesirable behaviour at the beginning of extinction may make an extinction programme inappropriate or dangerous. For example, if the undesirable behaviour in question is self-injury or injury to others, the introduction of an extinction programme may result in added physical harm to individual(s). It is true that many extinction programmes have not resulted in a temporary increase in responding at the beginning of extinction (e.g., crying in Figure 2b in Duker, 1975; speech initiation of teachers and peers in Figure 2 of Sajwaj *et al.*, 1972; finger-feeding in Figure 1 of O'Brien *et al.*, 1972) and this phenomenon may be a result of the particular reinforcement schedule preceding extinction, as the schedule is known to affect response rates during extinction in animals (see Blackman, 1974). An absence of response rate increase cannot be relied on, however, unless the previous reinforcement schedule is certain; in clinical situations this is almost never possible, so that extinction is better not used for severely injurious behaviour.

(4) Extinction may be considered inappropriate where a quick result is required, particularly if there is evidence that the behaviour has been only intermittently reinforced. This situation may occur if an undesirable behaviour is particularly upsetting to parents, teachers or care agents, or if only a limited time is available for a treatment programme. Although it is 'hazardous to compare general procedures with each other', Holz & Azrin found that with lower animals punishment was a quicker method for reducing response rate than was extinction, after a continuous schedule of reinforcement (Holz *et al.*, 1963; Azrin & Holz, 1966). Similar studies do not seem to be available in the literature dealing with the treatment of undesirable behaviours in the retarded, but the same may be true. If, however, it is fairly certain that the target behaviour has been reinforced in the past on an

intermittent schedule and extinction still seems to be the method of choice for reducing the behaviour, it may be possible to speed up the extinction process by altering the reinforcement schedule to a continuous one before beginning extinction. It would presumably be difficult to convince untrained staff of the logic of this kind of strategy, but there is one report (unfortunately not a controlled trial) of the use of this procedure in the literature (Galvin & Moyer, 1975). The crying of the young child (of one of the authors) was reduced by first moving to a continuous reinforcement schedule for the crying and then to an extinction schedule.

(5) In some situations, although it may seem to be appropriate at first sight to use extinction to reduce undesirable behaviours, practical problems may arise which would make the use of this technique unwise. Gilbert (1975) has discussed the difficulty of employing extinction procedures effectively in institutions when the reinforcer in question is some facet of adult attention. He points out that unless the programme planners can control the behaviour of all staff (including domestics, porters, voluntary workers, visitors and others not normally included in treatment action) in response to the undesirable behaviour to be reduced, then this target behaviour may be reinforced, unwittingly, on a sparser schedule than in the past, may not be extinguished and may indeed be strengthened. Frankel (1976) has commented that, although this is a danger, the effects of intermittent reinforcement need not necessarily be disastrous as either the schedule could be stretched so much (if the majority of adults respond correctly) that the target behaviour does extinguish, or the child may learn to discriminate between 'reinforcing adults' and 'extinguishing adults', producing the undesirable behaviour only for the former. Unfortunately, it would be impossible to guarantee in advance that either of these conditions would hold, whereas it would be almost inevitable that someone not involved in the treatment programme would reinforce the target behaviour at some time. As Frankel (1976) says, it is probably unnecessary to recommend the abandonment of extinction procedures for attention-maintained behaviours in institutions; it is, however, important to be aware of the dangers and hence to maximise the chance of a successful programme.

A second, rather similar, problem which may arise but which has not as yet been documented is that of escalation of the intensity of the target behaviour. Again the difficulties apply mainly to attention-maintained behaviours on extinction programmes, but the possible consequences are probably more dangerous than those discussed by

Gilbert. Within a particular class of undesirable behaviours, such as biting others, there is a variation in the intensity of the behaviour (even within subjects), i.e., a child who bites others does not bite with exactly the same intensity or power every time. It is possible when an extinction programme is operating that adults will correctly ignore the majority of bites but will react in some way (a grimace, a cry, an orienting response even) to particularly hard bites. If their reaction is reinforcing to the child, the result will be that the average intensity of the undesirable behaviour will increase, as a result of differential reinforcement of 'high intensity' responses. Similarly, if the child happens to bite, by chance, in a particularly painful place on one occasion and the recipient reacts, instead of ignoring, then differential reinforcement of biting in painful places will result in the child's learning only to bite there (where he gets a reaction) and not to bite elsewhere (as he gets no reaction). An identical argument holds for many other undesirable behaviours which may be attention-maintained, such as hair-pulling, kicking, spitting, head-butting, pinching, self-injury and so on, all of which can vary in intensity. Again, it follows not that extinction should be abandoned for attention-maintained behaviours, but that a wary eye should be kept on the possible dangers and whenever feasible it should be checked that the extinction schedule can be stuck to even in the face of high intensity behaviours before beginning the programme.

Despite the practical problems which have been discussed above, extinction is often the method of choice for reducing undesirable behaviours. If the technique of restructuring the environment cannot be used (and this is often the case) then extinction, if it seems likely to be successful, is probably preferable to punishment because of the ethical and practical difficulties involved in the use of punishment (see p.110). It is normal to combine the positive reinforcement of appropriate behaviours with the non-presentation of reinforcement of undesirable behaviours (extinction) in clinical programmes and certainly if the target behaviour is still being reinforced in some way, then a programme involving merely the reinforcement of other behaviours is unlikely to be effective. Unfortunately, there appear to be few experimental tests of the importance of this combined approach in the literature. The principle can, however, be seen particularly clearly in a study designed to reduce finger-feeding in a child unable to spoon-feed (O'Brien *et al.*, 1972), where it was found that, in order to reduce the child's finger-feeding, it was necessary to employ not only extinction (involving prevention of edible reinforcement after finger-feeding) but also positive reinforcement of self-feeding skills.

## C. PUNISHMENT

The Oxford English Dictionary defines punishment as follows: 'the infliction of penalty, the subjection (of offender) to retributive or disciplinary suffering, to handle severely'. Thus the ordinary English use of the word seems to refer to the *procedure*, whereby the recipient is made to suffer.

The use of the word 'punishment' in operant theory was, for many years, parallel to this English usage but, more recently, it has been redefined as follows: 'a consequence of behaviour that reduces the future probability of that behaviour' (Azrin & Holz, 1966), and this new definition seems to be being accepted (Johnston, 1972; Kazdin, 1975). The present meaning, in operant theory and in the clinical field of behaviour modification, is thus in terms of an *effect on behaviour*, and not a procedure. The definition is indeed precisely opposite to the definition of reinforcement.

The colloquial use of the word punishment, with all its connotations, has resulted in a reluctance to use the term, with its new meaning, in the clinical field and thus some will refer instead to 'negative reinforcement'. This is of course, an incorrect use of the term (see Chapter 3). Here the word punishment will be used throughout to mean a consequence of behaviour that reduces the future probability of that behaviour.

A thorough functional analysis is invariably required to define a punishing stimulus for a particular child in a particular situation, and the only genuine evidence of its effectiveness will come from the results obtained from its use. Nevertheless, there are several common types of stimuli which are often effective:

(1) time-out;
(2) response cost;
(3) overcorrection;
(4) restraint;
(5) electric shock.

### 1. TIME-OUT

'Time-out' is short for 'time-out from positive reinforcement'. The procedure is as follows: contingent on the undesirable behaviour, positive reinforcement becomes unavailable for a short period of time. In the animal literature the procedure has been used in teaching matching-to-sample, time-out (unavailability of the edible reinforcer and switching off the house lights) being contingent on errors. In clinical work, time-out is used in various ways, most commonly when the reinforcer concerned is praise or social attention and time-out involves a short period of isolation (e.g., Wolf *et al.*, 1964; Burchard & Barrera, 1972; Clark *et al.*, 1973). It has also been used to correct inappropriate meal-time behaviour, time-out involving either removal of the meal from the child for a short time or removal of the child from the meal (e.g., Whitney & Barnard, 1966; Barton *et al.*, 1970), and it could be used, in principle, in any situation involving presentation of positive reinforcement, where undesirable behaviours are occurring (see, for example, Myers & Deibert, 1971; Lucero *et al.*, 1976).

A number of controlled studies in the clinical literature have been concerned with the characteristics of time-out (Zimmerman & Baydan, 1963; White *et al.*, 1972; Alevizos & Alevizos, 1975; Hobbs & Forehand, 1975; Clark *et al.*, 1973; Willoughby, 1969) and some of these studies are reviewed in MacDonough & Forehand (1973) and Hobbs & Forehand (1977). Varying the duration of time-out has shown that time-out from social events becomes more effective as the period of time-out is increased towards several minutes (Zimmerman & Baydan, 1963; Hobbs & Forehand, 1977). Time-out periods over several minutes were found not to produce an increased effectiveness, however (White *et al.*, 1972), and evidence from the animal literature suggests that excessively long periods of time-out result in a suppression of appropriate behaviours (Zimmerman & Ferster, 1963). It has also been shown in one study (White *et al.*, 1972) that if the duration of time-out is altered for particular individuals, order effects occur: specifically, if short (1-minute) time-out is used first and is then increased to 15 and 30 minutes, the rate of undesirable behaviour drops progressively. If, on the other hand, the long durations are given first and then changed to shorter durations there is an *increase* in the rate of undesirable behaviour. Thus, if unsure what period of time-out to employ, it seems advisable to begin with short periods and then, if necessary, to increase the duration, rather than the reverse. Similar findings have been obtained by Burchard & Barrera (1972) and Kendall *et al.* (1975).

Much as target behaviours increase most quickly when started on a continuous positive reinforcement schedule, it has been shown that undesirable behaviours decrease most quickly on a continuous schedule of time-out (Clark *et al.*, 1973). However, low ratio schedules of time-out such as VR2, VR3 and FR2 seem to be almost as effective as continuous schedules (Calhoun & Matherne, 1975; Clark *et al.*, 1973). High ratio schedules (such as VR8) are almost useless when used for high frequency behaviours which have not been subjected to previous low ratio schedules of time-out. It appears, though, that if a behaviour is first reduced on a low ratio schedule of time-out, the high ratio schedules can then be quite effective (Hobbs & Forehand, 1977).

Release from time-out could be considered to be a negative reinforcer of behaviour preceding the release, and consequently it is usual in the clinical situation to make the ending of time-out contingent on at least a very short period of good behaviour. There is evidence with normal pre-school children that this contingency results in lower rates of disruptive behaviour during the time-out period, as would be expected, and that it produces an increased efficacy of the time-out in reducing undesirable behaviours outside the time-out period (Hobbs & Forehand, 1975).

Finally, just as positive reinforcement of alternative behaviours is used in extinction programmes, the use of time-out to reduce undesirable behaviours is usually combined with reinforcement of other behaviours. There is some clinical evidence to support this. Willoughby (1969) showed that a partially effective time-out programme became fully effective only when combined with positive reinforcement of other behaviours. He concluded that 'if the punished response provides the only available means of reinforcement, it is unlikely that time-out will have lasting suppressive effects on the occurrence of the undesired behaviour'.

In one case, a 10-year-old retarded boy was screaming in the classroom at a baseline rate of about 29 times a day. The intensity of the screams had brought complaints from the residential area across the street and from other class teachers in the school, and of course the noise was disrupting the child's own class. A brief functional analysis suggested that the boy's screaming occurred when the teachers were not attending to him, and that it was reinforced by their consequent efforts to quieten him down (including allowing him to play on his favourite rocking horse). During the treatment programme, a five-minute period of isolation in an adjacent small room (time-out) was made contingent on even the smallest scream, while quiet working alone was reinforced approximately every 10 minutes with a teacher's praise and attention, and a short ride on the rocking horse. The results are shown in Figure 7.1. At 15-month follow-up the boy's behaviour remained excellent, with no screaming at all on most days and no more than one scream on the remaining days.

Before leaving time-out, it is important to note that when time-out involves exclusion from a situation, as it commonly does, care must be taken to ascertain that the child is already receiving positive reinforcement of some kind in the situation from which he is to be excluded. This is of course clear from the name for this technique (time-out *from positive reinforcement*) but seems to be frequently forgotten. Time-out from an aversive situation would in fact be negatively reinforcing and result in an increase in the undesirable behaviour. Two examples follow of clinical situations where this occurred. Further examples are provided by Vukelich & Hake (1971) and Solnick *et al.* (1977).

A 10-year-old deaf boy with a normal non-verbal IQ, but total absence of language, began to throw his food and hit his peers during meal-times. A brief time-out from the meal (exclusion from the dining room) contingent on such behaviour resulted in a reduction in this behaviour within a short period. However, the use of an identical procedure in a large-group situation resulted in an increase in his aggression. For this boy the large-group situation was in itself aversive and escape from it (brief isolation) was reinforcing. He did, however, love his food, so that brief exclusion from a meal-time was indeed punishing. This illustrates the dangers of a 'cook-book' approach: the use of a specific procedure (isolation) was effective in reducing one behaviour but ineffective in reducing another, for reasons that are clear on close examination of the two situations in which the behaviours took place.

A 7-year-old boy, on the borderline ESN(S)-ESN(M) range in IQ, with language at about a 3-year level, frequently threw his full plate at the beginning of lunch, and sometimes this was preceded by throwing other objects on the table (salt and pepper, vases of flowers). His behaviour at other meal-times was somewhat better, but still occasionally resulted in throwing. Exclusion of the child from the meal contingent on throwing, i.e., brief 'time-out', resulted in an increase in the undesirable behaviour, suggesting that he found meal-times so aversive that escape from them was reinforcing. The institution of a programme of positive reinforcement of appropriate behaviour plus time-out for throwing did result in elimination of the undesirable behaviour (see Figure 7.2). The programme involved the division of the boy's lunch into small portions with massive social reinforcement (plus stars) for appropriate behaviour which, to begin with, had to be

Figure 7.1: The Effect of Time-out on a Boy's Screaming in the Classroom

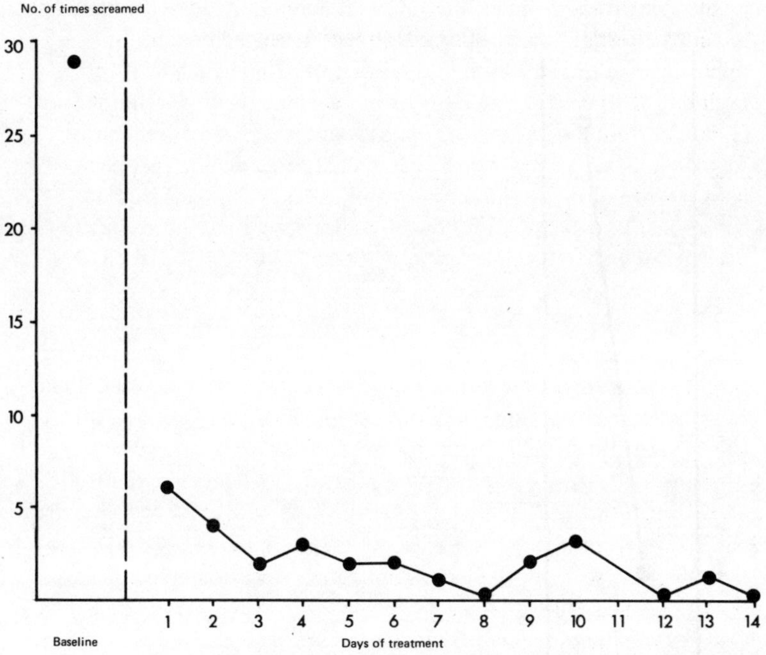


partially prompted. Gradually the prompting was faded and the size of portions increased as the boy learnt to eat his meal instead of throwing it. On the occasions on which he did throw, time-out was used and did seem, from his response to it, to be aversive, presumably because the meal-time was now positively reinforcing.

2. RESPONSE COST

Numerous reports of the use of token programmes, of various kinds, in the training of the mentally handicapped have appeared in recent literature (e.g., Lent *et al.*, 1970; Kaufman and O'Leary, 1972; Iwata and Bailey, 1974; Birnbrauer *et al.*, 1965). One way of dealing with undesirable behaviours which occur when individuals are on token programmes (points, stars, plastic discs) is to deduct a number of tokens, contingent on the undesirable behaviour. This procedure has been used

Figure 7.2: The Increase in Meal-time Misbehaviour Produced by Supposed 'Time-out' and the Effect of Introducing Positive Reinforcement Procedures during the Meal-time

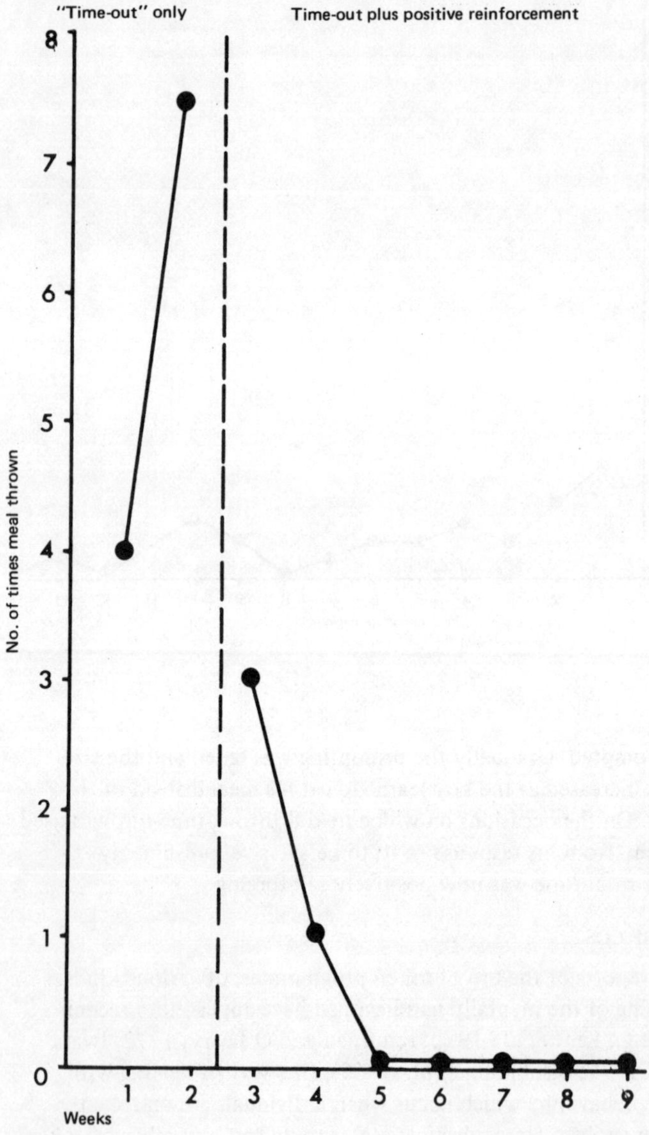

as a punishment contingency for swearing, property damage, aggression (Burchard & Barrera, 1972); being late for class or off-task (Kaufman & O'Leary, 1972; Iwata & Bailey, 1974); speech dysfluencies (Siegal *et al.*, 1969); and so on.

Many studies of response cost have not been concerned with retarded individuals and it is not known whether the characteristics of response cost differ in this population from the retarded population. Burchard & Barrera (1972) investigated the effects of amount costed in retarded adolescents already on a token system. They concluded that response cost was effective only if the individual had few tokens and/or little opportunity to earn more.

### 3. OVERCORRECTION

Overcorrection is a recently developed procedure which seems, judging by the published literature, to be gaining in popularity. The majority of studies involving the use of this technique have been carried out by Azrin, Foxx and their colleagues, mostly with severely retarded, institutionalised adults and children (Azrin & Foxx, 1971; Foxx & Azrin, 1972; Azrin *et al.*, 1973; Foxx & Azrin, 1973a; Azrin & Wesolowski, 1974; Azrin *et al.*, 1975; Foxx & Martin, 1975; Foxx, 1976) but occasionally with clients of normal intelligence (Foxx & Azrin, 1973b). The target behaviours tackled have included disruptive and aggressive behaviours, stereotyped and self-stimulatory behaviours, theft, coprophagy and pica, stripping, toiletting 'accidents'. In all the published reports the procedure has been astonishingly successful, with rates of undesirable behaviour plummeting down within a day (Foxx & Azrin, 1973a; Azrin, Sneed & Foxx, 1973; Azrin, Kaplan & Foxx, 1975; Foxx & Martin, 1975) or, at the most, a week (Foxx & Azrin, 1972; Azrin & Wesolowski, 1974) in the majority of reports.

The procedure of overcorrection is now seen by Azrin to involve two separate procedures : restitution and positive practice. For most target behaviours both procedures may be used, but for some it is only possible to use the positive practice part (for self-stimulatory behaviours, for example). Restitutional overcorrection involves 'restoring the disturbed situation to a vastly improved state' and positive practice overcorrection involves 'practising appropriate modes of responding. . . in situations in which (the subject) normally misbehaves' (Foxx & Martin, 1975). To give an illustrative example, for the treatment of coprophagy (ingesting faecal matter) restitution would involve a prolonged period (about 15 minutes) of mouth, teeth and hand washing with antiseptic solutions, contingent on the coprophagy, and positive practice (usually carried out after the restitutional overcorrection) would involve prolonged (about 15 minutes) practice of more appropriate ways to deal with faeces (flushing toilets, cleaning up faeces from the floor and so on). For disruptive behaviour like throwing furniture, restitutional overcorrection would involve setting to rights all the furniture disturbed and positive practice would consist, presumably, of practice in taking proper care of all the furniture. In the case of stereotypies and self-stimulatory behaviour there may be no disturbances of the environment to set right (so that restitution is impossible) and then overcorrection will consist only of positive practice which, for behaviours like hand flapping, would take the form of hand exercises, involving hand positions incompatible with hand flapping (see Foxx & Azrin, 1973a).

The procedure of overcorrection does have a certain attraction in that it makes 'the punishment fit the crime' and, according to Azrin and his colleagues it is a re-educative procedure in a sense in which other punishment techniques are not (see Foxx & Azrin, 1972; Foxx & Martin, 1975). Although Azrin & Foxx also see overcorrection as a mild punishment technique, they claim that it is 'relatively non-aversive' (Azrin *et al*., 1975) and that it is 'favoured by hospital ward staff as a humane and meaningful type of treatment' (Azrin *et al*., 1975). The usual definition of punishment (see p.99) does indeed require that overcorrection be classified as a punishment technique but there is no concrete evidence that the technique is re-educative (except in the sense that any punishment is). A close examination of the studies of overcorrection by Azrin and his colleagues, and by other workers, reveals no formal data demonstrating that overcorrection training results in an increase in the expected positive skills and it therefore seems best to designate overcorrection as a punishment technique at present (Murphy, 1978). This conclusion is supported by Epstein *et al*. (1974), who showed that a hand overcorrection procedure was effective for both hand stereotypies and topographically dissimilar inappropriate behaviours, as would be expected of a contingent aversive procedure acting as a punishment.

There is evidence that occasionally overcorrection has no effect on the rate of a client's behaviour or even worsens the behaviour (i.e., produces an increase in rate). Two subjects in Azrin & Wesolowski's (1975) study of floor sprawling did not improve and two of the self-injurers in Azrin *et al*. (1975) became worse as did one subject in Measel & Alfieri (1978). It seems likely that when a subject's behaviours worsen with overcorrection training, the procedure is acting as a reinforcer rather than as a punishment. The procedure is therefore open to the same dangers as other punishment techniques: if the subject does not find the overcorrection period aversive then the rate of the target behaviour will not reduce. Moreover, from the ethical point of view, overcorrection may not be less worrying than other punishment techniques as, although it is said to be only mildly aversive, it is apparently speedy in its effect (which suggests that to those treated the procedure is very aversive) and also appeals to staff (who think it more humane). There are dangers in a punishment technique which appeals to staff, particularly if the staff are led to believe that the procedure is especially 're-educative', in that it may then be applied unethically, without functional analysis, data collection and other safeguards.

### 4. RESTRAINT

The use of short periods of restraint, contingent on the occurrence of undesirable behaviour, has rarely been described as a punishment for such behaviours in the retarded. There is a report of its use, in slightly different form (i.e., extended periods of restraint) in reducing aggressive behaviour in a male psychiatric in-patient (Edwards, 1974). There are, however, few reports in the mental retardation literature, apart from the use of mild restraint in correcting undesirable behaviours at meal times (Henriksen & Doughty, 1967; Myers & Deibert, 1971; Lucero *et al.*, 1976), which could be construed as a form of time-out, and the use of two-minute periods of restraint to reduce undesirable off-task behaviours in a retarded boy (Salzberg & Napolitan, 1974).

Contingent restraint can, however, be very effective in reducing undesirable behaviours. The restraint itself can vary according to the individual; possibilities include a restraining chair (i.e., chair with straps), holding the child's arms down tightly to his side for a short period, holding the child's head tightly (between the trainer's palms) for a short period, keeping the child's head between his knees, etc. Some contingent restraints are at least partially equivalent to time-out from positive reinforcement, but they include a restriction of movement which can be additionally aversive.

A 9-year-old severely retarded girl was treated for her almost continuous masturbation (which her parents and teachers found offensive and which interfered with her learning of new skills) by contingent restraint. The girl was allowed to masturbate in her room but, when masturbating in public, she was told, 'No', and her arms were held tightly to her sides for about 20 seconds (a count of 20), and then released. The contingency seemed to be an effective punishment procedure, reducing her rate of masturbation to almost zero. Baseline rates were found by (10-second) interval sampling: masturbation occurred in 66 per cent of intervals when the girl was wearing a skirt and only 6 per cent of the time when wearing trousers. During the contingent restraint programme the amount of masturbation decreased markedly and, when tested 6 months later, the girl did not masturbate at all despite wearing a skirt.

Before leaving contingent restraint, a word of warning is necessary. It may not prove aversive to all patients and may actually be reinforcing to some; Lovaas and Simmons (1969), for example, found that restraint combined with talking resulted in increased self-injurious rates in their clients. Consequently, as for all punishment procedures, care is necessary before applying a technique to any undesirable behaviour.

5. ELECTRIC SHOCK

Contingent electric shock has been employed in the USA, in the past, for less than life-threatening behaviour problems (Lovaas *et al.*, 1965). Some writers now feel, however, that shock should be used as a punishment only where other training methods have failed to control an undesirable behaviour which threatens the life of the individual (Corbett, 1975). Many such behaviours can be called self-injurious behaviours, for example, severe head-banging and self-biting, while other life-threatening behaviours are not primarily self-injurious, for example, persistent vomiting or uncontrolled climbing. Several reviews of the treatment of such behaviours have appeared (Gardner, 1969; Smolev, 1972; Bachman, 1972; Corbett, 1975; Frankel & Simmons, 1976) and the following conclusions seem to be generally accepted:

(a) Contingent shock is only one of many methods of treatment for life-threatening behaviours.

(b) In some cases none of the alternative methods of treatment (all are examples of procedures discussed here under extinction or punishment and/or reinforcement of other behaviours) is effective, so that the choice will be between trying a programme which includes contingent shock (see Romanczyk & Goren, 1975, for example) and keeping the individual in semi-permanent restraint. (This kind of restraint is in no way equivalent to the kind of contingent restraint used as a punishing consequence. Restraints preventing self-injury – such as arm-splints to prevent fist-to-head banging – become, almost invariably, *reinforcing* to the self-injurer and thus placement in restraints cannot act as a punishing consequence. This reinforcing effect of restraints in self-injury is, incidentally, hard to explain in operant terms.)

(c) Several studies show that a reduction in severe self-injurious behaviour can occur with as few as 5 or 12 shocks (Bucher & Lovaas, 1968). Few find any of the harmful side effects originally predicted from a theoretical stand-point, such as an increase in other undesirable behaviours in parallel with decreased self-injury, emotional responses to or avoidance of the staff dispensing the shock, suppression of appropriate behaviours (Risley, 1968a; Bachman, 1972; Lichstein & Schreibman, 1976).

(d) All find the effects of shock to be highly discriminated and to generalise only when part of the planned programme is to teach generalisation. Several studies have found relapses to occur (Kohlenberg, 1970; Birnbrauer, 1968; Jones *et al.*, 1974; Corbett, 1975; Paton, 1976) and although some of these relapses may have been the result of omitting to reinforce alternative behaviours (Kohlenberg, 1970; Birnbrauer, 1968) not all of the cases can be dismissed in this way.

In conclusion, contingent shock should be used to reduce life-threatening behaviours only when all else has failed, only as part of an extremely well-planned programme (involving both staff-training and such essentials as generalisation training) and only in combination with a programme for reinforcing alternative behaviours. Even when all such criteria are met it is not unusual for some of the adults (nurses, teachers or anyone involved in the programme) to feel quite unable to co-operate in a programme involving this kind of punishment. In such cases, if the feeling is general it might be impossible to institute the programme; if the feeling is that of a minority, it may be advisable to allow the minority not to be involved in the handling of the individual in question, at least until the end of the contingent shock treatment (providing of course that this minority is in agreement with such a policy). However, if the parents of a child cannot agree to a contingent shock schedule then clearly the programme cannot be carried out. If, however, they agree in principle, but feel unable to take part, then the best policy may be for them to opt out of the management of their child until after the completion of the programme, if they are agreeable to this.

Many other contingent aversive stimuli than those discussed above have been tried. For example, unsweetened lemon-juice was squirted into the mouth of an infant, contingent on life-threatening rumination.

and a successful reduction in rumination resulted (Sajwaj *et al.*, 1974); teaching items of increased difficulty were introduced contingent on a 9-year-old retarded girl's tantrums during language training sessions, with a consequent decrease in tantrums (Sailor *et al.*, 1968). The type of punishment employed does of course vary with the individual, the characteristics of the problem behaviour and the stimuli he or she finds aversive; it is not possible to state in advance which kind of punishment will suit which problem behaviour.

Despite the potential effectiveness of the punishment technique, it tends not to be used frequently in clinical work because of the ethical problems involved. A recent survey in the USA (Wallace *et al.*, 1976) showed that only 50 per cent of the state-run facilities surveyed used aversive procedures involving shock, physical punishment, chemical or auditory irritants under any circumstances. There is insufficient space here for lengthy discussion of the ethical issues encountered in the use of punishment but it is perhaps worth noting that one of the major dangers may be that the use of a contingent aversive stimulus in a very well-planned, well-controlled programme, if seen to be effective by staff, may be later used in an unplanned and uncontrolled way with a child who is similar or has similar problem behaviours to the one originally treated. Staff cannot be blamed, in a sense, for this kind of generalisation, particularly given the conditions in which many of them have to work. Clearly, though, the use of punishment must be very carefully controlled so that abuse does not occur and attempts to provide such controls (over positive reinforcement programmes too) have begun in the USA (see Wexler, 1973; Peek & McAllister, 1974; May *et al.*, 1974; Gast & Nelson, 1977a).

## D. PROGRAMMES INVOLVING POSITIVE REINFORCEMENT

### 1. DIFFERENTIAL REINFORCEMENT OF OTHER BEHAVIOUR

There is considerable evidence that any programme aiming to reduce the rate of undesirable behaviours is more effective when other behaviours are concurrently reinforced. Some of this evidence comes from controlled comparisons (for instance, Willoughby, 1969) while the remainder arises more incidentally (from, for example, the difficulty of discovering any reports of the successful use of extinction or punishment *alone* in reducing undesirable behaviour).

It is possible to use reinforcement of other behaviours without additional programmes to reduce the undesirable behaviours, although clearly if the undesirable behaviours also still elicit reinforcement they will certainly not disappear entirely. Strictly speaking, DRO (differential reinforcement of other behaviours) programmes involve reinforcement of some behaviour(s) but not others, so that if, say, an attempt to reduce masturbation (thought to be maintained by the sensory reinforcement involved) consisted only of reinforcement of eye contact (perhaps as a preliminary to other skills) then the programme would not strictly speaking involve a DRO schedule (except in the sense that both eye contact and masturbation were reinforced, but other behaviours were not) and the procedure would be unlikely to reduce the level of masturbation.

It is, perhaps, partly because of this problem (of completely eliminating reinforcement of the undesirable behaviour) that the most effective programmes have involved reinforcement of behaviour *incompatible* with the deceleration target behaviour. Young & Wincze (1974) have provided an excellent illustration of this principle in their treatment of a profoundly retarded adult patient who used to self-injure, both by banging her head on the bed-rail and hitting her head with her fists. To begin with, an alternative but not incompatible behaviour (eye contact) was trained. Despite an increase in eye contact, no reduction in the self-injury occurred. Then training was given to maintain a certain posture (sitting with hands by the sides). The posture was incompatible with fist-to-head banging but not head-to-rail banging and, with training, there was an increase in the time spent sitting (with the hands by the sides), accompanied by a decrease in fist-to-head banging, but an increase in head-to-bedrail banging. (Contingent shock was then applied to head-to-bedrail banging and a reduction in this class of self-injurious behaviour occurred, which did not generalise to fist-to-head banging.) Thus reinforcement of *any* other behaviour did not affect the rate of undesirable behaviour, while reinforcement of a particular incompatible behaviour resulted in the parallel reduction of the undesirable behaviour with which it was incompatible, but no decrease (indeed an increase) in other undesirable behaviours (even though the two undesirable behaviours seemed topographically and functionally similar). It is, as yet, unclear how general the results of Young & Wincze's (1974) procedures are. It does, however, seem advisable to search for incompatible behaviours, rather than merely reinforcing any other behaviour. It is particularly interesting that Young & Wincze gained control over an undesirable behaviour usually considered somewhat intransigent, using positive reinforcement methods, as often these are thought (particularly by those with only brief training in behaviour modification) to be less powerful than, say, punishment techniques. A further example, with a larger number of subjects (18), of positive reinforcement in the control of an undesirable behaviour often treated by punishment techniques, is that of Ashkenazi (1975) who treated encopresis by positive reinforcement of incompatible behaviour (elimination on the toilet) with the helpful addition of some discriminative training of rectal pressure. The technique used was extremely successful and the improvements were well maintained at six-month follow-up.

### 2. DIFFERENTIAL REINFORCEMENT OF LOW RATE BEHAVIOUR

An alternative method of decreasing undesirable behaviours, also involving positive reinforcement procedures, is that of reinforcement of low rates of undesirable behaviour, DRL schedules (see Deitz, 1977). As yet the use of the DRL schedule has been limited to the reduction of classroom misbehaviours in educational settings (Deitz, 1977; Deitz & Repp, 1973, 1974). These studies have demonstrated that it is possible to reduce the levels of undesirable behaviour by differentially reinforcing low rates of the undesirable behaviour, but it is not yet clear whether the use of DRL schedules is in any way preferable to the other techniques which have also proved to be effective in the reduction of such behaviours. It is possible, however, that such a procedure would be useful in reducing very high rate misbehaviours (which are extremely difficult to deal with) to a level where other techniques could then take over.

## CONCLUSIONS

It may seem that a bewildering variety of possible procedures has been described, any of which could be applied to an undesirable behaviour. It would therefore be useful to compare the various techniques so as to determine whether some are consistently more effective than others. This is, unfortunately, not really possible. Frequently, the different procedures are just not applicable to the same undesirable behaviour (as, for example, in the case of a self-injurious behaviour where the reinforcer is attention: extinction is dangerous, time-out in isolation may be dangerous if few injurious acts are required to produce severe physical damage, but other forms of punishment or reinforcement of other behaviours would be possible). Even where several alternative contingencies could be applied and comparisons made, it would be difficult to draw any conclusion beyond the specific individual with the specific problem behaviour and the particular dimensions of the contingencies used. Holz *et al*. (1963) did attempt, however, to compare punishment, extinction, stimulus change and satiation, using parameters for each procedure that would normally produce maximum effectiveness (in terms of reduction in response rate). They concluded that, at least for their sub-human species, punishment was the most rapid and effective method of eliminating the target response, being more rapid than extinction, and not showing a fast recovery, unlike satiation and stimulus change. This work has not, however, been repeated with retarded individuals and the conclusions should be treated with caution. There certainly is some evidence from studies with the retarded that punishment has more rapid effects than extinction (see, for example, Lovaas & Simmons, 1969) but, first, there are often very good ethical reasons for not employing punishment techniques (see page 110 and, second, relapses are known to occur after the reduction of a behaviour using punishment (see, for example, Kohlenberg, 1970). Furthermore, the recovery of response rate noted by Holz *et al*. (1963) after stimulus change techniques had been applied may not occur if other behaviours are concurrently reinforced, as has been suggested here (p. 93). It must therefore be concluded that no particular technique can be said to be generally more effective than any other technique.

It is more productive by far to approach the problem of choice of procedure in relation to the indiviudal case. In that restructuring of the situation may effect an instant improvement in the undesirable behaviour, it is probably sensible to consider this technique first. If there are clear discriminative stimuli setting off the undesirable behaviour, then it may well be possible to reduce the behaviour by removing these stimuli, then including positive reinforcement of other behaviours to ensure maintenance of the treatment effect. All too often, however, during the initial functional analysis the target behaviour will be discovered to be so generalised, presumably as a result of a history of contingent positive reinforcement in many situations, that removal of discriminative stimuli will be impossible. It will then be necessary to use extinction, punishment and/or positive reinforcement techniques.

Positive reinforcement techniques of the DRO type can be very effective particularly in combination with other procedures. Unfortunately, it seems to be more difficult to teach parents and care agents to administer positive reinforcement appropriately, if they do not already do so, than it does to teach them to punish an undesirable behaviour. This may be partly because positive reinforcement programmes tend to involve more effort, as even some of the most difficult children show more desirable than undesirable behaviours. Despite this problem, it is important to consider including positive reinforcement procedures in a treatment programme early in programme planning, even if only as an adjunct to one of the other procedures.

When it comes to considering extinction, there are unfortunately, some disadvantages (see pp. 95-8) which make it an unsuitable technique at times, especially when the putative reinforcer cannot be prevented from continuing to occur contingently (as when a behaviour is reinforced by sensory feedback, for example, as is often the case in masturbation) or where it would be dangerous for the behaviour to escalate in the short term (immediately after extinction begins) or long term (as a result of unavoidable reinforcement of high-intensity responses). Luckily these problems do not often arise, so that extinction will often be the technique of choice (normally in combination with a DRO schedule), when the use of stimulus change is not possible.

Punishment is usually the last class of procedures considered because of the ethical problems it involves, but it may at times be the only possible solution. When extinction is rejected because the reinforcer thought to be maintaining the behaviour is not preventable, then even punishment may be ineffective: it is possible for an aversive stimulus to become reinforcing if paired with a positive reinforcer (Bender, 1969). When extinction is rejected for other reasons, however, punishment techniques should not be unsuccessful. If punishment is the procedure of choice, then a decision also needs to be made about which particular kind of aversive stimulus is to be used. Perhaps because the removal of a positive reinforcer seems less ethically unjustifiable than the presentation of a noxious stimulus, time-out is the most frequent form of punishment employed. Alternative forms must, of course, be chosen to fit the individual, much as for positive reinforcers. It is unfortunately possible, even after lengthy functional analysis and careful planning, to choose a technique which turns out to be unsuitable or ineffective. Behaviour modification is, above all things, an empirical approach however and, provided full data are kept so that it is known for certain that a treatment programme is not working, an incorrect choice of technique is not normally a disastrous error. Few problem situations are so complicated and unfortunate as to fit only one possible programme; it is very rarely impracticable to design a new or adjusted programme which may turn out to be effective.

# 8 SELF-HELP SKILLS – WASHING, DRESSING AND FEEDING

Janet Carr and Barbara Wilson

Normal children become increasingly independent as they grow older, acquiring the self-help skills we are discussing here through a combination of imitativeness and iron-willed determination to be independent. The only one of these skills likely to cause the mother of a normal child any concern is toiletting (discussed in Chapter 9). Washing, dressing and feeding he learns effortlessly and almost before his elders have realised what is happening. For the handicapped child, however, the acquisition of these skills may not be so easy; without special teaching he may remain dependent on help from others at almost every moment of an ordinary day. With special teaching most children, even the profoundly handicapped, can learn at least some of the self-help skills. With every skill that the child acquires he becomes more nearly 'normal', and this can result in a change for the better in people's attitudes towards him; the child himself may gain great satisfaction from his own prowess, which he can demonstrate repeatedly throughout the day; the work-load of those caring for him, whether parents, nurses, teachers, hostel or training centre staff, is lightened; not least important, his ability in these areas may determine to some extent whether or not he can continue to live in the community.

For all these reasons, the self-help skills are ones that we want to teach to the handicapped child. Behaviour modification methods can improve the effectiveness of our teaching.

## WASHING

Children need to wash or be washed not only at the beginning and end of each day but also before meals, after using the toilet and at other times when they are particularly dirty, for instance after playing in the garden or in sand. Washing then can occupy a considerable amount of time in the day, and a child's inability to wash himself may be an added burden to those caring for him. However, amongst the self-help skills washing is the one that has been the least discussed in the literature.

Only one experimental paper on washing (apart from those on tooth-brushing) has been reported in sufficient detail to allow for replication. Treffry *et al.* (1970) trained eleven severely or profoundly retarded girls whose average age was 14 and average IQ about 20 (none was above 30). A 12-stage scale for washing and drying hands was used and the girls were trained by a forward-chaining method, using sessions of 5 to 15 minutes after meals for a 9-week period. One girl made no progress, four showed varying increase in skill and six were able to wash independently at the end of the programme.

Other papers have mentioned washing amongst various self-help programmes but have not discussed it (Mackowiak *et al.*, 1978) or have referred to scales devised and used (McDonald *et al.*, 1976) and results achieved (Song *et al.*, 1976) but without giving any detail of the programmes.

Manuals written for parents of mentally handicapped children are, like the Treffry *et al.* paper, more helpful, giving detailed instructions for teaching washing including backward-chaining scales for hand and face washing, bathing, hair washing, etc. (Baker *et al.*, 1976, Baldwin *et al.*, 1973, Carr, 1980). The number of steps in a scale, for example for hand washing, varies from 8 (Baker *et al.*) to 12 (Treffry *et al.*) to 16 (Carr) to 26 (Baldwin *et al.*), the latter including separate steps for washing each separate finger. Treffry *et al.*, whose 12-stage scale includes drying, point out that the majority of the steps they give had to be broken down into smaller ones for effective teaching; although not all of these smaller steps are described, it is clear that in practice the scale was considerably longer than that given. Baldwin *et al.* (1973) present programmes for washing hands, cleaning teeth and combing hair only, and say that these may be extended to washing face and bathing; Baker *et al.* (1976) give separate programmes for these. Other programmes for drying hands and for hair washing are set out in Carr (1980) and in Baker *et al.*, who also give one for hair brushing, while Carr includes one for teaching the child to be aware of the need for a wash.

Many of the chaining scales may seem not entirely appropriate for a particular child, either because they are over-detailed or because the steps are not small enough, or because some other approach to the task is preferred. No one scale can be expected to suit everybody, and readers of all three parent manuals are encouraged to regard the scales given not as a sacred text but as a guide, and to be prepared to adapt them to suit themselves. The following is an example of one scale, for hand washing (Carr, 1980):

1. Go to basin.
2. Put in plug.
3. Turn on cold tap.
4. Turn on hot tap.
5. When sufficient water in basin turn off hot tap.
6. Turn off cold tap.
7. Take soap.
8. Put hands and soap in water.
9. Take soap and hands out of water, rub soap between hands.
10. Put soap down.
11. Rub palms and fingers together.
12. Rub hands together, interlacing fingers.
13. Rub palm and fingers of right hand over back and fingers of left hand.
14. Rub palm and fingers of left hand over back and fingers of right hand.
15. Rinse hands in water.
16. Pull out plug.

At first the child is physically prompted, the adult's hands moving his hands, through the whole sequence, and reinforcement is given as soon as the plug has been pulled out. After some repetitions the teacher may sense that the child is beginning to participate in the task; he may then begin to fade the prompts, starting with those for pulling out the plug. When the child can pull out the plug by himself it will be time to begin fading the prompts for rinsing hands. And so on.

There is a special problem with teaching washing, which is that it involves quantities of water. Children often love playing with water, and this may be an advantage in teaching washing, in that the child enjoys it. However, what he enjoys doing with the water may be quite unconnected with washing – over-filling the basin, drinking from the tap, smacking the water in the basin or pressing a hand under the tap to make the water fly everywhere. The teacher may have to continue with a certain amount of prompting or at least of shadowing of the child's hands, even when he has become quite skilful at some of the steps in the chain, to ensure that he does not make an almighty mess. (It may also of course be an excellent idea to allow him to indulge in this messy water play at other times when he and his surroundings are suitably prepared.)

Because hand washing is relatively enjoyable to most children it may be better to regard it as one complete task, while the less enjoyable hand drying may be regarded as another, to be taught separately. Baker *et al.* insist that drying should be taught before washing, presumably because they see the two as a single chain of events. However, there seems no need for this, and indeed there may be some advantage in teaching, and reinforcing, the two tasks separately; if chaining scales are better constructed in really small steps it may also be helpful if the scales themselves are not too extended.

## TOOTH-BRUSHING

Cleaning teeth has received more attention in the literature, perhaps because it seems technically more demanding than washing. Abramson & Wunderlich (1972) trained nine boys (mean CA 12.4, mean PPVT MA 2.8). Out of a maximum possible score of 19 the mean pre-training score for the eight boys who completed the programme was 11, while the post-training mean was 16. The boys were trained first to select their own brush and paste, then to apply paste to brush, finally to brush the left, middle and right sides five times each. The major change was found on the last stage – pre-training they brushed only 10 per cent of the time, while in post-training checks they were observed to brush 81 per cent of the time. Wehman (1974) used a token system to improve tooth brushing by15 institutionalised retarded women. Stars, exchangeable for a variety of treats, were given for proper tooth brushing, which was checked by an independent observer. Over a 60-day period the success rate was 92 per cent (831 stars earned out of a possible 900) and at the end of the period other women on the ward had asked and been allowed to join the scheme. Smeets *et al.* (1976), in a replication of the study by Horner & Keilitz (1975), used a 14-stage tooth-brushing programme with four severely retarded young adults, all of whom had some speech. Observations of normal ward procedure showed that attendants would turn on a tap, put toothpaste on the brush and then leave the residents to get on with it. Some residents, however, 'would just dispose of the toothbrush, swallow the excess water and toothpaste and wait for the attendants to wipe their mouths'. The programme, using verbal instructions, demonstration and physical guidance which was gradually faded, resulted in considerable improvement in the performance of all four subjects.

Other tooth-brushing programmes are given in the parent manuals, with the number of steps ranging from 5 (Baker *et al.*) to 22 (Carr) to 29 (Baldwin *et al.*), the differences being accounted for by differences in the size of the steps and in the extent of the programmes; Baldwin *et al.* and Carr include putting the toothpaste on the brush while Baker *et al.* suggest this be done by the mother. Carr points out that the most difficult part to teach will usually be the brushing of inner surfaces, and this was found to be the case in the study by Smeets *et al.*

Electric toothbrushes are commended (Baldwin *et al.*) and an earlier study (Aronwitz & Conroy, 1969) found that an electric toothbrush was more effective than a conventional one in reducing gingival inflammation and in cleaning the teeth, but was slightly less effective in reducing plaque (the substance responsible for the destruction of tooth enamel). A plaque-identifying material may be bought at chemists which, used as a mouth-wash, shows up plaque as a cherry-red substance on the teeth, and this may then be removed by scraping or brushing with a conventional toothbrush – probably both kinds of brush have a place in the dental care of the mentally handicapped.

## DRESSING

While dressing is not the most important of the self-help skills, a child who can manage his clothes by himself has taken another step towards independence and one that he may find very gratifying. Although the major dressing occasions are limited to morning and evening the skills may also be practised at toiletting times and when changing, for games, swimming, going out and so on.

As with other self-help skills, teaching dressing relies on observation and functional analysis, prompting, fading, breaking down the task into small steps, chaining and reinforcement. The first step is to observe what the child is able to do for himself and where his difficulties occur. In making these preliminary observations it may be helpful to use a chaining scale for each garment, either one of the published scales (Baker *et al.*, 1976; Baldwin *et al.*, 1973; Carr, 1980; Martin *et al.*, 1971; Minge & Ball, 1967; Moore & Carr, 1976) or one devised for the occasion, and to note at which stage the child fails to complete the task. Supposing it were decided to look at the child's ability to put on his vest and to use the scale given in Moore & Carr. The teacher will start at the beginning of the task, at Stage 6; he will lay the vest on the bed and say to the child, 'Put your vest on.' If the child does not carry out the instruction the teacher moves to Stage 5, and then if necessary through the whole scale, as follows:

Stage 5. Vest handed to child.
Stage 4. Vest handed to child rolled up ready to go over his head.
Stage 3. Vest put over child's head.
Stage 2. Vest put over child's head, one arm pulled through armhole.
Stage 1. Vest put over child's head, both arms pulled through armholes and vest pulled down to rib level.

If the child succeeds at any stage then the following stage is the starting point for teaching. Let us say that the child can manage Stage 1 – that is, that he can pull the vest down from rib level – and that the teacher has decided to use backward chaining. The teacher then begins by putting the vest over the child's head and putting one arm through an armhole. He or she then tells the child, 'Put your vest on' and prompts the child to put the second arm through its armhole; after this, the child pulls down the vest and is given his reinforcement. Subsequently, the teacher fades the prompts on Stage 2 and, when the child has mastered this stage, moves on to training Stage 3. And so on through the stages until eventually the child is able to put on his vest with no help from start to finish.

Other garments, pants, socks, shirt, trousers, dress, jumper, cardigan, etc., may be taught similarly, using available scales or, if preferred, drawing up new ones. The teacher who wants to draw up a new scale should herself go through the process of putting on or taking off the garment, working slowly step by step, and noting where in the process difficulties are likely to occur. (It is a salutory experience; normally we dress and undress so mechanically that we have little idea of how we go about it.) Undressing may be taught in the same stepwise fashion and as a rule is rather easier to teach. If at any point difficulties arise in teaching either dressing or undressing the teacher should check, first, whether the reinforcer is really an effective one for the child; and second, whether the step he is teaching is too big. For example, supposing that the child learning to put on his vest made little progress at Stage 2 (putting the second arm through the armhole). The teacher would break this step down into a series of smaller ones: 2a, teacher puts second arm halfway through armhole; 2b, puts wrist of second arm through armhole; 2c, puts hand up to but not through armhole, 2d, doubles arm up against ribs under vest. When the steps are smaller the chances of the child's success are greater.

Many people prefer to teach dressing and undressing at the normal times for these activities – morning and evening – and to give only one trial of each garment on each occasion; so the child learns in a way similar to that for normal children. This will probably save the child from becoming bored with the task but may mean that, because of limited practice, the teaching is spread over a long period. If the teaching cannot be carried out at normal times it is worthwhile using training sessions at other times (Martin *et al.*, 1971, Minge & Ball, 1967), while teaching may still be successful even if not carried out every day of the week (Moore & Carr, 1976).

When a child is being taught to dress himself the teacher has to decide how far the teaching should go. Is it enough to ask that the child should simply get the garments onto his body or should he also be expected to do up fastenings – buttons, poppers, zips, buckles, laces? Should he start with his clothes laid out for him or be expected to get them out of the cupboard? Should he be told what to wear or choose his clothes himself? All of this will depend partly on the child's ability and partly on how his progress goes. Fastenings often seem impossibly daunting to teach but even severely handicapped children can master buttons and zips. Even shoe-laces, which at first sight seem to demand a near-genius level of combined manipulative and spatial skills, can be taught providing the steps in the task are small enough, while the use of broad football-boot laces, each of a different colour, also helps in the early stages. Programmes for tying shoe laces in a knot and bow are given in all three parent manuals and in Martin *et al.*; all four use different approaches, so there is ample choice. On the printed page, even with illustrations (Martin *et al.*, 1971; Baldwin *et al.*, 1973) these programmes are difficult to follow, but they become clearer when the instructions are tried out in practice.

Besides programmes for basic garments and fastenings, others are described which are less usual but potentially useful – threading and buckling a belt, and hanging up clothes on a hanger (Baker *et al.*, 1976), knowing inside from outside (Martin *et al.*, 1971; Carr, 1980), putting on a bra (Martin *et al.*, 1971), knowing which shoe to put on which foot (Carr, 1980).

All the studies and manuals draw attention to the fact that a particular part of a particular dressing programme may cause difficulties and that this may be different with different children. Minge & Ball found that some girls had great difficulty in learning to remove a dress when given only a spoken direction, and some to take and put on a dress – the difficulty here being apparently in grasping the garment. Martin *et al.* found that over two-thirds of the total average time (10 hours 54 minutes) spent in teaching girls to put on a sweater went in teaching them to discriminate inside from outside. For the boy in

Moore & Carr's study the major difficulty was in pulling up a sock placed half-way over his heel. Responses that occur later in a chain have been found more difficult to teach than those which occur earlier (Kazdin, 1977), perhaps because they are further removed from reinforcement. This explanation could apply to the results of Minge & Ball, who used backward chaining, but not to those of Martin *et al.*, who used forward chaining and found the greatest difficulty with the first step; nor to that of Moore & Carr, for whose subject the major problem occurred in the second step of the (backward) chaining scale. It may be that although some parts of a process are generally found especially difficult – getting a pullover over the head (Baker *et al.*) or the second arm in a jacket (Carr, 1980) – other difficulties may arise idiosyncratically, and teachers should be prepared for and ready to tackle these.

Although dressing skills can be taught, it is not always easy to do so and the group programmes reported (Martin *et al.*, 1971; Song *et al.*, 1976; Minge & Ball, 1967; Monaco *et al.*, 1968) describe limited success in the limited time for which the programmes ran, although it is possible that within the groups there were individuals who became independent in dressing, as has been described elsewhere (Moore & Carr, 1976). Minge & Ball's programme, with six girls chosen because they were 'amongst those with the fewest self-help abilities in the hospital', ran for six months, each girl receiving two 15-minute training sessions a day. Mean scores, on a situational test, improved significantly from 7.88 to 19.75, the comparable figures for a control group being 13.4 and 15.6. However, the greatest improvement was found on attentional items (Look at me', etc.), with virtually no change in the girls' ability to put the garments on. Martin *et al.* used 15-30 minute training sessions each day; the average number of sessions per garment varied from 36 (lacing and tying shoe on foot) to 3 (putting on undershirt). Not every girl was trained on each item, and the percentage of the number undergoing training (ranging from 8-2 girls) who reached competence varied from 100 (e.g., putting on undershirt) to 50 (putting on sweater). Much greater success was achieved by Azrin *et al.* (1976). In a characteristically 'rapid' programme seven profoundly retarded adults were taught to dress and undress themselves. The average time taken in training to reach criterion was 12 hours over three or four training days (compared with a minimum estimate of 65 hours over 6 months in the study by Minge & Ball). The students in the study by Azrin *et al.* had an average CA of 31 and an average MA under 1½ years on the Stanford Binet. Each student had two training sessions a day, each session lasting two to three hours; undressing was taught before dressing; a 'forward sequence' was used, with the student participating fully in the early as well as in the later stages of each dressing process; each trial involved all garments, instead of concentrating on one at a time; and emphasis was laid on the use of physical prompting and on the use of near-continuous praise and stroking as reinforcers. A dressing-undressing test showed that, before training, students averaged less than 10 per cent success, while the average score after training was 90 per cent. This study demonstrates remarkably effective teaching of very severely handicapped people. It will be interesting to see whether other workers using these methods are able to replicate these results.

Azrin *et al*. excluded from their study twelve students with physical disabilities, and it seems probable that while some children will be able to attain high levels of competence others will have particular difficulties. For them it may be unrealistic to aim for the most advanced skills, and we may instead try to give them as much independence as possible, while not making too many demands on them. This may mean using clothing adapted to their needs (Waters, 1970) – loose garments and simplified fastenings, jumpers with wide necks, trousers with elasticated waists, slip-on shoes. Even for potentially capable children these may be valuable in the early stages of teaching (Azrin *et al*., 1976); for more limited children they may make the difference between incompetence and independence.

## FEEDING

Self-feeding is one of the most enjoyable of the self-help skills to teach, partly because it is a relatively simple skill and partly because most people like their food, so that the food itself may be a powerful reinforcer. Before starting a feeding programme it is necessary to find out just what the retarded person can and cannot do for himself during meal-times. Indeed the problem may be not that he cannot feed himself but that he engages in some inappropriate behaviour during the meal such as spitting out food, stealing food from others or hurling his plate across the dining room. The checklist in Table 8.1 shows one way of making a preliminary assessment of assets and deficits (others are also available – e.g., Gunzburg, 1963).

It is not possible to cover all these problems in detail but some

Table 8.1: Self-care at Meals

| A. Eating skills | Cannot | Can with help | Can by self but messy | Can by self neatly |
|---|---|---|---|---|
| Chews adequately | | | | |
| Tries to feed self with fingers | | | | |
| Eats with spoon | | | | |
| Eats with spoon and fork | | | | |
| Eats with fork alone | | | | |
| Uses fork and knife | | | | |
| Uses knife as pusher | | | | |
| Cuts with knife | | | | |
| Spreads with knife | | | | |
| Drinks from cup | | | | |
| **B. Social Training** | | | | |
| Finds own place and sits | | | | |
| Sits still during meals | | | | |
| Waits for others to finish | | | | |
| Lays table | | | | |
| Pours from jug | | | | |
| Serves with spoon | | | | |
| Carries plate | | | | |
| Passes plates | | | | |
| **C. Behaviour problems** | **Often** | **Sometimes** | **Rarely** | **Never** |
| Uses fingers unnecessarily | | | | |
| Tips drink over | | | | |
| Throws or tips food | | | | |
| Grabs other people's food | | | | |
| Regurgitates food | | | | |
| Faddiness about food | | | | |
| Bolts food | | | | |
| Excessively slow | | | | |
| Eats from plate with mouth | | | | |

examples will be given from each of the three areas – self-feeding skills, social training and behaviour problems.

Before beginning to teach the child to feed himself, it is important to see that he is comfortably seated, with his feet resting on the floor, or if he is not tall enough for that, on a box or other support; the table top should be at his waist level so that he can see and reach over the table easily. For children who have difficulty in manipulation a number of aids are available, such as rubber handles to slip onto cutlery for easier gripping, suction mats to prevent crockery from slipping and plateguards to help scooping (for a selective list of aids and stockists, see Carr, 1980). During assessment the child's food preferences should emerge, and it is of course best to start training using foods that the child is fond of. Some foods may be selected as being specially appropriate to some stages in training; for instance in teaching finger-feeding pieces of toast, apple, biscuit or banana are good, while in teaching spoon-feeding soft rather glutinous foods which are easy to scoop and keep on the spoon, like mashed potato, mince and apple sauce, are best.

## TEACHING SELF-FEEDING

### Spoon-feeding

This task may be seen as a series of small steps:

(1) holding the spoon;
(2) loading the spoon;
(3) taking the loaded spoon from the plate to the mouth without spilling;
(4) taking the food from the spoon into the mouth;
(5) returning the spoon to the plate.

The teacher should position himself behind the child rather than to the side of or facing him, so that the teacher's hand can move the child's hand in a natural hand-to-mouth movement. The teacher closes his hand over the child's hand (not over the spoon) and prompts the child to load the spoon, take it to his mouth, tip the food into his mouth and return the spoon to his plate. Having prompted the child in this way for several mouthfuls the teacher can begin gradually to fade the prompts as he feels the child begins to participate in the action. This procedure is known as graduated guidance (Westling & Murden, 1978). Since for many children the food itself is the reinforcer for taking the spoon to his mouth, it is often preferable to regard replacing the spoon on the plate as a separate task. In this case the prompts will be faded first on step (4), the teacher releasing his grip on the child's hand just as the spoon is going into the child's mouth, so that the child completes this last step himself. When the child is able to do this successfully, the teacher now slackens his grip when the spoon is very slightly further from the child's mouth. There are in fact a number of sub-steps between steps (4) and (3) and it is important not to try to go too fast or the child may fail. The most difficult part to teach in the spoon-feeding chain seems to be step (2), loading the spoon; as a rule, this may be overcome by very slow, careful fading of the prompts, though again it may be worth giving extra reinforcement (a word of praise perhaps, or a stroke of the child's cheek) immediately the scooping has been accomplished. Where the difficulty has an unusual cause, an unconventional remedy may be called for. One boy who persistently failed to learn to scoop his food was found to be failing because he would use his fingers to push the food onto his spoon (Song & Gandhi, 1974). This was dealt with by tying one hand to his side and putting a sock over the other, the spoon being then tied to the sock-covered hand in a convenient position for scooping. The boy then successfully learnt to scoop the food, and when two weeks later the sock was no longer put over his hand he continued to use the spoon appropriately.

In the following example we describe how a thirteen-year-old with an estimated mental age of six months was taught to feed himself within 5 days. Tony had been fed all his life. At 13 he was admitted to a special unit on a short-term basis and it was decided to try to teach him to feed himself. As Tony was particularly fond of ice-cream he was given this as a dessert and, after having been fed his first course as usual, he was prompted to feed himself the first four spoonsful of ice-cream, the rest being fed to him as before. Initially the nurse teaching him had thought to use praise as an additional reward but each time she said, 'Good boy, Tony!' he turned round to look at her for several seconds. She stopped using praise, and the teaching progressed faster. Over the next two days Tony progressed from feeding himself four spoonsful of ice-cream to feeding himself the whole course, and by the third day he needed help only in loading the spoon. The nurse gradually faded her prompts on this part of the action, letting Tony take over more and more of the scooping. At first Tony often used his unoccupied hand to play with the food so the nurse held this hand on the edge of the plate, which also helped to steady the plate. By the end of the fifth day Tony was eating independently and without a great deal of mess.

Using the same methods of prompting, fading and backward chaining other self-feeding skills, such as drinking from a cup, using a fork and cutting and spreading with a knife, may be taught; programmes for these are found in the parent manuals (Baker *et al.*, 1976; Baldwin *et al.*, 1973; Carr, 1980). An additional technique, also aimed at fading prompts but in a rather different way, is that of 'tactile cue fading' (Westling & Murden, 1978), in which prompts given first to the child's hand are gradually shifted to the wrist, then if necessary up the arm to the elbow and shoulder (Larsen & Bricker, quoted in Song & Gandhi, 1974). Alternatively, modelling may be considered as a teaching method, and was used by Nelson *et al.* (1975) and by O'Brien & Azrin (1972), although both studies found prompting to be superior. Modelling may also be useful for those children who are averse to prompting, though some of these may be helped by desensitisation.

**Teaching Chewing**

For children who will only eat very smooth liquidised food it may be possible to introduce first very small and then larger lumps into their food, or to make the food gradually thicker. Four-year-old autistic Lisa only ate liquidised food or else sucked food such as biscuits until it dissolved in her mouth. For a few days her food was made very slightly thicker each day, then, when the consistency had become fairly solid, it was thoroughly mashed with a fork rather than being liquidised. At this time only foods that could be easily mashed were used, such as potatoes, and peas mixed with gravy. Then a few small pieces of minced beef or carrots were added. In this way Lisa progressed to being able to accept a more normal meal although her food was always cut up into small pieces. Concurrently, Lisa was given long pieces of food to hold in her fingers such as carrot sticks and hard rusks that she could not dissolve by sucking, and she was encouraged to bite off a piece – one end was placed in her mouth and the teacher prompted Lisa to pull gently at the other end. When a piece was bitten off Lisa's jaws were gently moved up and down to encourage her to chew the piece of food. A child who imitates well may watch and imitate the teacher's chewing – sometimes letting the child watch himself in a mirror helps.

When appropriate eating skills have been learnt care must be taken to ensure that they are maintained; without post-training, both staff and children may revert to pre-training levels (Albin, 1977; O'Brien *et al.*, 1972).

## TEACHING APPROPRIATE SOCIAL BEHAVIOUR AT MEAL-TIMES

Although some retarded people will not be able to learn all the skills listed in the assessment chart, most should be able to learn to sit still between courses or wait to be served, perhaps to lay the table, help serve the food, stack the plates and clear away after the meal. Indeed these tasks may even be used as reinforcers for appropriate meal-time behaviours; twelve-year old Joey, who enjoyed clearing away, was allowed to do this if he did not throw food during the meal. Other more severely handicapped children may need to learn to sit at table or wait their turn to be served. Timmy would not sit at table and so was fed by an adult who followed him round the room popping in a spoonful whenever he was stationary enough to receive one. Staff tried prompting Timmy to sit at the table but he reacted with tantrums and aggression, so it was decided to use a shaping procedure. Instead of being fed wherever he happened to be, Timmy was only fed when he wandered within three feet of the dining table. When he was spending most of his time within three feet he was fed only when he was within two feet, then one foot of the table. Following this the teacher sat at the table and Timmy had to come to her when he was ready for his next mouthful; then he was required to touch his own chair before being fed, then have his arm over the chair, then his arm and one leg. Within two months Timmy was sitting at the table for all meals, and was then ready to begin learning to feed himself.

A different problem was presented by Sam, a large fourteen-year-old who would sit down at the table as soon as he was taken to the dining room but, if his dinner was not given to him immediately, would scream, kick the table over and flail about. Similarly if his second course did not appear as soon as his first was finished he would go through the same procedure, and as soon as he had finished eating he would leave the table. These problems were tackled by very gradually increasing the length of time that Sam had to wait. At first his dinner was always ready for him when he sat down, but when he had finished that a helper held him still for three seconds, praising him for sitting before giving him his pudding. Over two days the three seconds were extended to five, then to seven, and so on until Sam would cheerfully wait three or four minutes for his second course. Later on, waiting at the beginning and end of meals was dealt with in the same way.

An important feature of the programmes for both Timmy and Sam was the fine grading of the steps by which they progressed. Each new requirement of the child was only marginally more difficult than the last, thus maximising the chances of the child's co-operation and success.

## OTHER MEAL-TIME PROBLEMS

The most frequently encountered undesirable behaviours are inappropriate use of fingers; troughing, or pigging (putting the face down to the plate or eating food spilled onto the table); eating too fast or too slowly; stealing; throwing or tipping plates; and excessive faddiness. A number of studies have described procedures to deal with these (Barton *et al.*, 1970; Henriksen & Doughty, 1967; Martin, McDonald & Omichinski, 1971), the most often used technique being time-out (Westling & Murden, 1978). Time-out (from access to food) is effective in reducing undesirable meal-time behaviours if the food itself is a reinforcer (although it is unlikely to be useful for those children who do not like or are indifferent to food). If on the other hand it is attention from adults or peers that is maintaining the undesirable behaviour, then time-out from this type of reinforcement may solve the problem. Overcorrection and brief restraint may also be considered, but what techniques are used in any one case will depend on the child, and the programme should always be evaluated in the light of his response to it. More rapid learning of appropriate behaviour may be achieved by using the 'mini-meal' method (Azrin & Armstrong, 1973). Each meal is divided into three portions and the child is given hourly training in feeding throughout the day. Not only does this enable the child to have more teaching sessions each day but satiation problems are reduced. The 'mini-meal' method may be used to teach self-feeding skills as well as to reduce unpleasant eating behaviour.

Helen, a seven-year-old with Down's syndrome, exhibited a variety of unacceptable eating habits but all were eliminated over a period of seven weeks. The main problem was food stealing; as soon as Helen finished her own meal she helped herself from other children's plates, and when the meal was being served she would grab food from the serving dishes. In addition she would push food onto her spoon with her fingers, and she gobbled, shovelling in one mouthful after another. The result was unsightly and unpleasant meal-times for everybody around and particularly for her mother, who felt that Helen should eat with the rest of the family. Stealing was tackled first. As soon as

Helen attempted to steal food, any that she had managed to get was removed and her hands were held to her sides for a count of twenty. Food stealing rapidly decreased. A fork in her other hand solved the problem of Helen's using her fingers to push food onto her spoon. When gobbling was the target behaviour time-out was considered (removing her plate for twenty seconds) but as brief restraint had been so successful in eliminating stealing this was used again. Each time Helen attempted to put food in her mouth before she had swallowed the previous mouthful, she was told, 'Hands down', and her hands were held as before. Helen gradually learnt to put her hands down when she was told to without the need for restraint. Eight weeks after the start of the programme Helen's mother reported that meal-times were no longer a nightmare, and that the family could sit down at table knowing that Helen would eat without making much mess and only from her own plate.

## CONCLUSIONS

Teaching self-help skills to mentally handicapped people takes time and effort. It is not surprising that some parents and other care-givers are slow to embark on it, the more so because the mentally handicapped themselves tend to accept help and do not, as normal children will, insist on trying to do things for themselves. Specialist teaching using behaviour modification methods can enable even severely handicapped people to attain some of the skills, though many questions remain as to the most effective ways in which these methods may be applied. No research exists to show, for example, whether forward or backward chaining is the more effective. Until such research is done we prefer backward chaining, since this teaching leads directly to completion of the task and hence to reinforcement; others, however, have specifically preferred forward chaining (Azrin, Schaeffer & Wesolowski, 1976).

The skills discussed in this chapter and the next are the essential ones for daily living but others may also be seen as potentially valuable and worth attempting. Amongst the programmes described in the literature are those to teach mentally handicapped people to use public transport (Gunzburg *et al.*, 1968; Hughson & Brown, 1975); to differentiate between coins so as to be able to go shopping (Wunderlich, 1972); to swim (Bundschuh *et al.*, 1972); to use a telephone (Leff, 1974); and to live independently in an apartment (Perske & Marquiss, 1973). These studies show that skills that might have been thought too advanced for the people concerned have been successfully acquired through systematic teaching.

The area of self-help skills is one in which parents are often keen to be involved with the teaching, and one in which they have been seen as particularly appropriate teachers (Baker *et al.*, 1976 ; Baldwin *et al.*, 1973). It is not always easy for parents (or others) to see how they should set about teaching these skills, and the published accounts and scales should be helpful. In future studies it is to be hoped that not only group results but also individual programmes will be reported and that not only successes but also failures and the reasons for them, difficulties and how these were tackled, will be described. Such details are often more informative than the more usual bland descriptions of plain sailing and a good deal more encouraging to others who have to contend with set-backs in their teaching.

# 9 TOILET TRAINING

Barbara Wilson

Toilet training is arguably the most important single self-help skill for the mentally retarded to master. Not only does the incontinent child run the risk of skin infections, but he is also socially unacceptable and causes a great deal of unpleasant work for those caring for him. In addition, incontinence is a major factor in determining whether or not a child is admitted to long-term care (McCoull, 1971; Wing, 1971). For these reasons toilet training is seen as an important skill which we will wish to try to teach to virtually all mentally retarded people.

Toilet training involves several different skills. In addition to learning bladder and bowel control and appropriate voiding, the child needs to learn to ask to go to the toilet and eventually to take himself to it. He may also need to learn skills such as pulling his pants up and down, wiping his bottom, pulling the chain and washing his hands.

## TO TRAIN OR NOT TO TRAIN?

Normal children are usually dry during the day by about two years of age and by three years normal urinary control should be established (Muellner, 1960; Campbell, 1970). In general, when devising behavioural programmes, the developmental level of the child should be taken into account but, although many severely retarded people may never reach a mental age of two years, they may yet be capable of becoming toilet trained. Subjects with IQs below 20 were excluded from Sloop & Kennedy's study (1973), but Azrin & Foxx (1971) successfully toilet trained nine adult retardates with a mean IQ of 14 and a range of 7 - 45. An adaptation of Azrin's procedure has been used with handicapped children having a mental age of less than two years at Hilda Lewis House, Bethlem Royal Hospital, a unit for specially handicapped children. A recent programme was with a 13-year-old boy functioning at a 5-6 month level on the Bayley Scales of Infant Development. Baseline data over 6 days showed that he used the toilet only once and was wet 14 times. At the end of two weeks' intensive toiletting, he was using the toilet between 5-13 times each day, and was wet less than once a day. He was discharged before completion of the programme, but his mother toiletted him at home every half-hour during the day, and for two weeks he averaged one accident daily. The number of accidents then increased somewhat, but not to the baseline level. The findings suggest that children with a mental age below one year can be toilet trained even though greater success may be possible with those of a higher developmental level. Smith & Smith (1977) found it quicker to train people below the age of 20 than those over 25, and to train those with a Vineland social age of two years or more rather than below two years. Nevertheless, with longer training the older, duller group reached comparable levels of success, achieving an 80 per cent reduction in accident rate in an average of eight to nine weeks, compared with five to six weeks for the younger, brighter group.

## GENERAL PRINCIPLES

### 1. OBSERVATION AND RECORDING

As with other skills, baseline data are needed prior to any training programme, on such questions as the timing and frequency of toiletting accidents, presence or absence of constipation and so forth. A typical observation and recording sheet used at Hilda Lewis House is shown in Table 9.1. For some purposes simpler record charts may be adequate, recording, for example, for one week whether or not the child remained clean and dry over the morning period and again over the afternoon period.

Table 9.1: Toilet Chart

NAME. . . . . . . . . . . . . . . . . . . . . Week Beginning. . . . . . . . . . . . . .

CODES

Urine:

Dry = dry pants
Wet = urinated in pants
UT = urinated in toilet
NU = not used toilet

Bowels:

BOP = bowels open in pants
BOT = bowels open in toilet

| Time | Sunday | Monday | Tuesday | Wednesday | Thursday | Friday | Saturday |
|---|---|---|---|---|---|---|---|
| 7.00–7.30 | | | | | | | |
| 7.30–8.00 | | | | | | | |
| 8.00–8.30 | | | | | | | |
| 8.30–9.00 | | | | | | | |
| 9.00–9.30 | | | | | | | |
| and so on through the day | | | | | | | |

### 2. THE PRINCIPLES OF REINFORCEMENT

All appropriate behaviour should be reinforced. Depending on the level or stage the child has reached, reinforcement may be given for approaching the toilet, pulling down his pants and sitting on the toilet, as well as for elimination in the toilet. Effective reinforcers should be sought (see Chapter 3). Some children, for example, find pulling the chain highly enjoyable and, for this reason, should only be allowed to do this following appropriate behaviour. A musical potty may also be an effective reinforcer and, in addition, will inform the trainer as soon as the child has urinated. It may also serve to draw the child's attention to what he is doing.

### 3. PROVIDING THE MOST SUITABLE CONDITIONS FOR LEARNING

This includes making sure the child is comfortably seated, so that his feet reach the floor or a platform, and seeing that he has something to hold on to if necessary. It may also mean choosing the best times, those at which the child is most likely to wet or soil, for toilet training – record charts are often useful here. It may further mean providing extra opportunities for urination to occur, by giving the child extra fluids in order to increase the frequency of urination.

### 4. MAKING USE, WHERE NECESSARY, OF THE BASIC TECHNIQUES

Shaping, fading, prompting and backward chaining may be necessary for teaching the additional skills needed for independent toiletting behaviour, for exampie, pulling down pants and wiping bottoms. Training pre-toiletting skills may also be necessary. This may include teaching the child to sit on the toilet for several minutes at a time and, if a pants alarm (a device worn by the child to signal inappropriate elimination) is being used, it may be necessary to shape the child's behaviour so that he does not destroy, dismantle or switch off the alarm.

## DAYTIME ENURESIS

### HABIT-TRAINING

One of the most commonly used methods for eliminating daytime wetting involves taking the child to the lavatory every half-an-hour or forty-five minutes and sitting him on the toilet for several minutes. If he urinates he is rewarded and this procedure alone may result in the child becoming toilet trained. This is not unlike the method used by many a mother, who puts her baby on the potty after every feed and thus manages to avoid several wet nappies. In both situations the child is given the opportunity to urinate in the appropriate place. With some children this method is successful, the child often urinates in the right place and gradually becomes able to wait for longer periods before needing to urinate. Alan was a seven-year old Down's syndrome boy who had never been toilet trained. A five-day baseline period during which he was toiletted every 30 minutes showed that he was dry 87 per cent of the time. It was decided, therefore, that an intensive programme was not necessary and that it was sufficient to continue toiletting Alan every half an hour. Following two accident-free weeks the intervals were gradually increased, first by five and then by ten minutes, with continued success.

Other children may use the potty each time they are taken but are also frequently wet in between times. In this case it may be better to change to a shorter interval, say 15 minutes, and then gradually extend the time. Other children may never 'perform' on the potty or toilet and can, therefore, never be reinforced for elimination in the appropriate place.

As this 'habit-training' method is so simple, it may be worth trying before beginning a more intensive type of programme. The trainer must decide how often to toilet the child and how long to leave him there each time. Information on this point may be derived from baseline records. If the child is wetting roughly every 20 minutes then the trainer would begin by taking him just before the next 20-minute interval was over. How long to wait each time is more difficult. If the child urinates into the potty straight away there is no problem, but if he does not then three to five minutes seems a reasonable period for him to remain seated – if indeed he will stay seated for that long. Martin, the thirteen-year-old mentioned earlier, had to be taught to sit on the lavatory for five minutes at a time before toilet training proper could begin. Initially he stood up every 30 seconds or so but, with prompting and reinforcing, learned within four days to remain on the lavatory for five minutes.

## INTENSIVE PROGRAMMES

The 'habit training' method does not work with all mentally retarded people, and other methods may be needed. The procedure used by Azrin & Foxx (1971) with institutionalised retarded adults can be very effective. Two pieces of apparatus are required by this programme – a pants alarm which sounds whenever the trainee wets his pants and a toilet alarm which sounds whenever he urinates into the toilet. The main features of this programme are greater opportunities for correct toiletting through the use of extra fluids, immediate and consistent correction or reinforcement (made possible by the pants and toilet alarms), reprimands and time-out from positive reinforcement following any 'accidents' and a post-training maintenance procedure to ensure continued success.

Azrin & Foxx's method has been adapted slightly at Hilda Lewis House for use with the severely handicapped children seen there. The adapted procedure is as follows:

PRE-PROGRAMME ARRANGEMENTS

(1) Baseline observations and recordings are taken for five days.
(2) The child's day, from 9.00 a.m. to 3.30 p.m., is broken up into half-hour periods and a rota of volunteers is drawn up, each volunteer taking on one or more half-hour periods at a time. The volunteers are drawn from nursing staff, occupational therapists, teachers and psychologists. The child is taken off the programme for lunch (i.e., from 11.30 a.m. to 12.30 p.m.) with the other children.
(3) The toilet area is prepared. If a musical potty or potty chair is to be used, this is taken to the area along with the child's favourite drinks, toys, sweets and other reinforcers, spare pants, pencils, a seat for the trainers and materials for cleaning the child and cleaning the floor. Record sheets and instructions for the trainers are prepared and pinned up in the toilet area. An example of a record sheet is given in Table 9.2.

INSTRUCTIONS FOR TRAINER

(1) Give the child as much to drink as he will accept. Record the amount on the chart.
(2) After one minute seat the child on the musical potty/potty chair.
(3) If he urinates the music will start. We hope this will reinforce the child as well as informing the trainer. In addition give lavish praise (or whatever social reinforcement child likes) plus edible or other reinforcer if necessary. Remove child from potty/toilet chair.
(4) If he does not urinate, remove him after 20 minutes with no reinforcement.
(5) During the time the child is not on the potty he can play with toys, with the trainer or do whatever he likes. This period may

Table 9.2: Example of Record Sheet

INTENSIVE TOILET TRAINING

| TIME | 9.00 9.30 | 9.30 10.00 | 10.00 10.30 | 10.30 11.00 | 11.00 11.30 | 11.30 12.00 | 12.00 12.30 |
|---|---|---|---|---|---|---|---|
| Amount of fluids drunk (number of cups) | | | | | | | |
| If used toilet (✓ or X) | | | | | | | |
| Time from sitting on toilet to using it | | | | | | | |
| Reinforcer given for using toilet (✓) | | | | | | | |

IF DOESN'T USE TOILET, GET CHILD OFF AFTER 20 MINUTES (NO REINFORCEMENT)

| | | | | | | | |
|---|---|---|---|---|---|---|---|
| If wet pants once off toilet (✓ or X) | | | | | | | |
| Time from getting off toilet to wetting pants | | | | | | | |
| No. of dry pants checks (with reinforcement for this) | | | | | | | |

Signature. . . . . . . . . . . . . . . . . . . .

Comments:

last 10 minutes or may be almost 30 minutes, if the child used the potty immediately.

(6) At five minute intervals during the time that he is not on the potty the child should feel his pants. If they are dry make a big fuss of him and say, 'Dry pants, good boy'. If they are wet say, sternly, 'Wet pants, bad boy' and change the pants. (This procedure is sometimes changed. If, for example, the child is one who finds a scolding very reinforcing, then, 'Bad boy' is not used. Instead his pants are changed without the trainer saying anything).

(7) At the end of half an hour the next volunteer will take over and repeat the procedure. Each volunteer should fill in the chart as appropriate throughout the session.

(8) At the end of the day, the chart is taken down, the observations graphed and the chart for the following day pinned up.

## ENDING THE PROGRAMME

If, after two weeks, there is little or no improvement the teaching is discontinued at least for some weeks. If, after two weeks, the findings are ambiguous, the intensive toiletting will be continued. If there is substantial improvement, the intensive training will gradually be faded out and replaced by a more normal toiletting procedure. How this is done will depend on the child but it is almost always necessary to ensure that generalisation takes place. To hope that this will occur of its own accord is to invite trouble. The following examples illustrate how intensive toilet training programmes were faded out for two children.

Following a successful intensive programme for Benjamin, it was decided that he should spend the mornings, i.e., until lunch time, in the toilet area and continue the intensive programme but he should spend the remainder of the day with the other children. During this time Benjamin was taken to the toilet area every half an hour, given his drinks and seated on the toilet. Following elimination, which always occurred within a few minutes, he was taken back to the group. Later Banjamin spent all day with the other children. He was toiletted every half an hour, but had no extra fluids. For the three months since then Benjamin has averaged one 'accident' each week and takes himself to the toilet when he needs to go. Benjamin learned very quickly but with many children it is necessary to proceed more cautiously. Alex, for example, after two weeks' training was taken just outside the toilet area when he was not seated on the potty. The trainer played with him there until the next toiletting was due. Over the next few weeks the distance from the toiletting area was increased by a few feet each day. Meanwhile the dry pants check occurred every ten minutes, instead of every five minutes, then every fifteen minutes and so on. The extra liquids were gradually reduced over the two weeks following the intensive programme and the schedule of edible reinforcement changed from continuous to partial, although Alex was always praised. Finally the interval between one toiletting and the next was slowly increased from 30 to 35 to 40 and more minutes. If Alex went to the toilet spontaneously and used it, he was praised. When he did wet his pants, which was not often, he was scolded and made to wash his pants. The fading procedure took about three weeks and after this Alex was toiletted in the ordinary way with the other children, although occasionally his pants were checked too.

Besides teaching the child to generalise his toiletting skills so that he is able to recognise and respond appropriately to the signals from his bladder when he is outside the immediate toilet area, it may, in some cases, be necessary to teach the child to use different toilets. In this case it may be necessary to repeat the teaching process in other toilet areas and with other toilets, although it is usual to find that the teaching time becomes progressively shorter as the child finds more toilets acceptable and becomes increasingly able to use them.

It may seem rather appalling that a child should spend long periods each day sitting on a potty or lavatory but, in practice, many children seem to blossom during intensive programmes. They have the undivided attention of an adult and may well enjoy the finger games, singing games, musical toys and so on. Some trainers only use these games as reinforcement of appropriate urination while others play with the child while they are waiting for him to eliminate, using the games to reinforce the child for remaining seated on the toilet for fairly lengthy periods of time.

Smith *et al.*, (1975) describe a toilet training procedure which is also based on Azrin's work. Like Azrin and Foxx, Smith *et al.* used a pants alarm as well as a toilet alarm. The pants alarm is further described in Dixon & Smith (1976). A recent study by Smith (1979) compared three different toilet training programmes. The first was 'intensive individual regular potting', i.e., each child was toiletted every half an hour or some other regular interval. The second method was 'intensive individual timing' in which the trainer predicted when elimination was likely to occur and toiletted the child around that time. The third method also used regular potting but taught several children at once. Both the individual methods resulted in greater reduction of incontinence and greater independence in toiletting than the group method. Of the two individual methods, regular potting was preferred to timing because it was easier to administer and all staff concerned preferred this method, but little difference was found in the results of the two individual programmes.

## NOCTURNAL ENURESIS

Like daytime wetting, nocturnal enuresis is a widespread problem among the mentally retarded. It has been reported that 79 per cent of four-year-old Down's syndrome children wet the bed at least once a week compared with 27 per cent of non-handicapped four-year-olds (Carr, 1975). Among the institutionalised retarded it is estimated that 70 per cent are enuretic (Sugaya, 1967). Some of the main methods for dealing with this problem will be described.

### 1. BELL-AND-PAD

Meadow (1977) describes this method whereby the child sleeps on a mesh or foil mat connected to an alarm buzzer which is activated when the child urinates. Meadow also describes some of the common problems which arise in using the method with normal children and which may also occur with the mentally retarded. The biggest problem with severely retarded people is probably their tendency to disconnect, damage or otherwise interfere with the equipment. It may be worthwhile shaping the child's behaviour so that he will accept the apparatus, but the method itself needs reasonable co-operation.

There are several studies of the use of the bell-and-pad method with normal children summarised by Doleys (1977), while others have explored the effects of overlearning (Young & Morgan, 1972) and of intermittent schedules (Finley *et al.*, 1973; Abelew, 1972; Taylor & Turner, 1975), both of which appear to result in lower relapse rates. Sloop and Kennedy (1973) found that a group of retarded children treated with the bell-and-pad showed superior results to those treated by being potted several times a night. In an earlier study (Kennedy & Sloop, 1968), four out of eight children reached the criterion of fourteen successive dry nights after a seven-week training period. In both these studies all subjects had an IQ of above 26 and the age range was from eight to eighteen years.

Parents of mentally retarded children are often reluctant to use this method. In part this seems to result from fear of the procedure due to lack of understanding of the principles and mechanics of a bell-and-pad system. In addition, parents may be unwilling to have the child woken and perhaps remain awake for some time or disturb another child in the same room. It is possible to have the buzzer ring in the parents' room to avoid disturbing other children. It is also possible to purchase a device which vibrates instead of buzzing when the child urinates and thus avoids noise altogether. If parents and others working with the mentally retarded wish to use this method then, as Sloop & Kennedy have demonstrated, the bell-and-pad can be an effective treatment for some retarded people.

### 2. RETENTION CONTROL

Retention control aims to increase the amount of urine the child will retain before voiding and has been used to treat diurnal enuresis in a normal child (Doleys & Wells, 1975). The child is reinforced for not urinating once he has reported the need to go to the toilet and the intervals between wanting to go and urinating are gradually increased – thus leading to an increased functional bladder capacity. Doleys (1977) summarises eight studies of the effect of retention control training on night wetting. He found that six studies reported success, one no success and one partial success. It may be worth trying this method with some mentally retarded people, particularly those for whom a bell-and-pad is unsuitable for one reason or another. Doleys, however, feels that there is not yet strong support for the use of retention control as a treatment for enuresis.

Progressive retention, another method of treating nocturnal enuresis, may be similar to retention control. Progressive retention (Carr, in preparation) involves lifting the sleeping child earlier and earlier in the evening until a time is found at which he is usually still dry. After the child has been lifted at this time for several nights, the time at which he is lifted is very gradually increased, with the aim that he shall become accustomed to being wakened when his bladder is increasingly full (but before voiding). This method was used with Nicky, a nine-year-old Down's syndrome boy, after a star chart had been unsuccessful and his mother had adamantly refused to venture on a trial of the bell-and-pad. Nicky was first lifted at 9.30 p.m. and this was gradually increased over four months, with variable evening success, to 10 p.m. when Nicky, for the first time in his life, began to be occasionally dry in the morning. Nine months later, Nicky was dry through the night approximately 70 per cent of the time and six months later again this increased to 100 per cent. Progressive retention, as described here, has been used, so far as is known, with only the one child and the factors leading to his successful training are quite unclear. Nevertheless the method may offer another avenue to explore if other methods fail or are seen as impracticable.

### 3. DRY-BED TRAINING

This procedure, described by Azrin, Sneed & Foxx (1973), is similar in many respects to the intensive daytime toilet training described by Azrin & Foxx (1971). It requires considerable effort from the trainer over a short period of time but may solve the problem very rapidly. The main features of the programme are:

positive reinforcement for having a dry bed and for using the lavatory at night;
practice in getting up during the night to urinate;
extra fluids to provide more opportunities for urination to occur;

alarm systems to enable immediate detection of correct toiletting; and

punishment for accidents in the form of reprimands and cleanliness training.

Initially, the trainee is given extra fluids before going to bed, woken every hour and led to (or asked to go to) the toilet. If he uses the toilet within five minutes he is rewarded, taken back to bed, praised for having dry sheets and allowed to go back to sleep for the remainder of the hour. If he does not use the toilet he is taken back to bed and reinforced for having a dry bed. Reinforcement in both situations includes extra fluids. If the trainee wets his bed he is woken, scolded, taken to the toilet and then made to change his sheets. After this he is given positive practice in using the toilet: he returns to bed for three minutes, is then taken to the toilet, returns to bed for another three minutes and so on for a 45-minute period. When there is one accident or less a night and the trainee uses the toilet on at least 50 per cent of occasions, he moves on to the second stage of monitored post training. During this stage, wet beds result in reprimands, cleanliness training and positive practice but there are no extra fluids and hourly awakenings. Stage two continues until there are seven consecutive accident-free nights when treatment is discontinued although the trainee's bed is inspected each morning and, if wet, he is required to change the sheets and remake the bed. Stage two is re-introduced if two accidents occur within a week.

Azrin and his colleagues used this method with twelve profoundly retarded adults (mean IQ 12) all of whom wet the bed at least four nights out of twelve but were accident-free during the day. Eight of the patients reached criterion after one night of training, three after two nights and one after three nights. Following this brief period of training, bedwetting for this group occurred at an average rate of 9 per cent during the first week compared with a 50 per cent baseline. This was a reduction in incontinence of 85 per cent during the first week which rose to 95 per cent by the fifth week. There were no relapses during a three-month follow-up period. The method seems promising in that it works quickly and with individuals who are functioning at a very low level. More studies are needed, however, especially perhaps with parents of mentally handicapped children as the trainers, although Azrin *et al.* (1974) report the successful use of this method when parents of normal children acted as the trainers. It would be interesting also to know whether or not the procedure would be as effective if some of the aversive elements, such as positive practice in toiletting and cleanliness training, were omitted.

## ENCOPRESIS

Enuresis and encopresis are physiologically and behaviourally different (Neale, 1963) although sometimes teaching bladder control will indirectly result in bowel control (Epstein & McCoy, 1977). However, behavioural treatments of the two conditions have much in common. Positive reinforcement, for example, is an important part of treatment for both the enuretic and encopretic child and maintains inappropriate bowel habits as well as establishing correct ones (Lal & Lindsley, 1968). It may be more difficult to 'catch' the child's bowel movements than it is to 'catch' him urinating, as the former occur less frequently. However, just as we can give extra fluids to provide increased opportunities for bladder training, it is possible to provide extra opportunities for bowel training, for example, with the use of a suppository (Lal & Lindsley, 1968). Ashkenazi (1975) treated a group of encopretic children aged three to twelve years, using positive reinforcement together with suppositories, and pointed out that a suppository may serve as a discriminative stimulus for correct toiletting. Other studies have employed a variety of medical and behavioural treatments for encopresis in normal children (Neale, 1963; Tomlinson, 1970; Crowley & Armstrong 1977; Wright & Bunch, 1977). Studies using retarded children (and some of those using non-retarded ones) often find that some kind of punishment procedure is necessary for inappropriate toiletting behaviour. Giles & Wolf (1966) taught five severely retarded boys to be continent of both faeces and urine by a combination of shaping, positive and negative reinforcement, suppositories and aversive consequences. Their method, however, involves procedures which are unacceptable to those working with the severely handicapped in this country – for example, depriving the child of meals until appropriate toiletting occurred (although each child was fed at least one large meal a day) and tying one boy to the toilet seat for 36 hours over a three-day period. This same child was placed in a restraining jacket and blindfolded following inappropriate responses. Barrett (1969) describes how parents taught their five-and-a-half-year-old retarded non-verbal boy to use the toilet for bowel movements by a combination of praise and edible reinforcement when he did open his bowels in the toilet, together with contingent isolation and restraint when he defaecated in any other place. The restraint and isolation involved placing the boy in a restraining chair and leaving him alone in his room for 30-45 minutes. The period of restraint and isolation, also used with a non-retarded twelve-year-old by Edelman (1971), would now certainly be considered too long and Hobbs & Forehand (1977) suggest that four minutes is an optimal period for a time-out procedure. In Edelman's case, punishment alone resulted in a decrease but not a cessation of soiling, which only occurred when the girl was negatively reinforced by being allowed to avoid washing up in the evening if she had not soiled.

Doleys & Arnold (1975) successfully treated an eight-year-old retarded encopretic boy by using a procedure based on Azrin & Foxx's intensive toilet training methods. This procedure, called Full Cleanliness Training, requires the child to clean himself and his clothing following inappropriate toiletting behaviour. The boy's parents checked his pants every fifteen to twenty minutes, reinforcing him for dry and clean pants. They also took him to the toilet each hour for about ten minutes, reinforcing him for any attempt to defaecate. On the way to the toilet they asked him if he wanted to open his bowels in order to draw his attention to the discriminative stimuli that precede a bowel movement. Star charts were also used. Any soiling resulted in:

(1) his parents' displeasure;
(2) the boy washing the soiled clothes for at least 15 minutes;
(3) the boy cleaning himself.

A mild laxative was also used during training. Soiling was eliminated by the sixteenth week, although there was some relapse after this when the parents became careless about the Full Cleanliness Training.

To summarise, if simple 'habit training' proves ineffective, there are three methods for dealing with encopresis, positive reinforcement used alone, positive reinforcement used with a suppository or laxative (if these are to be used, the advice of a doctor should be sought) and positive reinforcement used with punishment for inappropriate toiletting responses. 'Habit-training' and positive reinforcement were both tried with Daisy, a five-year-old moderately retarded girl seen regularly by a paediatrician for this. It was felt, however, that a behavioural treatment might be effective. During the first visit to the home, Daisy's mother described how she had recently taught her to overcome her fear of sitting on the toilet by giving her sweets. Daisy had never been known to defaecate into the toilet. For the first month of treatment, Daisy's mother sat her on the toilet each day after breakfast, as soon as she returned from school and before bed. Again, at no time did Daisy defaecate into the toilet. A star chart and reward system were discussed – Daisy's mother was asked to record every day for two weeks where Daisy had her bowel movement (i.e., in her pants, on the floor, in the toilet). A chart was left for this purpose. Still Daisy did not open her bowels into the toilet although she urinated in the toilet quite happily. By this time Daisy had finished school for the summer holiday. It was explained to her that if she used the toilet for a bowel movement she would get a star on her chart. Each star could be exchanged for a packet of sweets and, if she had any stars at all by the time of the psychologist's next visit, she could go to the shops with her and choose an ice-cream or something else that she liked. During the first week Daisy used the toilet twice and, by week 8, was only defaecating into the toilet. Figure 9.1 illustrates Daisy's progress. A side effect of treatment is that Daisy is now dry at night, although this problem had not been tackled directly.

Figure 9.1: Daisy's Toiletting Programme

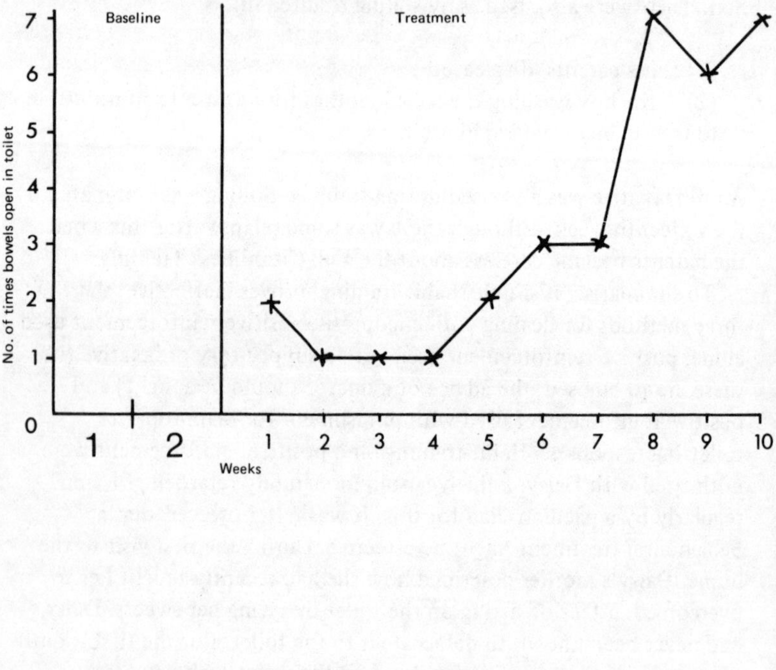

## OTHER INAPPROPRIATE TOILETTING BEHAVIOURS

Not all toiletting problems result from primary enuresis or encopresis. Many retarded people, even though they are able to use the toilet correctly, engage in various inappropriate toiletting behaviours because they like the consequences. Danny, for example, frequently smeared faeces in the classroom. A functional analysis of his smearing showed that it was being maintained by the attention he received each time he smeared, being taken from the classroom by an assistant, bathed, talked to, dressed in clean clothes and, often, given a cup of tea. For this and similar problems, the main treatment method is to remove the positive reinforcement maintaining the behaviour, while ensuring that plenty of positive reinforcement is available for other more acceptable behaviours (Balson, 1973). In Danny's case it was important to see that, as far as possible, he did not receive warm baths, cups of tea and conversation with adults consequent upon his smearing although he was receiving a great deal of adult attention at other times. In this and similar cases it is easier said than done to pay no attention to the smearing. Parents and staff will, naturally, become angry and want to scold the child, which may be extremely reinforcing for certain children (see Chapter 3). Furthermore, if the child is not changed immediately, it is difficult to carry on working in the midst of such an unpleasant smell. With Danny, the programme was as follows.

(1) Dress him in a catsuit each day to reduce opportunities to smear.
(2) When he soils his pants, pay no attention for fifteen minutes. Staff agreed that it would be worth putting up with the smell in the short term in order to eliminate the problem altogether.
(3) After fifteen minutes take Danny to the bathroom, wipe him down with a cold flannel without speaking to him.
(4) Bath and change Danny just before he goes home, i.e., not contingently on soiling or smearing.

Soiling and smearing stopped within a matter of two weeks. A very similar programme was used with John, who soiled in his bedroom and appeared to enjoy all the fuss that this produced. When he was removed and cleaned up calmly and the room cleaned in his absence, the smearing stopped.

Overcorrection and restitution may sometimes be used to reduce these kinds of problems (for a description of this method see Chapter 8). If overcorrection is used, the child cleans up any mess he has made plus cleaning the surrounding area or cleaning the same thing over and over again. This may mean, for example, that the child washes his pyjamas and the sheets, scrubs the floor and remakes the bed. Positive practice in this case would include showing the child the appropriate place for faeces, placing faeces in the lavatory bowl, seating the child on the lavatory and similar procedures. A cat-suit or pyjama trousers buttoned to pyjamas tops may help to reduce opportunities to smear but, with a child capable of toiletting himself, has the disadvantage of making him unable to use the toilet unless he has some means of communicating his need to an adult. The advantages and disadvantages of any procedures have to be weighed carefully for each individual.

Other punishment procedures which may be considered include positive reinforcement for not soiling. Again, time-out and restraint must be used for no longer than a few minutes, the child should be under continuous observation and records should be kept. Furthermore, continuous observation and records should be kept. Furthermore, time-out and restraint should be used contingent on the problem behaviour occurring, and so if the smearing or soiling is discovered sometime after the child has actually done it, these methods should not be used.

For certain problems and with some children 'changing the environment' may provide a solution. Maria, for example, a seven-year-old partly toilet-trained girl, defaecated on the floor in her bedroom approximately twice a week. She did not smear the faeces but covered them with her bedclothes, causing almost as much mess as if she had smeared. Her mother felt that she was frightened to go to the lavatory during the night even though the hall light was left on and a night light left in Maria's bedroom. Maria's mother tried leaving a potty in the bedroom, but Maria usually knocked this over either by accident or by design. Eventually a heavy wooden commode chair was made by a local carpenter and an eight-week follow-up showed that Maria had defaecated on the floor only once.

Sometimes the problem may be not that the child will not use the toilet but that he uses it too often. This may, of course, be due to an infection or some other physical cause and these should be thoroughly investigated first. There are children, however, who urinate very frequently for no apparent physical reason. Lucy, for example, caused great concern to her teachers by constantly dashing to the toilet and often staying there for ten or fifteen minutes until an adult went to find her. A week's baseline was taken during which Lucy went to the toilet on average 30 times a day. Lucy's teachers had tried several methods to reduce her visits to the toilet – locking the classroom door, slapping her leg and energetic persuasion – but these had created a number of new problems and had had little effect on the frequency of Lucy's trips to the toilet. No physiological explanation had been found for her frequent micturition and it was felt that the attention she received from staff for going to the toilet was maintaining the behaviour. An extinction programme was considered but rejected as being impracticable. After discussion with the teachers involved it was decided:

(1) to allow Lucy to go to the toilet no more than once every fifteen minutes. This interval would be increased gradually;
(2) to reward Lucy by attention and approval at frequent intervals so that she would be rewarded for staying in the classroom

Figure 9.2: Treatment

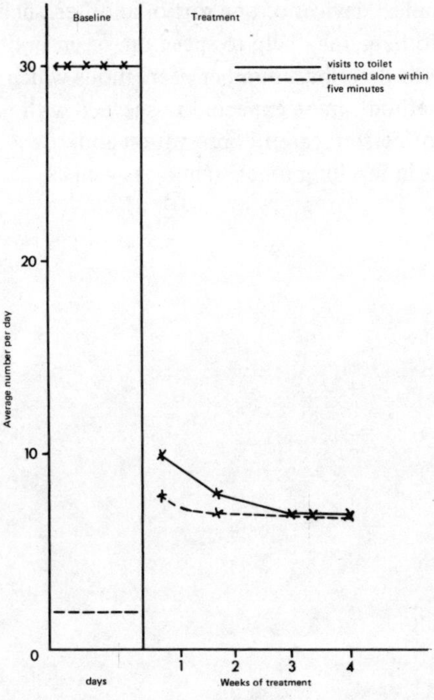

rather than for going to the toilet;

(3) that when she did go to the toilet, if she had not returned within five minutes, the teacher would collect her, saying once only, 'Time to get off, Lucy', and physically prompting her if necessary. There would be no further verbal communication or eye-to-eye contact on the way back to the classroom.

Figure 9.2 shows that Lucy's visits to the toilet dropped from 30 to 7 a day and she returned alone within five minutes on the vast majority of occasions.

## CONCLUSIONS

Toilet training is an important skill for mentally handicapped people to acquire because it increases their independence, decreases the workload for caretakers and appears to be a major factor in determining a retarded child's admission into long-term care. Behaviour modification methods can be successfully used to teach toiletting to even profoundly handicapped people while technical devices of one sort or another, such as alarm systems and special clothing, may help to speed up, or ensure, success. The aim here has been to describe a number of methods which may be useful, but no single method can be expected to succeed with every mentally retarded child or person; careful observation and analysis must always come first in teaching toilet training as well as other kinds of behaviour.

# 10 LANGUAGE TRAINING

Patricia Howlin

It is not a simple task to establish precisely the frequency of language deficits in the severely retarded, since both definitions of language handicap and survey methods differ widely. Nevertheless, it is clear that the rates of language and speech difficulties are extremely high. Schlanger & Gottsleben (1957), in a survey of 516 residents in a New Jersey Training School, found that no less than 79 per cent had 'varying types and levels of speech defectiveness'. Spreen (1965), in a review of studies on the relationship between IQ and speech and language disorder, reports that the frequency of language handicap is 100 per cent below IQ 20, around 90 per cent in the 21-50 IQ range and about 45 per cent in the mildly retarded groups. Gould (1977) found similar levels of language disability in retarded children. Over 50 per cent of those with an IQ below 70 showed severe language handicaps, and in children with an IQ below 20 comprehension and spoken language were almost always absent.

It is obvious from such statistics that there is a considerable need for specific help in improving the communication skills of the mentally retarded, and over the past fifteen years operant training programmes have had great impact on the development of language in both subnormal adults and children.

## LANGUAGE TRAINING PROGRAMMES

One of the earliest studies to demonstrate the effectiveness of reinforcement techniques in the remediation of language skills was that by Isaacs *et al*. (1960). Using cigarettes and chewing gum as reinforcers, first for lip movements and later for any vocal behaviour, they were able to reinstate speech in two schizophrenic patients who had been mute for 14 and 19 years respectively. Later, Sherman (1963, 1965) used similar methods to re-establish speech in institutionalised psychotics. It was about this time, too, that work on the development of speech in non-verbal children began to appear (Hingtgen & Trost, 1966; Wolf *et al*., 1964; Hewett, 1965; Salzinger *et al*., 1965; Lovaas, Berberich *et al*., 1966).

Many of these early language training programmes were generally designed simply to increase *rates* of vocalisations, rather than complexity of utterances. Reinforcement (usually with bites of food) would be given for random vocalisations made by the patient, thereby increasing the frequency of such sounds. Subsequent reinforcements would then be given for closer approximations to the sounds required by the therapist.

Lovaas, Berberich *et al.* (1966), however, found that although children could learn a few words in this manner, such procedures, despite prolonged training, generally resulted in only a very restricted growth in vocabulary. The *direct* training of imitative responses, rather than merely reinforcing chance vocalisations, resulted in much greater progress.

Wolf *et al.* (1964) described the effective use of imitative training in developing speech in a 3½-year-old, brain-damaged, autistic and mentally retarded boy. Lovaas, Berberich *et al.* (1966) report on the establishment, within 26 days, of a large imitative vocabulary in two initially mute autistic 6-year-olds. Kerr *et al.* (1965), Cook & Adams (1966) and Sapon (1966) also used direct imitation training successfully with language deficient children.

## THE TRAINING TECHNIQUES USED

The techniques used in these studies, and in the very large number of investigations which have followed them, have been well summarised by Lovaas (1966) and Sloane *et al.* (1968). Although the methods described have generally been used with language handicapped *children*, they are based on the same techniques of modelling, prompting, fading and reinforcement as described in previous chapters, and as such can be readily adapted to suit the needs of adults.

Typically, the training of an imitative vocabulary in a mute subject might proceed along the following lines. Sessions should be kept very brief at first, and conducted in as quiet and undistracting an environment as possible – a small, barely furnished room is ideal for this purpose. At first, rewards may be given for simply looking at the therapist's mouth when instructed. This is necessary for the subject to see the shape of the mouth movements involved in making particular sounds, and physical prompts, such as guiding the child's head towards the therapist, may be needed initially to establish this behaviour. Once attending to the therapist is well established, training on specific imitations can begin. To start with, these would usually be sounds already emitted very frequently by the child and therefore relatively easy to bring under control. For example, in the case of a child who constantly repeats the sound /Ba-Ba-Ba/ the therapist might echo this sound after him, and then reinforce the child when he makes his /Ba/ sound again shortly afterwards.

Using sounds which already appear frequently in the child's repertoire increases the likelihood of his 'copying' the therapist's vocalisation and being reinforced for this, and thus also increases the likelihood of his making such sounds more frequently thereafter.

If the child makes very few spontaneous vocalisations, an alternative procedure is to begin by training sounds which can be easily prompted and demonstrated by the therapist.

Sounds such as /B/ or /OO/, which have clear concomitant visual components, are easier to learn than gutteral sounds such as /K/ or /G/. They also have the advantage that they can be physically shaped – by pushing the child's lips together, or pulling them forwards, for example. At first, *any* sound which the child makes following the therapist's stimulus-sound should be immediately reinforced, even if this bears little resemblance to the therapist's vocalisations. Once the frequency of verbalisations has been increased in this way, subsequent reinforcements should only be given for increasingly closer approximations to the therapist's sound. Physical prompts should be gradually faded until the child is able to repeat the sound without help. New sounds can then be introduced. Initially it is wisest to work on sounds which differ clearly from each other, so that the child does not become confused. Later, however, less discrete sounds can be introduced. It is often found that the first few sounds can take many hours of training to achieve, but thereafter subsequent imitations tend to emerge more rapidly.

At this stage of training, the main aim is to increase the number of sounds which the child can imitate and it is not necessary that the sounds have any particular meaning for the child. He is simply learning to imitate the therapist.

Later, however, when the child is able to imitate a variety of different sounds, he can be taught to 'chain' these together to form simple words or word approximations, which are related to objects in his environment, and hence will be more meaningful for him. For example if the child can make the sound /Ba/ clearly, he can be taught to imitate /Ba-Ba/ as an approximation to 'baby', when shown a picture of a baby or a doll. /Ma-Ma/ for 'Mummy', or /Da-Da/ for 'Daddy' might also be taught in the same manner. Similarly if the child is able to make the sounds /K/ and /Ah/ these can be chained together to form the word 'car'. At first, each of the pair of sounds may need to be prompted separately by the therapist and the child rewarded for imitating one at a time. Then, very gradually, the time interval between the presentation of the two sounds should be reduced, until reinforcements are obtained only for production of the two sounds together. Later three- and four-sound chains can be introduced. Once chains of 2 to 3 sounds have been mastered, imitation of the names of many simple objects can begin. In order to maintain the child's co-operation at this stage it is necessary to select items which the child is particularly fond of or interested in, and if this is done the items themselves, rather than any external and possibly distracting rewards, may be used as reinforcements. Thus, as soon as the child makes an attempt to say 'Car' he can be given the car to play with for a few moments.

It is always important to ensure that the words taught are those referring to objects familiar in the child's environment. Words such as 'lift' or 'car' are much more appropriate for a child living in a high-rise block of flats in town than are the words 'cow' or 'daisy'. As in the very earliest stages of teaching, rewards should be given consistently for even very poor approximations to the therapist's prompts at first; later, only more accurate imitations should be reinforced.

## DEVELOPING SPONTANEOUS NAMING

Once the subject is able to imitate many simple words, he should be encouraged to use these spontaneously, in the absence of direct prompts by the therapist. At first, prompts will need to be faded slowly. For example, taking an object whose name the child can already imitate with ease, he should be asked clearly, 'What is this?' and then prompted immediately with the appropriate answer, such as '*Ball*'. Gradually these prompts can be faded and a typical sequence might be: (1) Ball; (2) Ba--; (3) B---, leaving the child to supply the missing sounds. Later, merely mouthing the initial letter of the word should be sufficient until eventually the child is able to answer the question in the absence of any prompts. Sometimes a child will imitate not only the correct response, but also the preceding question. So instead of responding with, 'Ball', he will say, 'What is this – ball.' It may help if the question is said in a quiet voice or even a whisper and the response loudly and clearly; or it may be necessary to interrupt the child as he attempts to reproduce the question, and only allow and reinforce him for responding correctly. New nouns and then other single words such as verbs or adjectives can be taught in a similar way.

A very successful way to teach verbs is to do this in the context of a play situation. The child might be prompted verbally, or physically if necessary, to carry out an action such as, 'Push the car', or 'Jump up and down'. The therapist should then ask, 'What are you doing?' and immediately and clearly supply the appropriate response – such as, 'Jumping' or, 'Pushing'. When the child is responding accurately to such prompts, they should be faded in the same manner as described above. Again, using activities which the child particularly enjoys will ensure increased co-operation on his part, and may also obviate the need for any additional reinforcers. If the child does not respond correctly to prompts at first, he should be prevented from continuing the activity until he does so.

Adjectives can be rather more of a problem to teach, since even young normal children can have difficulty in distinguishing correctly between pairs of adjectives such as big and small, or fat and thin, despite the fact that such words may appear frequently in their spontaneous language. Colour names, however, usually appear relatively early in children's speech, and are acquired without too much difficulty. Having first established that the child can match colours easily he can be taught at least primary colour names using the same techniques of prompting and fading as discussed above.

It is also useful to teach children to use proper names such as 'Daddy' or 'Mummy' or their own names. These are obviously necessary to enable him to name people in his environment, but in addition they can be used later in simple phrase speech. Eventually the child should also learn to ask for objects which are not immediately visible.

As well as learning to name objects or actions or people on demand, it is necessary for the child to learn to request items he wants. This will often prove more difficult to teach than simple naming, but is an extremely important stage in the development of spontaneous speech. Many authors in fact regard the progression from reflex labelling to symbolic naming, or the requesting of objects which are *not* present, as the first stage of true language development (Lewis, 1951; Rutter & Bax, 1972).

Using a particularly favoured object, perhaps a special toy or even if necessary an object to which the child is obsessionally attached – a piece of string or a bit of paper – this should be held in front of the child but just out of his reach. He can then be asked, 'What do you want?' and prompted with the correct response. Again prompts should be gradually reduced until the question is answered without help. Later the child can be taught to select and ask for the item he wants from a range of different objects, until eventually he is able to express his needs spontaneously and without necessarily being questioned first.

## TEACHING PHRASE SPEECH

Once a fairly extensive single-word vocabulary has been established two-word chains, such as noun-verb, or adjective-noun constructions, can be taught. This may be done in a manner similar to that described for the building up of sound chains, using words which are already in the child's repertoire. If he has already been taught colour names, for example, he can be taught to join these to familiar nouns to form phrases such as 'Yellow hat' or 'Green bag'. When the child has learned to use verbs in isolation, he can be taught to use these in association with nouns to form phrases such as 'Bobby clapping' or 'Mummy eating'.

The study of early phrase speech in normal children has revealed a striking similarity, across cultures, in the semantic relationships expressed in these utterances (Slobin, 1970; Bloom, 1970; Bowerman, 1973). Given the relative ease with which normal children learn to use particular semantic structures, it is probably wise when working with retarded children to restrict training to similar relationships. The most common relationships expressed in early two-word uttereances are those of:

| | |
|---|---|
| locatives | (play bed, pillow here) |
| possession | (Mummy('s) shoe) |
| action | (kick door, Daddy go) and |
| quality | (pretty boat, big chair) |

When the child has progressed beyond the two-word stage, longer phrases may often be successfully taught by using a 'backward chaining' technique, as described in previous chapters. Thus, the subject will be initially required to provide the final word to the trainer's prompt. For instance, the therapist, following the question, 'What is it?' might prompt with the cue, 'It is a red. . .' and the child would then be reinforced for supplying the word 'ball'. The prompt may then be further reduced so that the penultimate word, too, must be supplied.

This process would continue until the child was able to answer using a complete, if simple, sentence. When teaching in this way it is often useful to train a number of very similar or 'pivotal' type phrases to which a variety of different ending can be attached. This helps the subject to learn to use with ease certain basic phrases such as, 'I want a. . .', or 'It is a. . .' or 'I have a. . .'.

It occasionally happens that children who *can* use simple sentence structures may be unwilling to use more than one- or two-word utterances as they are perfectly able to make themselves understood in this way. Such children may sometimes use quite long sentences under stress – as in the case of one eight-year-old who, after getting no response to his continued screams for 'Glass orange, glass orange', suddenly came out with 'Oh for heaven's sake, please may I have a glass of orange juice. Please!'

With such children 'backward chaining' techniques may be less successful, and the child may simply refuse to provide more than one- or two-word answers. In these cases it may be necessary to prompt (and insist that the child repeats) each word of the sentence in turn before he is rewarded.

With more capable children, 'telegraphic' utterances such as, 'More dinner' or 'Want ball' should not be reinforced, and children should only be supplied with what they want when they use a complete phrase, such as 'I want the ball', or 'I want more dinner.' If the child learns that one- or two-word utterances are *not* sufficient to get what he demands, and that he must use simple but complete sentence structures, phrase speech should develop fairly rapidly.

As soon as the child has reached the level of two- or three-word utterances, different constructions can be taught. For example, pronoun-verb or pronoun-noun combinations such as, 'I have', 'You are', 'My hat', 'Your cup', can be taught. Dolls or puppets can be very useful in teaching third person pronouns since these enable the therapist to demonstrate various pronoun cases. For example, a female doll can be shown carrying a bag, and the child taught to respond correctly to questions such as, 'What is she doing?' or, 'Whose bag is it?' Male dolls, or pairs of dolls, can be used to teach masculine and plural pronouns, and children frequently show great enjoyment in playing with such materials. The therapist's or the child's own actions can be used to teach the various forms of 'I' and 'You' and again this can be turned into a play situation. For example, if the child is sitting on a swing or throwing a ball back and forth, he can be prompted to respond to questions such as, 'What are you doing?' or, 'What am I doing?' This game is then only allowed to continue if the child answers appropriately. To avoid confusion over pronouns, it is usually advisable to teach one pronoun at a time to begin with, and only when this is well established to progress to new ones. As with normal children, the pronouns 'he', 'she' and 'it' are usually easier to acquire than 'I' and 'you'.

## INCREASING CONVERSATIONAL AND HIGHER LEVEL LANGUAGE SKILLS

Other useful structures to teach, in order to introduce as much flexibility and range as possible into the child's use of language, are prepositions, different verb tenses, singular and plural endings and other simple inflections. Teaching responses to questions which typically occur in social interactions such as, 'What is your name?, 'How are you?', 'Where do you live?' also help the child to take part in very simple conversations, as well as being important if he should get lost. Later training in more complex verbal skills – such as asking questions, carrying messages, reporting on past events and so on – can also be undertaken, again using the techniques of prompts and rewards and the gradual fading of prompts.

Generally, the guiding principle of any language training programme is to proceed always in a step-by-step fashion, teaching the child to master one particular sound or word or concept before progressing to another, and then eventually training him to combine simple elements in his repertoire to form increasingly more complex utterances. Using old familiar forms in this way to build up new structures ensures that teaching progresses steadily and smoothly towards achieving the goal of normal or near-normal language. In addition, there is now evidence to show that normally developing children acquire language skills in a similar manner – using two relatively simple constructions together to express novel ideas, before developing new structures to express the same ideas (Slobin, 1973). For example, before children begin to use plural phrases such as, 'They are green', consistently, they will tend to use two singular phrases instead, such as 'That one is green and that one is green' (Bloom, 1973); or, before three-word utterances such as subject-verb-object are acquired, these are often preceded by a number of two-word utterances in rapid succession which, in fact, express the same functions. Thus, shortly before the emergence of three-word phrases as in, 'Adam hit ball', the child will produce utterances such as 'Adam hit. . .hit ball. . .Adam ball' (Brown, 1973).

The methods described above are, of course, meant only as general guidelines for a language training programme and will, of necessity, be modified according to the needs and skills of each particular child. If the child already uses a few spontaneous words one would not start right at the beginning by teaching him to imitate single sounds. Some children, on the other hand, may be so globally retarded that much greater emphasis will need to be placed on the teaching of simple receptive skills. Basic instructions such as, 'Sit down', 'Look at me', 'Do this', which are necessary parts of the training programme, may need to be learned before teaching can progress further. Alternatively, for children who possess good use and understanding of simple, concrete ideas, the goal of the programme may be to increase their command of more abstract, imaginative language skills.

## DECREASING INAPPROPRIATE SPEECH

In cases where echolalic or stereotyped jargon utterances are a problem the first aim is to reduce these forms of speech. This can be done most effectively by consistently ignoring *all* echolalic or stereotyped verbalisations, whilst at the same time prompting the child to use correct forms of speech. As long as the child receives no response to his echolalic remarks and is attended to only when he uses appropriate constructions, egocentric utterances can generally be very rapidly brought under control. Such methods do not, as some parents fear, result in the child becoming discouraged and refusing to talk at all. Instead, socially appropriate speech tends to increase rapidly, while inappropriate echolalia shows a steady decline. Other children, as already mentioned, may be quite capable of using well-formed sentences or phrases, but prefer to communicate non-verbally, or by means of telegraphic utterances such as, 'Want out' or, 'Go toilet'. Again, prompts for the correct response should be provided at every possible opportunity, whilst all inadequate or non-verbal forms of communication – whether these be simply placing an adult's hand on the desired object or screaming loudly until someone manages to divine the child's wishes – should be consistently ignored.

It can often be very difficult for parents, nurses or teachers to deal in a consistent manner with such behaviours, because many children are extremely adept in making their wishes known even though they may use very idiosyncratic means to do so. Constantly correcting the child when it is perfectly clear to parents or teachers what he means is not always easy, but those who are familiar with the child need to be aware that strangers will not necessarily understand him in the way they do. For the child's sake, therefore, it is necessary to insist on the use of correct grammatical utterances. Even the occasional response to an echolalic or stereotyped utterance – perhaps laughing at a particularly funny jargon phrase, or giving the child something he has asked for in an echolalic way – is likely to result in a rapid increase in his use of such phrases and make them very resistant to extinction. Figure 10.1 shows the rapid upsurge in jargon utterances during an extinction programme following any attention for these. The child's utterances were of an extremely provocative kind which his mother had great difficulty in ignoring. Finally, however, she did succeed in consistently ignoring him, and jargon utterances have since remained at a very low level.

## MODIFYING THE PROGRAMME ACCORDING TO THE INDIVIDUAL CHILD

In order to ensure that the programmes implemented are appropriate to the child's level of ability, prior language skills need to be carefully assessed. Formal language tests such as the Reynell Developmental Language Scales (Reynell, 1969) are useful in obtaining standard measures of the child's use and understanding of language. If the child is functioning at too low a level to score reliably on such tests, they should be supplemented by observations, made in the child's everyday environment, of what he does say, whether this is spontaneous or echolalic, whether he uses meaningful sounds or single words or phrases, and of how much he can understand in the absence of gestural or other cues. Baseline measures of how much the child is speaking or understanding prior to treatment need to be taken in order to assess the effectiveness of subsequent treatment.

During training, regular measures of the numbers of new sounds or words or constructions acquired are needed to ensure that progress continues to be made. If treatment fails to be effective for any reason this should be easily discernible from records. Treatment procedures may then be modified accordingly. Assessment measures need to be simple enough for those in charge of the child to fill in the records quickly and easily, and in the early stages counts of sounds or words used should be adequate. When larger numbers of words are being acquired, daily frequency counts may no longer be feasible, but instead

Figure 10.1: Extinction of Jargon Utterances Used by Seven-year old Mildly Retarded Boy (IQ 74)

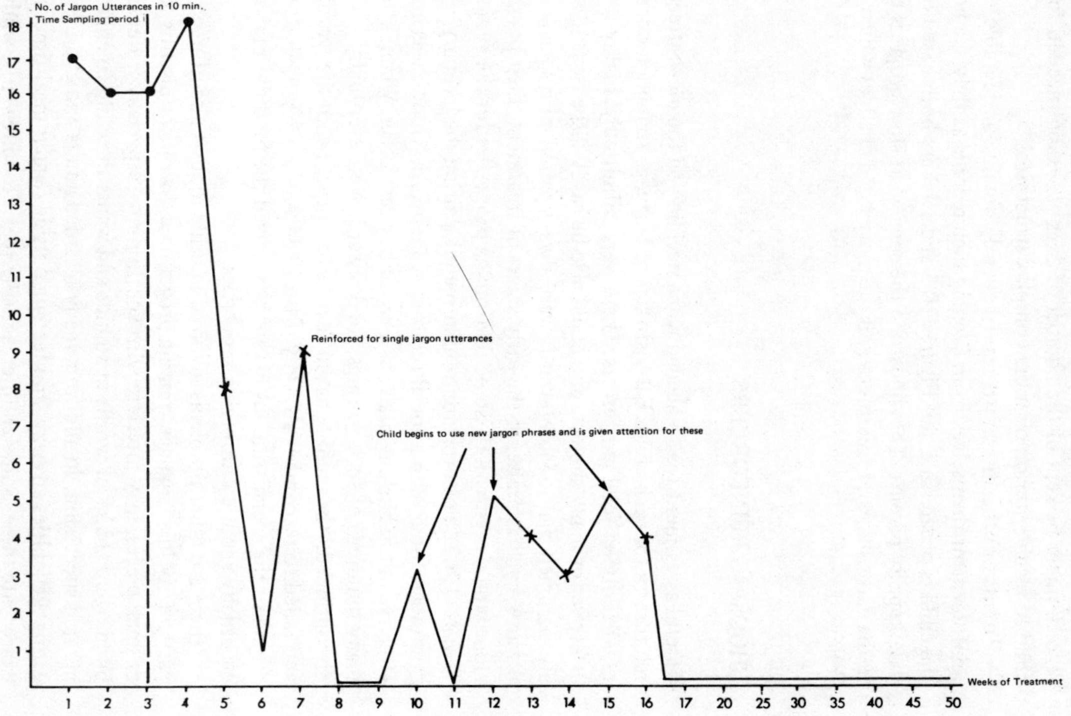

records might be kept of the number of days or sessions needed for the child to reach criterion on more complex structures.

Parents or other therapists can frequently obtain considerable reinforcement themselves from keeping such records as they see how the child is progressing and Figures 10.2 and 10.3 are both based on data kept by parents. They illustrate the somewhat slow progress made in the early stages of treatment and the more rapid changes which followed.

## CHOOSING REINFORCERS

Careful assessment is also needed when deciding on the most effective reinforcers for each child. Early studies of language training tended to rely heavily on food reinforcers. These were, admittedly, highly effective for many subjects and could also be easily dispensed. It was also assumed that if food rewards were always paired with social rewards, such as praise, in the early stages of treatment, then praise alone would eventually assume reinforcing properties for the subject. Lovaas (1967), however, found that merely pairing the 'primary' reinforcer, food, with a social reinforcer, the word, 'Good', was not effective in establishing praise as a secondary reinforcer. When, after many hundreds of such pairings, food rewards were eventually discontinued, 'the child behaved as if he had never heard the word', and failed to respond at all. Only if the child was actively made to attend to the social stimulus before he received the food did praise eventually acquire reinforcing properties.

There are other problems involved in using food as a reinforcer, particularly in a language training programme. Sweets or biscuits, even in small pieces, may interfere with vocalisations, especially if one is building up chains of words or sounds and wants the child to emit these in rapid succession. In addition, many retarded adults and children have eating difficulties anyway, and feeding outside regular meal-times may exacerbate these. Some children actually reject food rewards, whilst others may react very strongly to attempts to fade these out, thereby disrupting sessions.

Nevertheless, particularly with severely retarded subjects who show very little interest in their environment, food may well be the only effective reinforcer. If food is used, this should be given in very tiny portions to ensure that training sessions are not interrupted unduly. Care should also be taken to fade schedules of reinforcement gradually

Figure 10.2: Short-term Training Project with Retarded Six-year-old Boy (IQ ~ 50). Only three words were used prior to training.

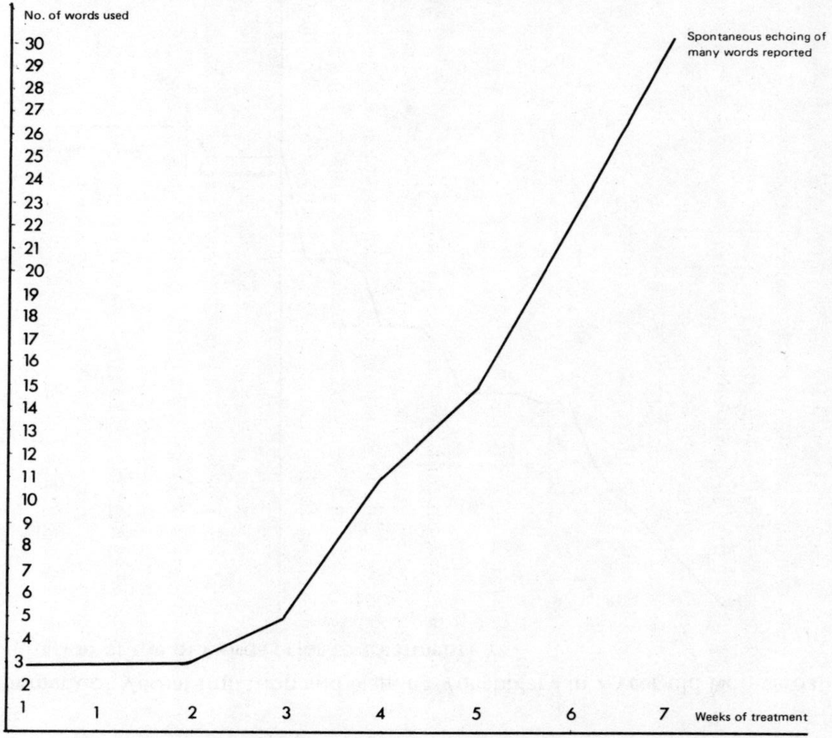

Figure 10.3: Development of Verbal Imitation and Naming Vocabulary in 7-year-old Non-verbal Autistic Boy (No imitation or use of words prior to treatment)

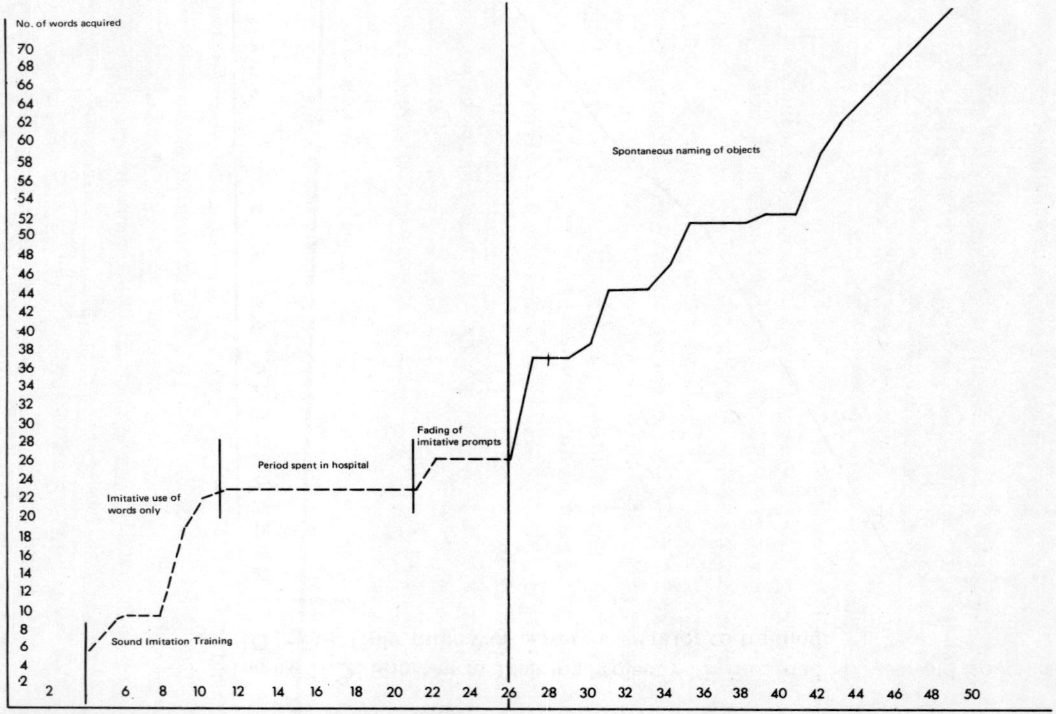

but steadily, so that the child quickly learns he must produce several correct sounds before receiving his reward.

Although food reinforcements will be necessary for certain subjects, the possibility of using other effective rewards should be investigated as part of a language training programme.

Since language is essentially a social skill, teaching the child to respond to social rewards is clearly the best means of ensuring that his attempts to use language are frequently and consistently reinforced by all those in his environment. There is then no need for therapists and others to go armed with stocks of Smarties and the like which are dispensed each time a word is uttered.

Praise alone can be very effective even with retarded subjects, although if it is not sufficient other social rewards, such as tickling or hugging or kissing, can also be employed. If social reinforcement is clearly ineffective, alternative methods will need to be tried, although these should always be accompanied by praise and attention. Toys, tokens and visual and auditory stimulation have all been used successfully in language training programmes. If the child shows no positive enjoyment of any particular activity or objects then rewards based on the Premack principle (see Chapter 3) may be utilised. In this case, any activity to which the child reverts when left alone can be used to reinforce attempts to speak. These may include obsessional or ritualistic activities, or simply allowing the child to sit alone doing nothing. Although many therapists, especially parents, may doubt the advisability of using such activities as rewards, they can be used very effectively in the early stages of treatment. Later, as the child's language and social skills develop, the need for obsessional or ritualised activities frequently declines markedly and more appropriate rewards can be substituted. Non-social rewards should be steadily faded out and replaced by social ones during training programmes, and as the child learns to use his newly acquired language skills effectively this alone may become a powerful reinforcer for him.

In language training, as with all other programmes, the reinforcement to be used is selected by careful observation of the child and of his preferences. If a variety of reinforcers can be identified it is possible to shift from one to another whenever the child shows some sign of satiation, thereby maintaining his willingness to work at the task.

## IMPLEMENTING FINDINGS FROM PSYCHOLINGUISTIC RESEARCH

As well as the need for assessment of the child's language level and of suitable reinforcers before embarking on language therapy, some consideration should also be given to the child's general developmental level. In normal children cognitive and linguistic development are closely linked (Cromer, 1974, 1978), and one does not expect a child to acquire a particular level of linguistic competence until he has reached an appropriate stage of cognitive development. Unfortunately, in work with mentally handicapped children, the influence of cognitive development on language acquisition has frequently been overlooked. In many cases the linguistic structures taught have been selected in an apparently arbitrary manner, with little assessment being made of, or attention paid to, the child's level of cognitive ability. However, studies of cognitive and language development in normal children have shown clearly that certain aspects of language are acquired at an earlier age than others, and the need to incorporate findings from normal psycholinguistic research into language training programmes for the retarded has now been recognised by a number of workers (Miller & Yoder, 1972; Morehead, 1974; Yule & Berger, 1975).

In normal language development the first sounds to appear after the initial babbling stage are vowels, and these are followed by the labial consonants /P/, /M/ and /B/. /N/, /W/ and /H/ appear between 18 months and 3 years. /K/, /G/, /D/, /NG/ and /F/, /Y/, /L/ and /S/ tend to be the next sounds to appear, whereas some sounds, such as /Θ/ (as in 'three') or /CH/ (as in church) may not be completely mastered until 7 or 8 years of age. The first sound combinations are usually in the order of the consonant-vowel, or consonant-vowel-consonant type, such as, 'Ta' or, 'Dad'.

When words begin to emerge, nouns almost always appear first, and these typically relate directly to the child's main interests: food, toys, clothes, animals, self and parents (Nelson, 1973). Verbs are usually acquired next, and later pronouns and prepositions (McCarthy, 1954). When children begin to use inflections on the ends of words the /ing/ ending of the present progressive (e.g., running, jumping, clapping) is used first, and without error. The /ed/ past ending on regular verbs (e.g., jumped, played, laughed) appears next and then the /s/ ending of the third person present (e.g., jumps, runs, claps). The latter two endings, however, prove much more difficult for normal children to acquire correctly, and they are frequently omitted, or used redundantly with irregular verbs (e.g., runned, sawed, wented). The next inflections to occur tend to be the plural /s/ and the possessive /ɪs/ endings (e.g., boats, Mummy's) although, again, many errors occur before they are finally used correctly. When pronouns emerge, 'it' tends to be used much earlier than 'I' or 'you'. 'In' and 'on' are the earliest prepositions to emerge. Indefinite and definite articles appear before other demonstrative pronouns (i.e., 'this', 'that', etc.). (For further discussions of morpheme acquisition, see Brown, 1973; De Villiers & De Villiers, 1973.)

Concepts of location develop much earlier than concepts of time, and this is reflected in the order in which normal children acquire adjectives and questions. 'In' and 'on' occur long before temporal prepositions such as 'before' or 'after'. 'What' and 'where' question forms are used and understood before 'why' or 'when' (Ervin-Tripp, 1973).

As already mentioned, normal children up to 5 years of age or later also have many difficulties with relational or dimensional terms such as big/small, more/less, different/same and even I/you, or with contrasting pairs of verbs such as come/go, bring/take. Experimental work has shown that young children frequently tend to confuse these terms and use them interchangeably. (For more detailed and highly readable discussions of stages in early language acquisition, see Clark & Clark, 1977; Menyuk, 1977.)

Children up to 8 years of age also have a marked tendency to process all sentences as if they were of a 'noun-verb-object' order. Sentences which violate this order, notably passives, are extremely difficult for them to use and understand correctly (Slobin, 1973).

In general, regular syntactic rules are easier for children to acquire than irregular rules. Mittler (1970) has shown that young children learn regular verb inflections, plurals, comparatives and superlatives more readily than the irregular forms.

Short-term memory span should also be considered in a language training programme. Several studies have shown that children are best able to process sentences which fall within their short-term memory span (Menyuk, 1964, 1969; Graham & Gulliford, 1968; Gamlin, 1971). However, although short sentences are clearly preferable as models there is evidence that normal children, at least, respond to full forms of a sentence better than to telegraphic utterances (Shipley *et al.*, 1969; Nelson, 1973; Love & Parker-Robinson, 1972; Scholes, 1969; Freedle *et al.*, 1970).

It has been suggested (Miller & Yoder, 1972) that during language training programmes therapists should 'reduce their syntax to telegraphic speech whenever possible while talking to the child'. This, they postulated, would make it simpler for the child to 'induce latent structures' from the utterances he heard, thereby facilitating his processing of language. Yule & Berger (1975), however, have suggested that limiting language models presented to the child in this way may actually inhibit the development of more complex syntactical forms. Although conclusive evidence on this point is still lacking, data from normal children would seem to indicate that it is wisest to use short but grammatically correct and fully expanded utterances as models for language learning.

The points made in the preceding section depend, of course, on the assumption that language in retarded children follows essentially the same course as language in normal children.

There remains, however, some disagreement as to whether the language of retarded children is merely delayed or is qualitatively different from that used by normal children. Cromer (1974) suggests that different sub-groups of language handicapped patients may possess very different language skills and that to refer to them as a homogeneous group is almost bound to produce conflicting results. At present the main weight of evidence tends to suggest (although there are some conflicting data) that the language of many retarded subjects is quantitatively, rather than qualitatively, different from that of normal subjects; that is, it is delayed but not deviant (Lenneberg *et al*., 1964; Newfield & Schlanger, 1968; Freedman & Carpenter, 1976; Leonard *et al*., 1976). Until there is firm evidence to the contrary, it would seem most profitable, therefore, to make use of as much information as possible from psycholinguistic research when designing language training programmes.

To summarise, the following points are suggested as potentially useful guidelines:

(1) Teach sounds, words and later syntactical structures in the order in which they emerge in normal language development.
(2) Teach grammatically consistent rules before irregular rules.
(3) Teach simple, active declarative sentences which maintain a subject-verb-object order before sentences which violate this order.
(4) Teach semantic concepts which are appropriate to the child's level of cognitive ability and avoid concepts with which young,

normal children are known to have difficulties.

(5) Ensure that the utterances to which the child is exposed as models are simple and within his short-term memory span, but retain acceptable, grammatical forms.

## DEVELOPING GENERATIVE LANGUAGE

The ever-increasing number of well-controlled studies of operant language training demonstrates conclusively the effectiveness of these methods in developing speech in non-speaking and retarded individuals suffering from a wide range of disorders (e.g., in mentally handicapped children, Guess *et al.*, 1974; in autistic children, Hemsley *et al.*, 1978; and in children with specific speech and language difficulties, McReynolds, 1972). Operant techniques have also been shown to be more effective than other methods designed to improve communication skills, such as play therapy (Ney *et al.*, 1971) or general language enrichment programmes (Fenn, 1976). Serious doubts remain, however, as to how far speech taught by these techniques extends beyond simple, associative learning. Do retarded subjects trained in this way eventually acquire what Carrol (1964) has defined as the essential attribute of language, 'the capability of generating and understanding new utterances'?

Certainly the results of operant language training programmes vary enormously. Some subjects, after many hundreds, even thousands of trials, show depressingly little change, whilst others, after relatively short periods of training, are reported as achieving 'normal' language. To some extent, outcome seems to depend very much on the initial language level of the child. Mute children with little comprehension of language tend to make relatively poor progress following operant training programmes; children who are initially echolalic, or using a little spontaneous language, tend to do much better (Lovaas, 1977; Howlin, 1978; Rutter, 1978). However, many other variables within the training programmes, or within subjects themselves, which may influence outcome have still to be investigated. Although much more needs to be known about the factors which affect outcome, it seems reasonable to assume that teaching generative rules, such as those governing the use of inflections or simple transformations (for example, those required to form interrogative or imperative sentences) is of more value than training stereotyped phrases associated with particular objects or events.

Whether the child is able to generate at least simple novel utterances can be fairly easily tested during the course of training. For example, if he is learning verb endings, such as the present progressive /ing/, one can test whether he has learned the rules governing its usage by asking him to apply it to unfamiliar verbs. For example, one child who had been taught this construction suddenly remarked, on hearing a dog bark, 'That dog is woofing.' The use of a made-up word which he had never previously encountered in this way demonstrated that he had learned the rules governing the use of /ing/, and was not merely repeating taught responses.

At a simpler level, if the child knows the word 'yellow' and the word 'cup' but has never used them together, he might be shown a picture of a yellow cup to see if he is able to generate new phrases using adjectives and nouns already in his repertoire.

At a still earlier stage, the child's ability to generalise word-labels to objects other than those he was first taught should be tested. If he has learned the word 'cup' using a blue and white striped mug, for example, his comprehension of the general concept represented by the word 'cup' should be tested and, if necessary, trained with other cups, such as red china ones, or green plastic ones (see Chapter 6). It is always useful for this purpose to keep sets of objects which, though similar in nature, vary along many different dimensions. Large collections of pictures, especially those from mail-order catalogues, can be particularly valuable.

## THE VALUE OF PRIOR IMITATION AND COMPREHENSION TRAINING

In addition to more fundamental issues, such as the extent to which generative language skills can be acquired through operant training, there are a number of other methodological problems involved in setting up a language programme. For instance, the importance of training motor imitations prior to verbal imitations has been emphasised by several workers (Bricker & Bricker, 1970; Sloane *et al.*, 1968; Hingtgen *et al.*, 1967). Typically, the child is trained to imitate gross motor movements, then finer hand and finger movements and eventually mouth movements before verbal imitation training begins. Unfortunately, experimental studies of this procedure (Garcia *et al.*, 1971; Baer *et al.*, 1967; Risley, 1968b) have shown that there is little or no generalisation from training in motor imitation to verbal imitation. Since many retarded children have difficulties with motor skills, time spent training motor imitation as a direct precursor to language training may be unprofitable. Imitative behaviours which help the child to copy mouth movements, or which ensure that he can sit and look at the therapist, may be of some direct value to training programmes but, other than this, motor imitation training may well be unnecessary.

A similar problem which arises is the need to train receptive language skills before expressive language. This approach has been very much emphasised in traditional speech therapy but, again, recent experimantal work has failed to support this procedure. Guess (1969) and Guess & Baer (1973), working with retarded children, found very little, if any, generalisation from training in the receptive use of grammatical structures to the productive use of these structures, or vice versa.

What is needed is a well controlled study to assess whether children trained first in motor or receptive skills subsequently acquire expressive language more rapidly than children not trained in this way. In the absence of such a study, however, it would seem at present that many retarded children show no generalisation from one set of learned skills to related but dissimilar skills, and hence the value of independent comprehension training programmes prior to expressive training programmes remains in doubt. Ideally, training in both receptive and productive skills should be carried out in conjunction to ensure complete and appropriate learning of structures.

However, many mute, non-comprehending children will respond very slowly, if at all, to expressive training programmes and, for these children, helping them to develop their comprehension will be of major importance. Thus, rather than spending many fruitless sessions trying to teach them to imitate a few sounds, it will be more profitable to teach them to understand simple commands in the home or school which will at least improve social communications with their parents and teachers (see Figure 10.4).

## WHAT TO DO WHEN PROGRAMMES FAIL – ALTERNATIVE APPROACHES

Finally there is the problem of children who, after prolonged training and continued modification of programmes, still fail to show any improvement in the use of spoken language. Why certain children fail to respond at all to programmes which have proved extremely

Figure 10.4: Development of Comprehension in a Five-year-old Retarded Boy (IQ 60). The boy showed no response to any verbal imitation training, and at the start of treatment understood only 3-4 words.

successful with similar children is unknown, and is a problem requiring much more research, as well as more adequate descriptions of subjects involved in training programmes. Alternative forms of communication, such as American Standard Sign Language or the Paget Gorman system (Paget *et al*., 1972) or the use of written communication or systems using symbols to designate words or concepts, have been used successfully with a number of non-speaking children (Marshall & Hegrenes, 1972; McLean & McLean, 1974; De Villiers & Naughton, 1974; Bonvillian & Nelson, 1976; LaVigna, 1977; Murphy *et al*., 1977). Most of these studies, however, have only involved single cases, and whether many more children might benefit from such approaches is still unknown. A review of the research on alternative forms of communication appears in Kiernan (1977). It is difficult to determine when one should abandon spoken language training in favour of other forms of communication; whether there are some children who should be trained in alternative systems from the outset; and whether certain systems will be more suitable for some types of language handicap than others. All that can be advised at present is that adequate records of progress during training be kept, so that at least, if patients fail to respond, alternative forms of treatment can be attempted before boredom and frustration set in on all sides. If this is done, and if alternative strategies are borne in mind, one would hope to avoid the situation, recently reported by Lovaas (1977), in which one poor child was subjected to 'over 90,000 trials' to teach him two simple word approximations. Hardly a very economical approach to language training!

## CONCLUSIONS

Recent work on normal psycholinguistic development has demonstrated only too clearly (see Brown, 1973) that the acquisition of language is a far more complex process than that originally postulated by behaviourist psychologists. Few (with the possible exception of Lovaas, 1977) would still support Skinner's claim (1957) that 'a child acquires verbal behaviour when relatively unpatterned vocalisations, selectively reinforced, gradually assume forms which produce appropriate consequences in a given verbal community'.

Miller (1964), for example, in his discussion of operant theories of normal language acquisition estimates that, on the basis of reinforcement theory, it would take an English speaking child approximately 100,000 million centuries to learn 1000 sentences of twenty words in length.

Although the importance of an adequately stimulating environment for normal language development has been demonstrated in many studies (Lyle, 1960; Tizard *et al*., 1972; Elardo *et al*., 1977; Clarke-Stuart, 1973) evidence that the use of techniques such as prompts, corrections or reinforcement *directly* affects language acquisition in normal children is sparse and somewhat equivocal (Cazden, 1968; Feldman, 1971; Brown & Hanlon, 1970; Nelson *et al*., 1973). In fact, normal children often appear to be remarkably unresponsive to direct attempts by parents and others to increase or improve their language skills (McNeill, 1966). The development of cognitive and social skills in such children is as important for the growth of language as environmental factors, and the manipulation of the normal child's language environment has only limited effects.

In the language handicapped, however, where normal environmental influences have failed to counteract the effects of cognitive and linguistic impairment, additional stimulation is necessary. Thus, although operant methods may have only minimal impact on normal language development, the value of reinforcement techniques, together with corrections, prompting and shaping procedures in establishing communication skills in the mentally handicapped has been clearly established.

# 11 TEACHING PARENTS, TEACHERS AND NURSES

Maria Callias

One of the most important recent developments in behavioural treatment has been the move out of special settings into the everyday, real world. This trend has been especially significant for the mentally handicapped and the need to train parents, teachers, nurses and others who are in daily contact with the retarded to play a part in the treatment is clearly recognised and is reflected in the rapidly growing literature on this topic.

The reasons given for the increasing interest in parent training (O'Dell, 1974; Yule, 1975) are especially relevant in the field of mental handicap. These are: first, the difficulty in generalising success achieved in special treatment settings to the everyday environment and of maintaining changes; second, limited resources in terms of trained professionals and money; and third, the hope that widespread training will have a preventative function in enabling parents and others to cope with future problems before they become established. In addition, it has been found possible to teach behavioural management to people without a background in learning theory or psychology; and there has been pressure from parents themselves for more practical guidance with the problems they have in bringing up their chronically handicapped children.

The need for practical help to parents is recognised by the Court Committee in its recent comprehensive review, *The Child Health Services in Britain* (DHSS, 1976). The Committee recommends that it should be a function of district handicap teams to ensure that such practical help is provided and points out that the social worker and health visitor, who should visit families regularly, have an important role in this. If they are to be able to advise on practical management, these team members would need to have some training and experience in behavioural approaches and in how to teach them. At the very least, they need to recognise when to refer families on to other team members for such help. Parents have not usually found it helpful either to be given the commonly heard general suggestion, 'Treat him like a normal baby', or to receive, as one parent did, this somewhat idiosyncratic advice on how to get help: 'Take her to the park where someone is sure to see that she is handicapped and help you.'

The nursing profession has recognised explicitly the need to train experienced senior nurses in behaviour modification by establishing their JBCNS Course 700 (Joint Board of Clinical Nursing Studies, 1974). Graduates of this course are expected to play an important role in training other nursing staff in hospital and community services, in addition to using these skills themselves.

The different groups of professionals and parents have to some extent different training needs, because of their diverse roles and settings, but they also have many training needs in common. The aim of this chapter is to offer practical solutions to problems relating to training non-psychologists in the use of behavioural principles with the mentally handicapped. Suggestions are based on the research literature and, where this is lacking, on our clinical experience. The main emphasis is on teaching parents because not only are their needs pre-eminent but much of what is said applies also to training other groups. The literature and additional issues of particular concern to teaching nurses and teachers are discussed later in the chapter.

## PARENT TRAINING

There have been several comprehensive reviews of the literature on training parents (Berkowitz & Graziano, 1972; Doernberg, 1972; Johnson & Katz, 1973; O'Dell, 1974; Tavormina, 1974; Yule, 1975). These include references to work with parents of mentally handicapped children, and the issues raised in these reviews are directly relevant to work in this area. For example, can parents be taught to use behaviour modification procedures to change their children's behaviour? What are the most effective ways of training parents? Do training methods relate to success with their children? What exactly, and how much, do parents need to be taught? When are parents successful, and in which circumstances do they fail? What are the reasons for failure? The answers to such questions should lead to decisions about how best to help particular families. As the research to date has concentrated on some of these issues but neglected others, and most studies have serious methodological flaws (O'Dell, 1974), we still have a long way to go before our interventions can be said to rest on a sound empirical foundation. However, the problems will not wait and, in making our decisions about how and what to teach, it is important to remember that many of our views may be modified by future research.

As O'Dell (1974) states, effective parent training requires three steps:

parents must acquire modification skills and changes in their own behaviour, these changes must be implemented with the child and changes must generalise and persist. Only the second step, implementing change in the child's behaviour, has received sufficient attention, resulting in a relative neglect of systematic information on changes taking place in the parents. There has been an implicit assumption throughout the literature that parents need to learn new skills, essentially those of behaviour modification, in order to help their children. Thus the emphasis has centred around first, showing that parents can effectively change their children's behaviour, and second, dimensions of parent training.

Whether parents should be involved in the treatment of their children is no longer questioned. A wealth of studies shows quite clearly that parents can use behavioural methods effectively with their children (reviews cited above). Parents of mentally handicapped children have successfully taught their children a wide variety of skills, including self-help (Lance & Koch, 1973; Longin *et al.*, 1975), dressing (Norrish, 1974), language (Seitz & Hoekenga, 1974), play (Mash & Terdal, 1973); several developmental skills (Bidder *et al.*, 1975; Freeman & Thompson, 1973). More commonly, parents have been taught how to encourage a wide range of new skills and how to deal with unwanted problems (Callias & Carr, 1975; Cunningham & Jeffree, 1971; Doernberg, 1972; Galloway & Galloway, 1970; O'Dell, Blackwell, *et al.*, 1977; Rose, 1974; Tavormina, 1975).

Although parents have only been involved in behavioural treatments since the mid 1960s there has been a shift over time in the manner and extent of their involvement (O'Dell, 1974). In early studies parents were instructed to carry out certain parts of the treatment (Berkowitz & Graziano, 1972, p. 304); later they co-operated with the psychologist in devising and carrying out treatment programmes (Howlin *et al.*, 1973; Hemsley *et al.*, 1978; Callias & Carr, 1975); later still, especially where training took place in groups, they were taught the principles of behaviour modification, which they put into practice with minimal direct supervision (Callias & Jenkins, in preparation; Callias *et al.*, in preparation; Tavormina, 1975). The latter approach seems promising for parents with chronically handicapped children who are likely to need a strategy for coping with problems, or at least a succession of teaching tasks, in the future. It is not known to what extent parents have succeeded in practice in generalising their new skills or have been able to use them independently.

Most training in clinical practice is done in individual consultation with one set of parents (or the mother only), in the clinic or in the home (Callias & Carr, 1975). The case for working at home has been well argued (Hemsley *et al.*, 1978; Howlin *et al.*, 1973; Patterson *et al.*, 1973), two major advantages being that the therapist sees the situation 'for real' and that problems of generalisation are minimised. The main drawbacks are that it is time-consuming for the therapist to travel to the home and, occasionally, that some homes are so busy that parent and therapist are too readily distracted from their main purpose. In this case clinic-based teaching may be preferable. The clinic setting also enables special monitoring devices, like the 'bug in the ear' (Hanf, 1968) or videotape recordings, to be used for immediate feedback and instruction to the learner.

A recent development is that of training parents in groups. Parent group projects have varied in a number of ways. Group training has sometimes been combined with an individual approach, for example, work with families of aggressive antisocial children (Patterson *et al.*, 1973; Patterson & Reid, 1973; Patterson, 1974), and with pre-school handicapped children (Freeman & Thompson, 1973). In most groups for parents of handicapped children, the children have been seen for assessment only or not at all, and parents have met as a group in a clinic or other setting. Some projects have chosen to concentrate on a particular content area, such as play (Mash & Terdal, 1973) or developmental skills (Bidder *et al.*, 1975), but most have included a heterogeneous group of children and so have dealt with a wider range of problems and skills (e.g., Attwood, 1978; Tavormina, 1975). Training in behavioural skills has been the main purpose of several projects, but has been only one aspect of other more general courses.

Parents have been taught either to apply specific techniques to particular circumscribed problems or a more comprehensive range of concepts and techniques. There is very little guidance from the literature on how to decide what to teach. Parents we have worked with clinically and in special workshops have been equally concerned to develop their children's skills and to deal with problem behaviour. Hence, teaching should include: strategies for observing carefully, defining the problems or components of a new skill in behavioural terms, and conducting a functional analysis of problems as well as a knowledge of operant principles and techniques for teaching new skills. Parents may also need to know how to facilitate generalisation and maintain changes in their child (Kazdin, 1975; O'Dell, Blackwell, *et al.*, 1977). The curriculum for group training should include all these aspects, although in working with individual families, the psychologist can be more flexible and selective.

Parents have been taught behavioural skills by formal didactic methods (lectures, talks, discussions, films, programmed texts) and/or direct practical training (modelling, role play, supervised practice with their child). Practical training methods have been shown to be most effective in enabling parents to acquire the skills (e.g., Glogower & Sloop, 1976; Koegel *et al.*, 1978; Nay, 1975; O'Dell, Flynn & Benlolo, 1977). Knowledge of general principles facilitated the generalisation of these skills to other problems (Glogower & Sloop, 1976). These findings have obvious implications for both individual and group teaching.

## INDIVIDUAL WORK WITH FAMILIES

It is perhaps worth emphasising that the main reason for teaching parents behavioural skills is to enable them to deal with any difficulties they may have in helping their child learn or in managing problem behaviours. To ensure that this is indeed their main or only need, a careful history and assessment of the present circumstances of the child and family should be undertaken. There may be additional problems and stresses (e.g., maternal depression, housing difficulties) in some families that have to be dealt with too. There is not sufficient evidence to contraindicate the use of behavioural approaches in such families, unless other problems loom so large that it is simply not feasible for the child to remain in the family. Undoubtedly some families find it easier to use these approaches than others do, and certain parental and family characteristics may alert the therapist to potential difficulties and to the need to work carefully and realistically. However, most of the evidence cited is subjective and impressionistic, and there is at present no satisfactory way of anticipating which families will not be able to benefit from training. Individual parent training has the advantage of allowing the therapist to tailor the degree of his involvement, and the amount and nature of training, to the specific requirements of families.

There are several essential steps in carrying out a behavioural intervention. The therapist may carry these out jointly with parents, or advise them on how to do so relatively independently. These steps are:

(1) identification and behavioural description of the problems;
(2) deciding what to tackle first;

(3) carrying out a functional analysis of the problem, including the identification of potential reinforcers;
(4) ensuring that the parent has, or acquires, the relevant skills to carry out the intervention;
(5) implementation of the treatment/training strategy;
(6) monitoring progress;
(7) reviewing the programme if it is proving ineffective; and
(8) ensuring generalisation and maintenance of new behaviours or treatment changes.

The first four steps comprise the behavioural assessment of the problem. The information can be gained through careful behaviour interview. A home visit to observe the situation at first hand is invaluable. It also provides the opportunity of ensuring that intervention will be realistic. While it is usually desirable to work in the home setting, constraints of time and distance may preclude this. In such cases, care must be taken to ensure that parents can implement the treatment suggestions at home. All too often, for reasons of convenience or parental choice, only one parent, usually the mother, is seen. This works reasonably well provided parents agree on what to do, or one of them has the main responsibility for rearing the child. It is preferable to see both parents at least on some occasions. It is essential to do so if there are major disagreements about crucial aspects of a treatment plan, in order to work for some measure of consistency.

Teaching parents the necessary skills for enabling their child to learn new behaviours is usually relatively straightforward. It is usually possible to visit the home at a convenient time, to teach feeding, dressing, or language. The parent can be observed, improvements can be suggested by modelling and/or directly teaching the parent *in situ*. Principles can be discussed and demonstrated. The amount of direct tuition that parents need will vary from minimal to several sessions.

Dealing with problem behaviour is more difficult. Children do not always misbehave at convenient times, so it may not be possible for the therapist to observe the problems directly. Parents need to be taught, through discussion, how to make careful observations and carry out a functional analysis of the problem. This stage is very important, if the therapist and parent are to avoid common pitfalls such as assuming, for example, that all tantrums are 'attention-seeking'. Children can have tantrums for a variety of reasons: they may be fearful of particular situations; unable to understand or carry out demands made on them; tired and irritable – or they may even be trying to gain some adult attention. The intervention will be very different in each case.

Principles for reducing problem behaviours, such as extinction and time-out from positive reinforcement, sound so simple. They are, but their implementation may not be. It is important to discuss fully with parents exactly what they are doing when, for example, they are 'ignoring' Tommy's swearing or tantrum. 'I don't stop him, but tell him not to do it' is not 'ignoring' it in the sense of using extinction. Even when parents do understand and could implement an extinction or time-out procedure, they may not be able to in certain circumstances. It is highly unlikely that a parent will be able to ignore Adam when he throws things about in the living room. Removing him from the situation may be problematic, but a feasible intervention may well be possible with a little planning in order to ensure that the important treatment features of time-out from reinforcement are adhered to and that the punishment is not unnecessarily harsh (Hobbs & Forehand, 1977).

Where there is a choice, it is worth trying to plan treatments so that reinforcement or techniques selected are those that parents find most acceptable. They are likely to find it easier to implement such a plan, and to be enthusiastic about it, and therapeutic changes in the child's behaviour are more likely to persist (Kazdin, 1975). In dealing with problem behaviours, trainee therapists and parents often forget the importance of making sure that children are receiving parental praise, attention and other reinforcement for acceptable behaviour. In circumstances where it is dubious that this is happening in the normal course of events, parents could be encouraged to work on improving particular skills, or to developing play or language with their child, so that an opportunity for some positive interaction is created. Another common fallacy is to assume that the child could behave in a more acceptable way in a given situation, and that the task is simply one of decreasing the unacceptable behaviour. It is important to check on this. Take the complaint that Tom hits and pinches other children. Careful observation and questioning will reveal whether he can also play with them or whether his peer interaction is restricted to hitting and pinching. If the latter is true, it will be necessary to teach him how to interact more appropriately at some level, however simple, as well as, or instead of, aiming to stop the hitting and pinching.

When the parents are implementing projects appropriately, the trainer's role is to review progress, identify any snags or problems and help parents overcome them. It is often necessary to encourage parents to persist when change seems excruciatingly slow, or to change tack when necessary. The generalisation and maintenance phases often require more attention than they get. Trainers should alert parents to the fact that, all too often, their child will not spontaneously demonstrate his new behaviour in a wide variety of appropriate settings and that extending their treatment strategy to these new settings will usually facilitate generalisation. Similarly, parents will need to be aware of the reasons why new behaviour patterns may not persist of their own accord, so that they can ensure their maintenance. They need to be taught to fade special training procedures (like prompts) gradually and how to move from continuous to intermittent schedules of reinforcement in order to strengthen and maintain their child's new behaviour. If the same problems occur both at home and school, a consistent treatment approach in both settings should be attempted.

Ideally, the therapist should continue seeing the family for 'as long as seems necessary' – this varies considerably from family to family. If no improvements occur and problems become intolerable, residential observation and intensive treatment may be needed. More commonly, improvement takes place, and contact can cease. With some families of chronically handicapped children, further contact is often required later and parents should be encouraged to renew contact if they need to. A few may prefer regular infrequent appointments (even six-monthly or annually), simply to review their child's progress and needs. While this may not, strictly speaking, be training, it enables parents to continue fostering their child's development.

## GROUP TRAINING FOR PARENTS

Perhaps the main reason for the recent move to group courses for parents has been the lack of resources for meeting the needs of families on an individual basis. Professional time may be saved by working with groups rather than individuals (though this has been disputed for parents of non-handicapped children; see Mira, 1970). The group approach introduces several other positive features. It is easier to ensure systematic coverage of behavioural principles and techniques; parents welcome the opportunity of sharing with each other their experiences – both of problems and of potential solutions (Tavormina *et al.*, 1976); feelings of isolation, felt by many families, seem to be reduced; hearing about other successful projects often stimulates parents to try to change problems they previously considered immutable; the encouragement and support that parents offer to one another is sometimes more acceptable and sustaining than that offered by a professional because it is perceived as coming from someone who 'knows what it's like' to be in their position.

Possible limitations of group courses include: the amount of organisation involved in planning and running a workshop; insufficient time for discussing all projects fully at each meeting; the difficulty in offering more intensive training or discussion to those families who need more than can be provided in this context; the unavailability of further contact that many families feel they need at the end of time-limited courses; problems can arise if parents are receiving conflicting advice from other therapists. Many of these difficulties can be avoided or resolved by careful planning and consultation; others are related to the problems of patchy services. Despite these problems, time-limited parent groups do help to fill the enormous gap in the services and are all too often the only source of practical advice to some parents.

The following guidelines for running an effective behaviourally oriented parent group are based on our own experiences of group training, suggestions for improvements which arose out of these for future groups and reports in the literature (cited above).

### 1. RECRUITMENT

The need for a group may arise in a number of different ways, either as an extension of existing services or to meet a newly recognised need. Increasingly, as parents become aware of this form of practical help, professionals will be approached with requests to organise training groups. Such services might be advertised to increase recruitment (Cunningham & Jeffree, 1975), but not all parents, even of those who might be thought likely to benefit from it, will want to join a group (Saunders *et al.*, 1975). Where possible, it seems preferable that the groups should be locally based and part of the community services, for this facilitates travelling for parents and tutors, contacts with local services and follow-up meetings. However, where families are widely scattered or local services are limited, a group without all these advantages may be better than nothing.

### 2. SELECTION OF PARENTS

Some selection may be necessary if the numbers of parents applying for a course exceeds the number of places available. Our own solution to this was a first-come, first-served policy, and an offer of places on a subsequent course to those not accepted for the first. If more homogeneous groups are preferred, selection can be made on the basis of child characteristics (see Section 4 below). Since parents who apply for courses are usually unknown, selection on other criteria is rarely a possibility. Moreover, there is insufficient information about the relationship between parental characteristics and differential success (O'Dell, 1974). Some workers have found parents of low socio-economic or educational status less able to benefit from formal teaching (Salzinger *et al.*, 1970; Patterson *et al.*, 1973; Rinn *et al.*, 1975), while others using more direct teaching methods have found no such relationship (Hirsch & Walder, 1969; Mira, 1970). Similarly, parents with personality, psychiatric or marital problems have been thought difficult to work with (Wiltz, 1969; Bernal *et al.*, 1972; Ferber *et al.*, 1974), though our own study suggested that parents with these problems could have considerable success in teaching their own children (Callias & Carr, 1975). At present there seems to be no way of forecasting accurately which parents will or will not benefit from group teaching, the suggestions made in the literature being poorly documented, and based on little more than impressions.

There are no hard and fast rules about the size of the group; probably four or five families are the minimum, while groups have been run for much larger numbers (Cunningham & Jeffree, 1971), dividing into smaller tutor groups of five to eight families for discussion of projects.

### 3. PRE-GROUP CONTACT

It is helpful to circulate parents with a short letter outlining the aims of the project, and of the commitment that this would entail in terms of time and work, and to ask them to fill in a brief questionnaire giving demographic data about themselves and basic information about their child's skills and handicaps.

If at all feasible, the families should be visited at home, to discuss their problems and to assess the child. This acquaintance with the child proves valuable later in the course, when the parents are discussing their projects, while the formal assessment is also useful as part of the evaluation of the course.

### 4. GROUP COMPOSITION AND CHILD CHARACTERISTICS

Groups may be easier to run where the children of the parents participating have characteristics in common (Bidder *et al.*, 1975; Mash & Terdal, 1973), although it is perfectly feasible to run more heterogeneous groups. If numbers permit, it is probably preferable to choose groups which are homogeneous for age of the children and/or for their degree of handicap. These seem to be the more important factors on which to base the groups, rather than medical condition, type of problem or the teaching task chosen by the parents – teaching a child to feed himself requires the parents to apply a similar strategy regardless of the cause of the child's mental handicap. When the grouping is done on the basis of the child's age (for example, under-fives, 5-12, adolescents and young adults) the parents find each other's concerns directly relevant to their own, whereas when the age groups are mixed parents of the older children may find it boring and unprofitable to listen to discussions on topics like feeding or potty training which they have left far behind them. Degree of handicap is also important. It may be difficult for parents of profoundly handicapped children to maintain realistic goals without becoming too discouraged by their children's comparatively slow progress, especially if they see more able children of other group members advancing more rapidly. If all the children in the group are at roughly the same level, this discouraging effect can be minimised.

Parents of children with most kinds of disorders are potentially suitable for inclusion in a behavioural group, the only exception being perhaps those of children with degenerative disorders of known course and limited life expectancy. The main needs of these families are not met by this type of approach.

However the groups are constituted, some parents may drop out of training. Little is known of the reasons for drop-out, but in the case of groups run for parents of mentally handicapped children (Cunningham & Jeffree, 1971; Callias & Jenkins, in preparation; Callias *et al.*, in preparation) the rate seems to be lower than the 36 per cent reported for other parent groups (Rinn *et al.*, 1975).

### 5. GROUP TUTORS

Tutors should have had experience of working with handicapped children and their parents using behavioural approaches. In practice, at present, this usually means clinical psychologists but, hopefully, these skills are being acquired by members of other disciplines (social workers, health visitors, nurses, teachers, etc.). The parent group itself offers a training opportunity in that less experienced workers can collaborate with the more experienced in running the group.

### 6. LENGTH OF THE COURSE

Early in the planning stages of a course, a decision has to be taken as to how long it will last. Most have been time-limited, usually meeting about ten times, weekly at first for seven or eight meetings and then less frequently. Intervals between later meetings may be increased to two, three, four or six weeks. This allows for concentrated teaching and supervision of projects early on, and then for increasing independence, with an opportunity for discussing progress. If desired (and in our case it was), follow-up meetings can be arranged.

Evening meetings are preferable from the point of view of the parents, allowing fathers as well as mothers to attend. Two hours seems a reasonable duration for the meetings, though we often found it difficult to end on time.

7. FORMAT OF THE MEETINGS

It is useful to spend a short time at the beginning of the first meeting on introductions and a brief outline about the aims, format and content of the course. Then this and subsequent meetings are usually divided into two parts: part I contains the didactic teaching part of the course; in part II the participants divide, if necessary, into smaller groups of 5 to 8 sets of parents for discussion of the parents' individual projects.

In planning part I of the meetings, decisions will have to be taken about three related teaching problems. First, how far should the teaching emphasise theoretical principles on the one hand, or practical techniques on the other? Second, should the focus be on formal teaching or on direct training methods? Third, what should be included in the teaching programme?

There is little discussion in the literature on the question as to how much theory is necessary or helpful for parents or others in using behavioural techniques successfully. Baldwin *et al.* (1973), in the introduction to their delightful manual for parents, advocate that we should teach only as much theory 'as is needed' – but how much is that? O'Dell (1974), commenting on the diversity of what is taught to parents at either a theoretical or practical level, concludes that 'very few conclusions can be drawn concerning the desirability of particular types of content' (p. 423). A few studies suggest that formal theoretical teaching is unnecessary for parents who aim to acquire behavioural skills (O'Dell *et al.*, 1977; Koegel *et al.*, 1978). Other studies have shown that general didactic teaching in combination with discussion of specific problems seems to enable parents to generalise their skills better, carry out more projects with their children and to fare better at follow-up than parents who were taught only through discussion of their specific problems (Glogower & Sloop, 1976). Parents of mentally handicapped children face especially the long-term problem of helping their children, and their need is thus for knowledge and skills which they can adapt and generalise to meet new demands as their children grow up. It seems clear that some form of practical training is essential for parents to acquire behavioural skills, while the teaching of theory and principles should help them to cope with new problems independently.

In our groups, part I of the meetings consisted of a lecture-discussion plus videotaped examples on one of a series of topics (see below). Because of time constraints, we were usually unable to include direct practical training for our parents. On the few occasions when we were able to do so using role-play (see Chapter 13), both we and the parents thought this extremely valuable. It would be worthwhile setting aside time for this kind of exercise – either regularly in each meeting or, alternatively, to occupy, say, the whole of one or two meetings of the series.

Written materials or manuals seem to have a useful place in training (Bernal & North, 1978; Nay, 1975), though they have been found less effective than direct methods when they are used on their own (Nay, 1975). Several clear and practical books have been specially written for parents of mentally handicapped children (e.g. Baker *et al.*, 1976; Baldwin *et al.*, 1973; Carr, 1980; Perkins *et al.*, 1976), as well as programme guidelines (e.g., Lance & Koch, 1973; O'Dell, Blackwell, *et al.*, 1977). Many parents find a manual helpful as an introduction to concepts and to refresh their memories at a later date.

In part II of each meeting the large group divides, if necessary, into smaller groups for discussion of individual projects. Two trainers to a group work well but, at a pinch, one very experienced person can manage.

In the first meeting, parents are asked to describe their child to the group and then they select the areas they wish to work on and, for homework, begin careful observations on these areas. Thereafter, the main focus each week is on helping parents to carry out their projects. Each family selects and works on at least one specific project with their child, and each has a turn to report on progress each week (hopefully, showing off some data too!). They are helped to overcome any difficulties by discussion, role play, modelling, re-analysis of the situation or any other teaching approach that works. Time should be rationed so that all families have a turn, and different parents take a turn to start each week.

There will, of course, be times when the discussion broadens; parents may have other worries on their mind that they wish to discuss. Nondirective counselling, specific advice or suggestions on how to use other services are all appropriate. Such counselling is quite compatible with a behavioural approach (Tavormina, 1974, 1975).

8. PROGRAMME

If parents are to be able to deal with a wide range of problems and skills in the future, the teaching content of the first part of the meetings will need to include, first, teaching of several basic behavioural principles and techniques and, second, application of these to particular skills and problems. Our programme provides the following model.

Week 1: Observation and inference, defining tasks, simple data recording methods.
Week 2: Operant principles – reinforcement.
Week 3: Techniques for teaching new skills:
(a) shaping, prompts, fades, chaining.
Week 4: Techniques for teaching new skills:
(b) imitation, generalisation and discrimination.
Week 5: Techniques for decreasing behaviour:
extinction, DRO, time-out from positive reinforcement, other mild punishment.
Issues in the use of punishment.

In weeks 6-9, content areas that are of particular interest and relevance to the group can be selected for detailed discussion. It is useful to do so both from a developmental perspective, and from the point of view of how parents can apply the above principles and techniques to them. Important areas to consider are: language, play and occupation, self-help skills (including toilet training), adolescence and the future, social behaviour with adults and peers or in certain situations (e.g., shops, parks). If whole sessions are to be allocated to role play practice, this could be done after week 3 and/or week 5 in the above programme, resulting in 6 or 7 sessions being spent on this part of the curriculum.

Week 10 and other follow-up meetings can be spent on progress reports from the parents and in showing videotape of the children. During one of these meetings, it is helpful to elicit feedback from the parents and suggestions for improving future courses.

9. HOME VISITS

If it can be arranged, it is helpful to make a home visit after the fourth or fifth meeting to see what parents are actually doing with their children, and to sort out difficulties.

10. ASSESSMENT AND EVALUATION

There are no well worked out, fully satisfactory simple ways of evaluating group projects. Nevertheless, some attempts should be made at evaluation, at one or all of a number of levels, and using a variety of methods. We looked at changes in the child and in the parents, using parents' project data, formal assessments of the child and videotape observation of parent-child interaction before and after training, and asked parents for their views on the course using questionnaires.

## PROBLEMS IN BEHAVIOURAL TRAINING

Although the literature abounds with examples of success, problems do emerge when treatment is essentially carried out by the adults in their natural environment. Difficulties can arise at home, in spite of genuine concern on the part of adults to help children. If we accept that behavioural learning approaches hold the most promise for helping retarded children develop, it is important to consider what obstacles hinder their use, and what can be done about them.

Several parent trainers have bravely exposed their treatment failures to scrutiny, believing that an examination of cases and conditions in which difficulty or failure occur can illuminate key elements in particular settings which may well go unnoticed in successful interventions (Callias & Carr, 1975; Ferber *et al.*, 1974; Saunders *et al.*, 1975; Sajwaj, 1973; Tharp & Wetzel, 1969; Yule, 1975). These papers offer clinical suggestions for coping with some recurring thorny issues. Problems fall into three main areas: attitudinal, practical and those relating to the constraints of the social context.

Parental attitudes and values that lead to a rejection of or difficulty in implementing behavioural principles have been called resistances (Tharp & Wetzel, 1969). Resistances include a rejection of determinism, regarding positive reinforcement as 'bribery', and the expectation that children should behave appropriately for intrinsic reasons. We have found it helpful to avoid getting embroiled in philosophical arguments, and to discuss treatment in practical terms: the child is not behaving as the parents would like him to; we are offering ways they can try out to help him learn new ways of behaving.

The concept and use of positive reinforcement sometimes needs careful discussion. One common objection to the use of reinforcement stems from the notion that extrinsic reinforcement will dampen the child's intrinsic interest in activities (Greene & Lepper, 1974; Lepper *et al*., 1973). It is perhaps worth emphasising that, in behavioural approaches, extrinsic reinforcement is used precisely because children *lack* the intrinsic motivation to persist in learning skills that will be of intrinsic value to them later. When children enjoy activities for their own sake, extrinsic reinforcement becomes superfluous. A goal of behavioural approaches is that new behaviours should be maintained by intrinsic and naturally occurring reinforcers (Kazdin, 1975, 1977). Some parents may be reluctant to use reinforcers because they mistakenly think reinforcers are always edibles or sweets; others may only be willing to use events that they feel ought to be reinforcing whether this is so or not. Reinforcers should be chosen which are acceptable to the parents and, preferably, from among the things they naturally use. This is not always possible. The therapist's task is then to discuss qualms and objections and to suggest that the parents experiment to see whether or not certain events are better reinforcers than others. Most parents will find the evidence more convincing than any amount of theoretical argument. Reluctance to use positive reinforcement with one particular child often arises from the view that it is 'not fair' to single out one child for special favours. The objection to singling out a child for punishment is less often heard. Discussion of the issue in terms of teaching the child rather than giving 'just deserts', combined with empirical test, usually helps to alter these perceptions.

Other attitudinal problems can emerge in the process of implementing a behavioural approach. Parents may have difficulty in understanding their child's problems and their role in it. Behavioural approaches can raise feelings of anxiety and guilt because the explicit statement that parents can be effective in modifying the child's behaviour can convey the hidden message that they are to blame for causing the current state of affairs in the first place (Yule, 1975). Clinical impression suggests that anxiety about causation is not confined to parents of non-handicapped difficult children but is found, perhaps surprisingly, in some parents of handicapped children too. It is well worth discussing this issue openly at an early stage, making these points: the child definitely has an intrinsic developmental disorder (of known or unknown causation); it may not be possible to know why problems developed as they did but, in helping the child, it is more fruitful to focus on the present situation and to look towards altering things for the future than to dwell on the past; circumstances currently maintaining the difficulties, usually modifiable, need to be differentiated from the original causes which are often unknown and unchangeable; a child's temperamental characteristics and pattern of handicaps may well contribute to difficulties in bringing him up and, consequently, parents need to learn some special ways of coping with and rearing the child. Parents of handicapped children frequently feel they have lost a lot of time for helping their child develop. It is often important to give time to their concerns that 'if only' they could have had advice sooner – and to help them come to a realistic view of what can be achieved. Setting a series of short-term goals rather than one enormous target is frequently helpful.

Parental feelings of inadequacy can be aroused or strengthened by ill-chosen teaching techniques or by other excessive demands during training. For example, the use of modelling on its own may have the effect of decreasing parents' confidence if they see someone else cope so much better with their child. It may be better to train a hesitant, demoralised parent using other techniques such as shaping and direct feedback, which may be slower, but have the advantage of boosting confidence. These attitudinal and general aspects of behavioural intervention have received little systematic consideration and could usefully be investigated more empirically.

Several practical problems can arise in behavioural intervention by parents. Simply gathering data can create problems. In spite of the difficulties, some objective record is usually helpful as a device for monitoring progress, as well as for assessing and evaluating projects. Not enough attention has been given to the issues of how to train parents to collect data. Measures such as providing or helping parents to prepare data sheets and using simple but valid indices of change could ensure that data collection does not become an intolerable burden that is neglected (Callias & Carr, 1975). The possible adverse effects of data collection on the parents' perception of their problems need to be borne in mind. Though data collection is viewed as beneficial by therapists, this is not necessarily the case for parents of retarded children (Yule, 1975). Baseline recordings may be worse than expected, or rate of progress may be discouragingly slow. On the other hand, simply counting or recording specific targets may be therapeutic, either because the parents notice that the problem is less frequent or milder than they thought, or because their own behaviour changes while they are monitoring that of their child. (Behavioural change in the therapeutically desired direction has often been found when individuals are asked to keep records of their own behaviour; see Nelson *et al.*, 1975). The trainer should be on the alert for the effects of data collection, and prepared to discuss these when necessary.

It may be necessary to maintain parents' interest and enthusiasm at the initial stages, when the fruits of their efforts are not yet evident. This is helped if the parents work on a skill or problem that they perceive as important, whether or not the trainer agrees. If the parents select a very complex or difficult task (for example, self-injury), it may be worth suggesting that they work simultaneously on a simpler project which is likely to be more encouraging, such as imitation or a self-help skill. In addition, clear and repeated discussion about expected rates of change in the child's behaviour may be needed. Obviously, if the current intervention seems to be ineffective, re-evaluation and alteration are called for. Such decisions are at present a matter of clinical judgement rather than founded on clear criteria.

Finally, there is one important practical issue that has been almost totally neglected, that of gauging just how much a parent is able or willing to undertake. There seem to be enormous individual differences (Callias & Carr, 1975; Saunders *et al.*, 1975). With parents who are willing, there is little to go on, other than to follow our own advice of working in graded steps rather than tackling everything at once. Even if the child presents with numerous problems, it may be preferable for parents to begin by tackling only one or two tasks. One of these should be teaching a new skill, even if the parents originally sought advice over problem behaviours. This provides the opportunity for positive interaction between parent and child, which has often been overshadowed by the problem. Teaching alternative behaviour may be a vital part of dealing with problems, particularly when the child lacks acceptable ways of behaving in that situation. It may also be important to suggest that parents set aside a short period of time regularly every day to work in, rather than attempt to change all their behaviour all day long. Parents can teach some new skills, such as dressing or play, successfully in daily 10-15 minute sessions, while the parents of a child who screams virtually all day long may at first find it easier to carry out a treatment programme properly for shorter periods (e.g., during meals or a play session) than all day long. Although overall progress may be slower initially, this approach allows parents to learn new patterns of interacting with their children without finding it too exhausting or too disruptive to the family. Parents are less likely to opt out – one mother admitted that she nearly gave up trying because she found it so tiring to change her interactions. As parents gain skills and see desired changes, generalisation can be introduced, and other tasks can be tackled. On the other hand, it may be necessary from a treatment point of view to deal with problems as and when they arise in the course of the day, because they are relatively infrequent (such as, 2 or 3 temper tantrums per day) or are totally disruptive anyway (such as throwing furniture). Where teaching skills is concerned, many parents are willing to restructure daily situations such as meal-times, or bath time, as learning situations, rather than simply to continue with the chore of feeding or washing the child themselves. Clearly, flexibility is needed in working out practical details to suit the needs of each family.

The unexpected obstacles that can arise if due attention is not paid to the home circumstances are clearly highlighted by Sajwaj (1973). Parents were successfully taught to use behavioural principles to modify unwanted behaviour within a clinic setting, but the procedures adopted failed to be effective at home. Observations at home revealed that circumstances were different because of competing demands on the mother. Consequently, there was less attention and reinforcement for appropriate behaviour. A functional analysis done at home at the particular times of difficulty led to the implementation of different procedures, which were successful. Home circumstances need to be known, either by basing treatment there or by eliciting relevant information.

The effects of behavioural training with the handicapped child on other children in the family have been little discussed, though parents sometimes wonder whether giving extra attention or reinforcement to one child will adversely affect the others. In practice, we have not found this to be a problem. It may be that the other children are not surprised that the handicapped child is treated differently. Older children, of course, can understand the problems and frequently participate in the training. Parental concerns should be heeded and, if real problems arise, suggestions may be offered – for instance, a parallel (even if not strictly necessary) token programme and back-up reinforcers for a younger sib (Carr, 1980), or something to be given to both children for doing the same task, like reading or laying the table.

Families who have additional concurrent problems such as parental ill-health or marital discord seem to have the most difficulty in carrying out behavioural interventions for problem behaviours (e.g., Patterson *et al.*, 1973; Callias & Carr, 1975). Ferber *et al.* (1974), in a replication of the work of Patterson and his co-workers, found that their failures occurred when the child's problems occurred within the context of serious marital difficulties and pervasive hostility toward the child. Such difficulties frequently overshadowed recognition of the changes that occurred in the child.

At present there is little to show which is the best way of helping families with these multiple problems. In clinical practice, it is quite feasible to offer counselling and behavioural advice concurrently either by the same or different workers, though we have no evidence as to which approach is the more effective. Obviously, exposing families to conflicting advice is unhelpful, at best, and may be harmful. Whether the task of implementing treatment should be shared or not depends on the skills and experience of the therapist(s), and the way the clinic or service is organised. In our focused parent groups, we often found ourselves discussing related problems that concerned the parents, and this did not appear to interfere with the main behavioural aims of the group. Mothers in groups in which the treatment was designed to combine behavioural and counselling approaches did better on all kinds of objective measures (Tavormina, 1975), and felt that they both understood and could teach their child better (Tavormina *et al.*, 1976) than did those parents receiving reflective counselling only. It may be that a combination of methods could be most helpful for parents with multiple problems.

Further research is needed to clarify such issues as the role of behavioural intervention in such families; and the timing of various interventions – whether problems are best dealt with simultaneously or in sequence, and in which order. It is perhaps also important to remember that, for whatever family and attitudinal reasons, some families find they cannot or do not see it as their role to work with their children using behavioural approaches (Wing, 1975b; Saunders *et al.*, 1975).

It is important that we try to find ways of applying behavioural modification principles which parents can accept and make use of, though at present there is no way of predicting whether parents who initially express antipathy or experience difficulties will continue to do so.

It should also be recognised that working directly through the parents may not be successful and this need not be for lack of trying. Behavioural approaches must be viewed as an important part of services for parents of handicapped children, but not as a sufficient service (Wing, 1975b).

## TEACHERS

### 1. TRAINING

There is ample evidence that behavioural interventions can be applied successfully by teachers, within a classroom setting, to teach a wide variety of skills to mentally handicapped children, and to cope with their behaviour problems (Barton, 1975; Kazdin & Craighead, 1973; Kazdin, 1977; Ward, 1975). In addition to other problems that parents have dealt with, teachers have been especially interested in language training and work related skills. Behavioural methods have been used in hospital schools (Barton, 1975) as well as day schools in the community (Saunders *et al.*, 1975; Smith, 1977). Most of the interventions have been done by advising teachers individually over specific problems, but teachers have also been taught behaviour modification systematically in group courses similar to those for parents (Koegel *et al.*, 1977; Smith, 1977). Attempts have been made to increase collaboration between teachers and parents (Saunders *et al.*, 1975). Teachers, like parents, need to have practical as well as theoretical training in order to use behavioural principles and techniques effectively (Koegel *et al.*, 1977; McKeowen *et al.*, 1975; Smith, 1977).

2. PROBLEMS

Many of the problems encountered in training teachers are similar to those found in parent training. In addition, the school setting introduces its own problems (Saunders *et al.*, 1975) – some attitudinal, some practical – while legal and ethical issues relating to acceptable ways of treating children in school are also important (Gast & Nelson, 1977b).

Many of the attitudinal objections to the use of certain procedures (eg. time-out from positive reinforcement) can be overcome by avoiding confrontation, discussing the problems in pragmatic terms and emphasising the importance of trying out empirically the treatment intervention to see what happens. For example, the issue of giving special or extra attention to particular children can be dealt with by indicating that what is needed is often a change in the *nature* of attention, or its timing, rather than giving more to one child or depriving other children. Most teachers devote some time to individual teaching, and it is this time that can be set aside for 'special' teaching. It is occasionally necessary to invest extra resources to implement programmes in certain settings, like the playground or certain lessons. Where they see it as necessary, staff are often willing to organise themselves so that they can devote more resources or time to a particular child for a short period of time so that, in the long run, the child can be more independent and less demanding. Once again, it is important to try to devise treatment strategies that the teachers find acceptable, and sufficient time should be spent, at an early stage on discussion and demonstration in order to ensure this. If problems are occurring both at home and school, it may be important to ensure that contact is made between teachers and parents. Joint meetings can be useful in setting up a consistent approach, and contact can be maintained via a daily diary and informal meetings between parent and teacher. It may occasionally prove difficult to arrive at a mutually acceptable plan, or the same treatment strategy may not work in different settings. The trainer needs to be on the alert for these potential problems, and to be prepared to use a variety of approaches in trying to overcome them.

## NURSES

### 1. TRAINING

Most behavioural interventions with the mentally handicapped have been carried out in a hospital or institution and have been directed at both reducing maladaptive behaviour (Bates & Wehman, 1977) and increasing self-care, participation in work and activities, and language development of individuals, or of groups in token economy programmes (Kazdin, 1977; Thompson & Grabowski, 1972). Training of nurses, attendants and other staff has ranged from informal instruction to formal courses in the same way as for parents and teachers. Again, practical training in the form of role play (Gardner, 1973) or modelling (Panyan & Patterson, 1974) is more effective than a purely didactic approach. The problem of training new staff rapidly has been dealt with in various ways. Teaching materials covering a range of theoretical and practical aspects have been developed for training on an individual basis (Kiernan & Riddick, 1973). Short intensive group courses for new staff which use theoretical teaching and role play are held at regular intervals at units like Hilda Lewis House (Callias & Carr, 1975). Similar short courses have been run by itinerant trainers at different hospitals with the purpose of introducing ideas (Williams & Jackson, 1975). Though they meet a demand, such short courses or workshops provide only initial basic training, and staff need to apply and consolidate their knowledge under supervision, if behavioural approaches are to be implemented responsibly (Stein, 1975). A more ambitious staff training scheme is the intensive course in behaviour modification sponsored by the Joint Board of Clinical Nursing Studies (1974) for qualified nurses. This course aims to impart a sound knowledge of behaviour modification and of how to teach it, so that nurses become qualified to run units along these lines and to teach other hospital staff and parents. While there is ample evidence that nurses working with the mentally handicapped can be taught to use behavioural strategies successfully (e.g., Kazdin, 1977; Thompson & Grabowski, 1972), the extent of generalisation and the long-term effects of training have received little attention (Kazdin, 1977). In a rare follow-up study of extensive in-service training in a hospital, Keith & Lange (1974) found that only 57 per cent of patient behaviours were maintained 3 to 26 months after training. None of the reasons traditionally given for poor maintenance of change (time elapsed since training, degree of retardation in clients, staffing) related to relapse rates. There was some evidence to suggest a more complex interaction effect between degree of handicap and staff:resident ratio, such that more programmes were maintained in wards of mildly handicapped residents where there were relatively low staff:resident ratios of 1:8 to 1:11, compared with high ratios of 1:5. Fewest programmes were maintained on highly staffed wards of moderate and severely handicapped residents.

## 2. ISSUES IN HOSPITAL SETTINGS

Introducing behavioural interventions into hospital settings presents many of the problems already discussed in relation to parents and teachers, and raises additional ones.

Initially, the introduction of behavioural approaches may be met with numerous resistances and objections if it clashes with the existing treatment ethos of the hospital or institution. A common stereotype of mentally handicapped people is that they are incapable of learning and are thus in need only of total care and protection – a view incompatible with the behavioural emphasis on teaching and encouraging residents to become as independent as possible. Again, behavioural approaches may be rejected for different philosophical reasons, perhaps being seen as over-controlling. Little attention has been paid to attitudinal or personality variables in staff training projects, yet there is evidence that some of the brightest students resist or opt out of behavioural programmes (Gardner, unpublished; Watson *et al.*, 1972). The importance of adequate discussion, demonstration of efficacy and consultation in setting up the programme is illustrated in two descriptive studies where behavioural programmes were introduced into hospitals for autistic children (Morrison *et al.*, 1968; Davids & Berenson, 1977).

On wards or units where training programmes are introduced successfully, problems of maintaining staff behaviour are common. Such problems of staff motivations may be overcome by providing staff with feedback on their performance and extra incentives

(Bricker *et al.*, 1972), or by amusing reminders in the form of a telling cartoon conspicuously pinned on a noticeboard (Fielding *et al.*, 1971).

There are other difficulties too. The structure and organisation of the institution in which staff work impose limits on their efficiency. Major practical problems can arise from the way the staff shifts are arranged, the physical surroundings, timetabling of activities and staff shortages (Kiernan & Wright, 1973). If the goals of the institutions are to be those of educating residents and reducing their maladaptive behaviours, organisational and administrative changes are needed at all levels to facilitate effective programming (Kushlick, 1975; Toogood, 1977). Kushlick (1975) recommends a 'Mager' (Mager & Pipe, 1970) analysis of the service. That is, general aims or 'fuzzies' need to be translated into specific behavioural terms with clear specifications about what criteria should be used to evaluate outcome and the consequences – in other words, an extensive analysis of the structure of the institution and of the roles and functions of staff at all levels. In such an analysis, staff training has an important place – when staff lack the skills necessary for training the residents. Only recently has the question of how changes can best be introduced to institutions been considered, and Georgiades & Phillimore (1975) provide some useful guidelines for the novice.

Most behavioural interventions on wards have focused on the manipulation of consequences to change client behaviour. Appropriate as this is in most cases, there are times when more attention should be paid to the environmental setting conditions. Differences in behaviour are associated with a wide range of qualitative differences in the physical environment and in the way units are run (King *et al.*, 1971). Moreover, the same residents have been shown to behave more adaptively when they are in a richly equipped recreation room than in a sparsely equipped day-room (Tognoli *et al.*, 1978). Levels of aggression have been reduced considerably simply by enlarging the living space, and then still further by introducing non-contingent reinforcement, though not simply by the provision of more toys (Boe, 1977). Such studies serve an important function in reminding us that behaviour is not independent of the environmental and social context in which both residents and staff live and work. The ethos and physical and social organisation of a hospital or unit are perhaps more important than size alone, in providing a humane and purposeful living situation (Raynes, 1977). Behavioural interventions have a role in such environments, enabling residents to learn skills and to control their unacceptable behaviour so that their lives become richer. They are not a substitute for fundamentally humane living conditions.

Ethical and legal issues concerning the use of behavioural interventions in hospital settings are receiving increasing attention, and have been carefully considered elsewhere (Kazdin, 1975, 1977; Hall, 1978). Where mentally handicapped people in institutions are concerned, questions need to be asked. Who will benefit from intervention? Is it the handicapped person himself or his caregivers only? With clients who cannot give informed consent, and who may not have relatives around to do so, the questions of who decides on goals and how training should proceed are important ones, especially in relation to any plan to use aversive techniques or deprivation of normal rights. Such decisions, the choice of particular techniques and their implementation, need to be carefully considered and monitored. Responsibility for programmes should be made clear, and staff who implement programmes should be adequately trained and supervised. The extent of training needed to ensure competent use of behavioural approaches is unclear, but short courses or experience only in carrying out programmes under supervision, though useful, are unlikely to be sufficient to ensure that staff can implement programmes independently. One of the major strengths of behavioural strategies, the fact that they are simple to understand, is often a disadvantage too. Their implementation may seem easy, but in many cases a complicated behavioural analysis is needed, together with highly skilled intervention.

The issues over ethics, responsibilities and roles of different disciplines are often very sensitive ones in everyday life, but unless they are discussed and acceptable solutions are found, services will continue to be fragmented, and the potentially powerful and valuable contribution of behaviour modification may be abused in many ways (MacNamara, 1977).

## CONCLUSIONS

Parent and staff training is expanding rapidly to fill the vacuum created by need (O'Dell, 1974). A crucial question is whether developments will continue to be based on research findings rather than simply on theory or fashion fads. Methodological problems abound, and most studies are still relatively unsophisticated descriptive feasibility studies. Nevertheless, it has been shown that behaviour modification can be used by adults who look after the mentally handicapped. Research has also indicated the most effective methods for teaching behaviour modification. Very little attention has been directed to the question of what changes are made in the caregiver's behaviour or interaction with the retarded child or adult, because outcome measures have related almost entirely to changes in the retarded themselves. More attention could be directed towards identifying which particular skills need to be taught and which are already present in the caregivers 'natural' repertoire. For example, a small study of five attendants showed that they used verbal and physical prompts but not the other relevant behavioural principles necessary to be effective trainers (Mansdorf *et al.*, 1977). Such information can lead to a more effective use of training resources – and avoid the embarrassment of trying to teach people what they already know. Very few studies have compared behavioural intervention with control, 'non-intervention' or contrast treatments.

Three other areas have so far been neglected. First, the fundamental question of whether the need of parents, teachers, nurses is always or only for training. It may be that they have the relevant skills but that other factors, like attitudes to the handicapped child, constraints of the context or personal difficulties, interfere with their efforts to help the child; alternatively, these factors may occur together with ineffective coping techniques. Second, the issues relevant to maintenance and generalisation of changes, in both the mentally handicapped and their caregivers, still require empirical validation. Third, the place of behavioural training in parent counselling services and community services for the handicapped needs to be explored.

If behavioural approaches are to expand and flourish to meet a legitimate need, many questions will require answers based on accumulating research evidence. The danger of being carried away on the wave of enthusiasm is that indiscriminate use of particular technologies can lead to obvious misapplication, and then to wholesale disillusionment and rejection. It would be unwise to assume that training should be limited to behaviour modification skills, or that these approaches are always sufficient by themselves. 'Research is needed to compare and integrate effective techniques from other areas regardless of their theoretical source' (O'Dell, 1974, p.430).

These comments may seem to be somewhat harsh criticism of such a relatively new service. They are not meant to be, because I consider training for parents and staff to be one of the most important developments in the treatment and education of handicapped children and adults.

# 12 EVALUATION OF TREATMENT PROGRAMMES

William Yule

Most of the readers of this book will rarely find themselves involved in large-scale research projects of the sort which compare the efficacy of different treatments. If they find themselves in such a position, then they will know that the classical groups-comparison experimental techniques for demonstrating treatment effects are well described in most introductory books on research design (Maxwell, 1958). Equally, the discerning reader will know that such group studies have particular weaknesses which militate against their use when one wishes to know about the effects of treatment on one individual patient. The results of group studies are often reported only in terms of averages, and such summary statistics describe the whole group, not the individual within it.

What the clinician wants to know is how many individuals improved by how much, how many were unaffected by treatment and how many were made worse. Even these data are but a guide to deciding whether to apply a particular treatment to a particular patient. Such results cannot guarantee that any treatment will definitely benefit that patient.

At some point, the therapist will want to answer the question, 'Is my treatment helping this patient?' No amount of previously published studies can answer what is very much an empirical question. The way to answer it is to monitor the effects of treatment and, by using an appropriate methodology, to evaluate whether there is a demonstrable relationship between treatment and outcome. The appropriate methodology for such monitoring is the subject of this chapter – single-case research designs.

## DEVELOPMENT OF SINGLE-CASE METHODOLOGY

Every patient presents the therapist with unique problems. The job of the therapist is to investigate and understand whatever psychological processes may be at fault and, based on such an analysis of the problem, to develop ways of helping the patient. Somehow, the therapist has to reconcile his knowledge based on studies of large groups of patients with his understanding of the individual patient. This synthesis involves a great deal of clinical skill, but it can be made more powerful by applying experimental methods to the study of the single case.

Experimental studies of single cases have a long history in British clinical psychology, largely as a result of the influence of M.B. Shapiro (Shapiro, 1957, 1966, 1970; Davidson & Costello, 1969). The emphasis of the early studies was more on gaining useful *descriptions* of the patient's psychological functioning than directly on treatment possibilities. Nonetheless, the logic of the investigations is shared with all experimental studies of single cases – namely: define the problem in objective, behavioural terms, then bring those behaviours under experimental control. In other words, the experimenter/therapist searches for independent variables which can be applied so that the particular problem behaviour can be altered in a meaningful, lawful manner.

Once a behaviour is brought under experimental control, therapeutic possibilities are obvious. However, it was the largely American group of behaviour modifiers, coming to treatment problems from a different background of single-organism studies in the animal laboratory, who shifted the emphasis more directly on to the therapeutic possibilities of single-case experimental studies. The parallel in logic between the two approaches has been pointed out by Yates (1970) and by Leitenberg (1973).

## SINGLE-CASE STUDIES IN BEHAVIOUR MODIFICATION

Single-case experimental methodology is a-theoretical. That is, the methodology is independent of the theoretical framework within which a particular therapeutic technique is formulated. Whether 'treatment' consists of bed rest, catharsis, primal scream, Kleinian interpretation or contingency management, the basic question remains the same. Is there a demonstrable, causal relationship between intervention and outcome? Despite this universality of application, at present most applications of single-case methodology come from investigators working within a behaviour modification framework, and so most of the examples that follow are drawn from this field.

As has been argued in earlier chapters, behaviour modifiers seek to demonstrate a *functional relationship* between treatment and subsequent change in behaviour. Evans (1971) argues that, 'Given our present state of knowledge the functional analysis provides the key link between aetiology and treatment. . .the functional analysis involves identifying the sufficient and necessary conditions for a particular response to occur and persist, so that knowing these conditions allows one to predict behaviour, and manipulation of these conditions allows one to control it.' Kiernan (1973) discusses these issues with special reference to the mentally retarded. The argument that such investigators are putting forward is that an understanding of what makes the individual tick will automatically provide the therapist with a potential way of intervening therapeutically.

In one of the earliest elaborations of single-case methodology as applied to behavioural treatment, Baer *et al.* (1968) restate the problem as follows: 'An experimenter has achieved an analysis of a behaviour when he can exercise control over it. By common laboratory standards, that has meant an ability of the experimenter to turn the behaviour on and off, or up and down at will.' In a real-life, applied setting, the therapist cannot usually go on repeating this control. The patient, rightly, would not accept it. To demonstrate to his own satisfaction and that of his scientific peers, the therapist must judge how much control is sufficient. This element of judgement enters into all evaluation.

In essence, the problem of demonstrating a causal relationship between treatment and effect can be reduced to the following propositions:

(1) Is there a 'real' change in the patient's behaviour following the application of treatment?
(2) If so, can alternative explanations for the demonstrated improvement be ruled out?

As Birnbrauer *et al.* (1974) point out, the first question can only be answered if data are gathered reliably and repeatedly (see Chapter 2). To answer the second question, some form of experimental manipulation is usually necessary.

## SINGLE-CASE EXPERIMENTAL DESIGNS

### 1. THE A-B DESIGN

The simplest 'quasi-experimental' design is not really experimental at all. It involves measuring the target behaviour over a baseline period (condition A), followed by continued monitoring during condition B, or treatment. Let us say that a mildly retarded nine-year-old boy is referred because of severe distractibility in class, and that after a careful consideration of relevant data it is found that he is 'off-task' on 80 per cent of occasions over a 10-day baseline period. When the teacher alters her interaction with the boy so that settling to work is immediately rewarded, his off-task behaviour drops to an average of 20 per cent three weeks after treatment is started. Clearly a change has occurred, but was treatment responsible for the improvement?

The problem in this simple case is that there are too many competing explanations which could plausibly account for the change. If treatment lasts over a lengthy period, how does one allow for the effects of 'maturation'? Chance events outside the teacher's control may be important. For instance, in checking attendance records it might transpire that the boy normally sits next to a very interfering playmate, who, whilst present during baseline, was absent during 'treatment'. Campbell & Stanley (1963) discuss these and many other factors which behavioural scientists working with children ignore at their peril.

Many external events can influence the course of a problem. 'Spontaneous remission' (Eysenck, 1963) can occur, unwilling as we are to admit that patients can improve independently of treatment. It is all too easy in using the simple A-B design to commit the fallacy of *post hoc, ergo propter hoc.*

Recently, there has been a renewal of interest in the A-B design, with the application of time-series analysis to such data. These developments have been discussed more fully elsewhere (Yule & Hemsley, 1977; Hersen & Barlow, 1976). For present purposes, it is sufficient to note that, whilst such data analysis techniques allow one to conclude that there has been a significant *shift* in the previous pattern at the point at which treatment was introduced, all the same problems of separating treatment effects from chance effects remain.

2. THE REVERSAL DESIGN (OR A-B-A-B DESIGN)

Baer, Wolf & Risley's (1968) formulation leads almost directly to one of the commonly used single-case experimental designs – the reversal design. During an initial period, the patient is carefully observed and a basal or *baseline* level of the problem behaviour is obtained. Then, during the second phase, treatment is applied whilst the target behaviour continues to be monitored. During the third phase of the experiment, the treatment conditions are withdrawn – effectively, the independent variables operating on the patient are 'reversed' to baseline conditions. Finally, in the fourth stage, treatment conditions are reintroduced.

Baer, Wolf & Risley (1968) argue that, 'In using the reversal technique, the experimenter is attempting to show that an analysis of behaviour is at hand: that whenever he applies a certain variable, the behavior is produced; whenever he removes this variable, the behavior is lost.' In other words, when the observations of the target behaviour are graphed over time, the graph should show discontinuities at those points when the treatment was applied or withdrawn.

In an elaboration of their paper, Wolf & Risley (1971) use data from a study by Hart *et al.* (1964) to illustrate this design in action. The graph, reproduced here as Figure 12.1, records the number of times a normal four-year-old nursery school child cried. Initially, the child was regarded by the nursery teachers as crying excessively. A careful analysis of the situation suggested that the child's crying was being maintained by the understandable, extra attention it elicited from the teacher.

After the first ten days of baseline observations, treatment was introduced for ten days. Treatment consisted of teachers' ignoring the boy's cries, after assuring themselves that he was not crying because he had been hurt. Within five days, crying had dropped in frequency from around seven episodes per day to about one or two episodes per day.

Figure 12.1: Number of Daily Crying Episodes of a Nursery School Child

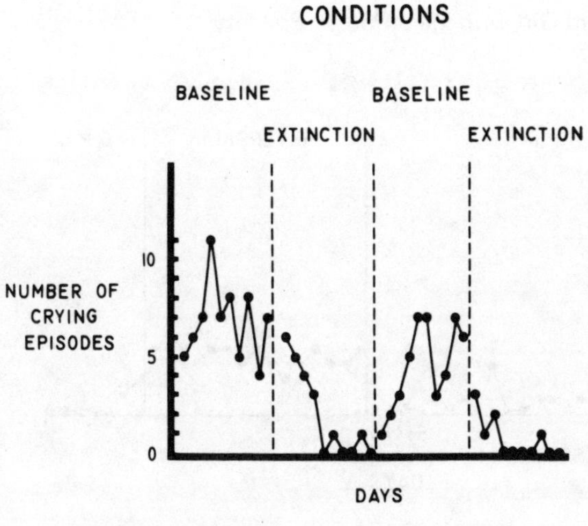


Source: Hart *et al.* (1964), p. 316. Reprinted with permission.

During the subsequent ten days, the teachers went back to giving continuous attention whenever the boy cried. As can be seen, the rate of crying quickly returned to baseline level. It was even more quickly extinguished during the last period when treatment was finally reintroduced.

A second example comes from a more recent study by Zlutnick *et al.* (1975), who report the case of a 17-year-old mentally retarded girl who presented with major motor epilepsy. She had daily seizures despite large doses of anti-epileptic medication. Careful behavioural observations revealed a characteristic 'chain' of events leading up to seizure, and so treatment consisted of interrupting this chain at a very early stage. As can be seen in Figure 12.2, during a five-week baseline period, seizures occurred on an average of 16 per day. This fell to near zero during the first treatment period. When treatment conditions were reversed, the number of seizures quickly rose, only to be controlled again when treatment was reinstated. A nine-month follow-up showed that the girl's seizures remained at a near-zero level.

In both these studies, the data provide convincing demonstrations of a functional relationship between the application of an active treatment (the independent variable) and the patient's clinical condition (the dependent variable). It can be seen that, under certain circumstances,

Figure 12.2: The Number of Minor Motor Seizures per Day for a Seventeen-year-old Girl with Major Motor Epilepsy

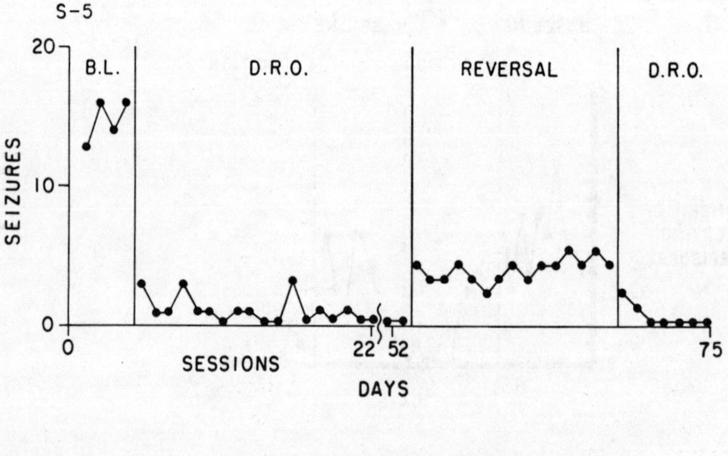


Source: Zlutnick *et al.* (1975), p. 10. Reprinted with the permission of the author and editor. Copyright © 1975; the Society for the Experimental Analysis of Behaviour, Inc.

this is an elegant yet simple design to employ in evaluating the effectiveness of treatment in an individual case.

As with traditional group experimental studies, there is an intimate relationship between the problem under investigation and the research design which is most appropriate to demonstrate experimental control. Thus, as the reversal design has been used more frequently, so its limitations have been documented (Leitenberg, 1973; Yule *et al.*, 1974; Gelfand & Hartmann, 1975). It is unreasonable to ask a parent or nurse or teacher to withdraw an apparently effective treatment which appears to have resulted in the child ceasing some unpleasant activity such as spitting, smearing faeces or hitting. Desirable as reversal may be on scientific grounds, such a request will appear bizarre to the caretakers.

More importantly, there are some behaviours which, once established, will not reverse. For example, when a non-talking child is trained to use some language meaningfully, that skill will probably become self-reinforcing, and similarly with the acquisition of other skilled behaviour such as reading, writing, swimming or riding a bicycle. It is probable that the reversal design is not appropriate for demonstrating experimental control over the acquisition of new skills. Its value is probably greatest where the frequency of occurrence of an already existing skill is being manipulated.

In passing it is as well to note that, if a behaviour change is so quickly reversible, cynics may question the value of the initial intervention. Such cynicism is, in part, misplaced. It is increasingly being recognised that changing behaviour is but the initial step in treatment. Maintenance of change over the longer term presents a different set of technical challenges. To be able to demonstrate that even the initial change has been effected rationally must be seen as a major advance in evaluating therapeutic intervention.

### 3. MULTIPLE-BASELINE DESIGNS

An alternative set of designs was introduced by Baer, Wolf and Risley (1968) which they termed the 'multiple-baseline' technique. As originally conceived, the therapist identifies a number of different responses which are troubling the patient. Each of these responses is monitored simultaneously. Then, whilst continuing to monitor all the selected behaviours, treatment is applied to one behaviour only. After an appropriate length of time, treatment is next applied to a second behaviour, leaving the others still untouched, and so on in sequence. By this means, 'The experimenter is attempting to show that he has a reliable experimental variable, in that each behaviour changes maximally only when the experimental variable is applied to it' (Baer *et al.*, 1968). This is an ingenious way of demonstrating a one-to-one relationship between intervention and outcome, utilising the well-known observation that troubles rarely present singly in real-life cases.

When appropriate, this design is relatively easy to apply, although it must be admitted that there are very few published examples. Hall *et al.* (1970) report the case of a ten-year-old girl whose mother was finding difficulty in getting the girl to practise her clarinet, do some preparation for a Girl Guide exam and do some regular homework. The mother counted the time her daughter spent each evening on each activity. 'Treatment' consisted of making the girl go to bed one minute earlier for each minute less than thirty minutes spent in following the targetted activity. As can be seen from Figure 12.3, the introduction of this contingency on each occasion is correlated with a dramatic increase in time spent in the desired activity. This study is also noteworthy in that the mother herself acted as experimenter and was responsible for gathering the data.

Figure 12.3: A Record of Time Spent in Clarinet Practice, Campfire Project Work, and Reading for Book Reports by a Ten-year-old Girl. *Baseline* – before experimental procedures; *early bedtime contingent on less than 30 minutes of behaviour* – 1 min. earlier bedtime for each minute less than 30 engaged in an activity.

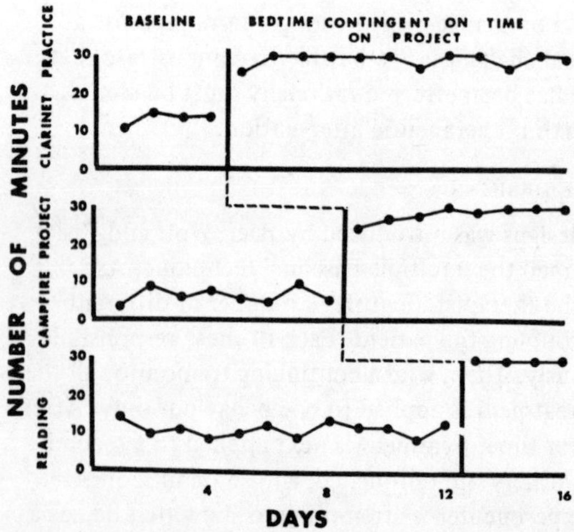


Source: Hall, Cristler, Cranston & Tucker (1970), p. 252. Reprinted with the permission of the authors and editor. 

For the multiple-baseline (across responses) design to be applicable, the therapist must be able to select behaviours which are (relatively) functionally unrelated. It is no use if the successful treatment of the first problem is associated with the disappearance of the second or subsequent problems, since this would fail to demonstrate the predicted experimental control (Leitenberg, 1973; Birnbrauer *et al.*, 1974; Gelfand & Hartmann, 1975). It would be all too easy to claim that the predicted effects did not occur, and *therefore* the behaviours must have really belonged to the same response class. Such special pleading should not become the behaviour modifiers 'reaction formation' or let-out clause.

A second variation of the multiple-baseline design takes cognisance of the fact that very often children's behaviour is situation specific. Children can be angels at school, yet devils at home. Johnny might urinate in the hall but never in the kitchen. It is now well recognised that treatment changes do not automatically generalise from one setting to another (Baer *et al.*, 1968; Patterson *et al.*, 1967). This observation is capitalised on in the multiple-baseline (across stimulus settings) design.

For example, a retarded child may be very whiny and demanding during play sessions with each parent. During baseline sessions, the amount of co-operative, constructive play is monitored in separate sessions with the father and with the mother. After this period, only one parent, say the mother, is instructed in ignoring the whines and in facilitating play using shaping and reinforcement. At this point, father does not receive such instructions. If co-operative play increases during mother's sessions but remains stable during sessions with father, this is some evidence that the treatment programme is having an effect. If, next, the father is given the same treatment advice, and if this is followed by an improvement in the child's behaviour, then the evidence that treatment is causally related to progress is strengthened.

A third variation on the multiple-baseline design is, strictly speaking, not a single-case subject design at all, in that it is the multiple-baseline across subjects. In other words, this is a design to apply across a small group of subjects. Nevertheless, this design already shows signs of being widely used, and may well prove to be the most useful in most real-life settings.

In this case, one selects two or more patients with closely similar problems. The target behaviours are monitored for baseline levels. Then, treatment is introduced to one subject at a time, maintaining all the others in baseline conditions. In other words, this is a sort of multiple-replication of AB designs across subjects. The point is that if treatment effects are repeatedly associated across subjects with the start of intervention, then chance factors are less likely to provide plausible alternative explanations.

Two examples will suffice. Flavell (1973) uses a multiple-baseline across subjects design with reversals to demonstrate that stereotypies could be reduced by training retarded children to play appropriately with toys. As can be seen in Figure 12.4, as each retarded child was reinforced in turn for playing with toys, so their amount of play increased and the amount of stereotypies decreased. Thus, the third subject showed no noticeable increase in play until this was specifically targetted during sessions 40 to 43. Such regularities in data are too strong to be merely coincidence, and so one is forced to conclude both

Figure 12.4: Rate of Toy Play and Stereotypies for Each Subject during Baseline and Reinforcement of Toy Play Conditions. The last few sessions in each condition are plotted.

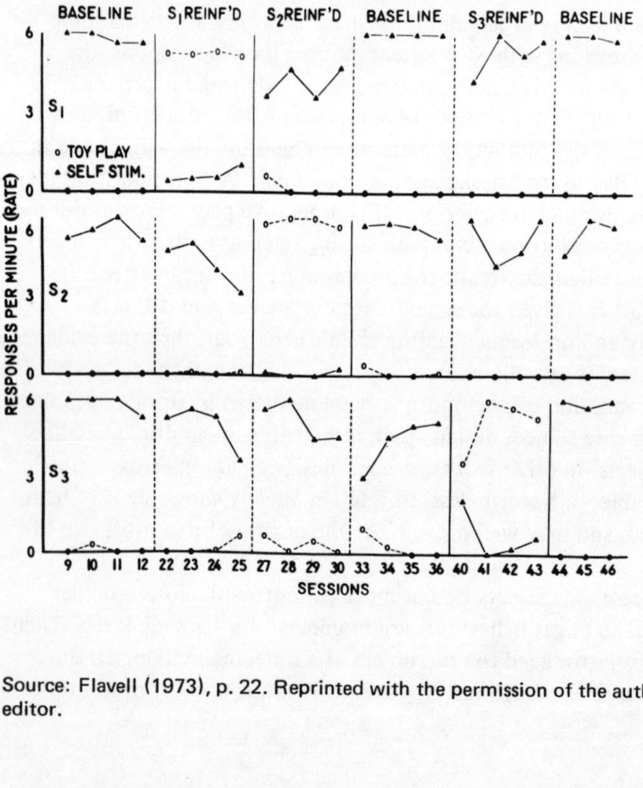


Source: Flavell (1973), p. 22. Reprinted with the permission of the author and editor.

Figure 12.5: Toilet Programme – Accidents per Week

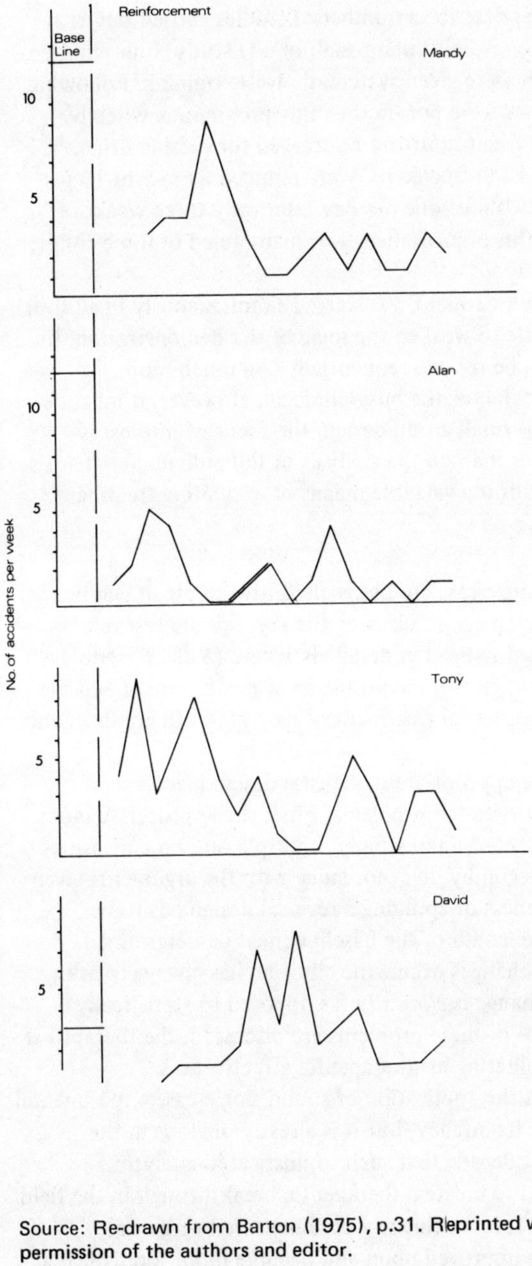


Source: Re-drawn from Barton (1975), p.31. Reprinted with the permission of the authors and editor.

that play did respond to positive reinforcement and that stereotyped behaviour was reduced as play was increased.

Barton *et al.* (1975) describe a number of studies carried out in a hospital school for the severely subnormal. In one study, four children in the special care unit were given systematic toilet training. Following a short baseline, all four were put on the same programme whereby they were potted every half-hour and reinforced for passing urine. As can be seen in Figure 12.5, 'accidents' were reduced from 5 to 10 per subject per day to only about one per day after only three weeks of intensive treatment. This improvement was maintained in three children at 12 months' follow-up.

In this last example treatment was started simultaneously in all four subjects. This does little to weaken the logic of the demonstration. In fact, subjects can even be treated sequentially – a much more convenient state of affairs for the busy clinician. However, it must be emphasised that in this small group design, the focus of interest is on the treatment rather than on the analysis of the individual patient's difficulties. Even so, this is a valuable means of evaluating treatment.

## CONCLUSIONS

Whereas the logic of single-case studies is elegantly simple, it can be seen that there is quite an art in selecting the appropriate research design. Moreover, as is discussed in detail elsewhere (Yule & Hemsley, 1977; Hersen & Barlow, 1976), the problems of measurement and the arguments about the statistical treatment of data are both complex and sophisticated.

The selection of the appropriate single-case design involves considering at least four related problems. First, the appropriate index of change has to be selected. Increasingly, multiple outcome measures are being employed. Secondly, in accordance with the arguments given above, the appropriateness of applying a reversal design has to be examined. Thirdly, the length of the baseline must be determined. Fourthly, even where changes occur, the clinician has always to ask himself whether the change is *clinically* (as opposed to statistically) significant. Provided all of these problems are discussed, the therapist is well on the way to evaluating his therapeutic effectiveness.

It is recognised that the application of sound single-case experimental methodology is still in its infancy, but it is already obvious in the publications of the last decade that such sophisticated analytic techniques have helped to create a therapeutic breakthrough in the field of mental retardation. It is confidently predicted that single-case reversal designs will be improved upon and become more sophisticated as applied research progresses.

# 13 THE ORGANISATION OF SHORT COURSES

Janet Carr

Behaviour modification is seen more and more as a valuable approach to teaching the mentally handicapped, and demand for courses on the topic is considerable. One of the aims of this book is to provide some practical help to those who wish to run such a course. Nobody, however, will want to rush into setting up a course without first determining certain basic requirements such as:

how long a course it should be – a day? a week?
for whom it should be intended – teachers? nurses? parents? psychologists? a combination of workers?
what the course should aim to achieve – increase theoretical knowledge? practical skills? both of these?
and how the organisers expect to draw conclusions on whether or not the aims have been accomplished – what methods of evaluation will be used?

## LENGTH OF COURSE

Most courses run in this country have been brief and concentrated, lasting from a few days to a week (Williams & Jackson, 1975); some, especially those for parents, have been spread out over a number of weeks (Bidder *et al.*, 1975; Callias *et al.*, in preparation; Cunningham & Jeffree, 1971, 1975).

Other courses have been much longer and more thorough, and have included written and practical examinations leading to the award of a certificate or diploma (Jackson, 1976; Murphy & McArdle, 1978; Speight, 1976). The basic content of these courses is similar (and is contained in the preceding chapters of this book). The essential difference between them lies in the amount of detail, practical experience and revision that can be included. Clearly the length of the course will constrain its objectives and the expectations of its participants. Different types of course, of differing lengths, will suit some people better than others. Course organisers may be in a position to offer one kind of course and not others. All these factors must be taken into account when a course is being planned. However, as a general rule, all short courses, up to and including those lasting six months, may be expected to be felt by the participants to be too short. It may be advisable for short courses to be explicitly described as offering no more than an introduction to behaviour modification (Williams & Jackson, 1975); for participants to be told that they cannot expect to gain a full working knowledge of the theory and skills involved; and for organisers to be prepared for a demand for follow-up meetings.

## COURSE STUDENTS

Many courses have been designed to cater for one type of student – for nurses or for psychologists, for teachers or for parents. In general, this approach seems an appropriate one, in that the course organisers know that the students share a common background of knowledge and experience. It may not, however, be essential to restrict membership of a course to one discipline. The courses run at the Institute of Psychiatry were designed for psychologists, but applicants from other disciplines – social workers, teachers, doctors, nurses – were also accepted; while the courses run at Hilda Lewis House deliberately include staff of all disciplines and also parents. The apparent success of these courses may be attributed to the fact that all students, of whatever discipline, are assumed to have virtually no knowledge of behaviour modification. With a very few exceptions this assumption seems, from the participants' performance on the courses, and especially where practical skills are concerned, to be justified; the basic principles and skills taught are relevant to all the students. Where different groups are known to differ markedly in their knowledge and experience of behaviour modification it may be advisable to offer different types of course.

## AIMS OF THE COURSE

Whether a course is to be aimed at increasing theoretical knowledge (for instance, with academic students), or at giving the participants skills which they can use to help and teach the mentally handicapped, must be decided at the outset. In our experience, the demand is almost entirely for the latter type of course. Some further suggestions for running this kind of course are given in the section on 'The Teaching Component' on p. 218.

## EVALUATION OF SHORT COURSES

Behaviour modification is becoming widely recognised as a useful approach, and the need for courses for psychologists, other professionals and non-professionals is acknowledged (Working Party on Behaviour Modification, 1978). Demand increases and courses proliferate. Some are carefully evaluated (Murphy & McArdle, 1978), but of the others, and especially of the mushrooming short courses, the question must be asked: what good do they do? Do the students who attend them learn anything? Or anything useful? Does attendance at a short course enable a student to do anything more or better than he was able to do before it? If a short course is less than ideal, is it better than nothing at all? It seems important that those who run these courses should try to provide answers to at least some of these questions, and that some attempt should be made to study the effectiveness of the course. Although a variety of evaluative approaches is possible the three to be discussed are by questionnaire; by written tests; and by assessment of practical skills.

### 1. QUESTIONNAIRES

This is the simplest level of evaluation and has been widely used (Cunningham & Jeffree, 1971, 1975; Smith, 1977; Tavormina, 1975). Participants are typically asked to record on a standard form their opinion of various aspects of the course, both didactic and organisational, and of the effect the course has had or is likely to have on their practising skills (see Appendix 3). Typically the response to these questionnaires is predominantly positive, as may also be other subjective reactions (Houston *et al.*, 1979). Gratifying as this response is to the course organisers, it should be viewed with some caution, especially where the course has been the only teaching experience to which the participants have had access. The organisers (the present authors among them) must reflect, particularly where courses for parents are concerned, that teaching of almost any kind might be welcome, and that the appreciation shown by the questionnaire respondents may not necessarily be due to the particular type of course undertaken. Nevertheless, questionnaires may be useful. Responses are not invariably favourable, and if the questionnaire is designed so as to elicit criticism as well as praise, it may provide helpful suggestions for future courses (Callias *et al.*, in preparation).

2. WRITTEN TESTS

Some form of written test of knowledge of behaviour modification has been used in a number of studies (Doleys *et al.*, 1976; Gardner *et al.*, 1970; Gardner & Giampa, 1971). A brief test was developed by one of us (JC) and used in the assessment of the Hilda Lewis House short courses; later this was expanded in collaboration with the other authors of this book, and this version of the test (The Behaviour Modification Information Test) was used in the evaluation of courses run at the Institute of Psychiatry (Carr & Yule, in preparation), of a course for teachers (Smith, 1977) and for nurses (Murphy & McArdle, 1978). The test is simple to administer and to score. It tests memory for technical terms and awareness of theoretical principles. The full test and scoring standards are given in Appendix 2. Results from the two Institute of Psychiatry courses showed that mean scores on the Behaviour Modification Information Test (BMIT) increased in each case by nearly 13 points (out of a maximum possible score of 51). Rank order correlations of BMIT scores before and after the courses were highly significant, showing that gains on the test were spread fairly evenly over those who at the outset knew a good deal about behaviour modification and those who knew very little. Rank order scores on the BMIT were also significantly associated with video ratings (see p.217), both before and after the course; thus, results from the BMIT can give some indication of students' probable performance on a practical test.

3. ASSESSMENT OF PRACTICAL SKILLS

If practical skills are taught it is important to assess how effectively they have been taught. In some courses students have been assessed in their real-life interactions with clients (Bricker *et al.*, 1972; Doleys *et al.*, 1976), while in others students have been assessed in role-playing situations (Gardner *et al.*, 1970; Murphy & McArdle, 1978; Smith, 1977). The student's performance is scored for the presence of appropriate responses (reinforcement given for positive behaviour, prompting and fading used correctly, etc) and for the absence of inappropriate responses (e.g., attention paid to undesirable behaviour).

A potential source of error in many studies is that students are rated by interested parties (course organisers), who are fully aware of where the students have got to in the course and whether the ratings being made are at the beginning or the end of the course. Although it is extremely difficult to avoid this situation when ratings are made *in vivo*, it seems probable that it would influence the outcome of the evaluation in a direction favourable to the expectations of the course organisers. In order to avoid this, where the assessments of the courses run at the Institute of Psychiatry were concerned, the role-play sessions were videotaped and were rated blind by independent raters. Although laborious and time-consuming, this method ensures that the benefits to be derived from a course are impartially evaluated.

Results from the two Institute of Psychiatry courses show that on the videotaped test of practical skills scored by blind raters, participants' scores increased in each case by about 8 points. When the ratings were done by course tutors, who were aware of which were 'before' and which 'after' tapes, the mean difference was 10.6 points. Participants who undertook the practical tests felt strongly that much of the improvement in their performance could be attributed not to what they learned on the course, but to familiarity with the test situation – on the second occasion they knew the layout of the video studio, the kind of behaviour the stooge could be expected to show, what they, themselves, would have to do and so on. All this they had had a week to think about, and it was this, they suggested, that made the major difference to their performance. Consequently, on two further courses (Murphy & McArdle, 1978), student nurses took the videotaped test at the outset and again a week later, before they embarked on an intensive course in behaviour modification, and again a week later following this course. Results showed that about half of the overall increase in scores occurred between the first and second tests – i.e., before any formal training took place.

This group of student nurses spent the intervening week between tests 1 and 2 working in Hilda Lewis House, and therefore had the opportunity to observe behaviour modification being carried out and, if they wished, to ask questions (how far they did so is unknown). It is not clear at present whether the same increase in pre-training scores would take place if the students were not in this kind of environment. Nevertheless, it seems that some of the improvement shown by students may be due not to learning but to familiarity with the test situation.

## THE TEACHING COMPONENT

Once the structural aspects of the course have been determined, the course organisers will need to decide how the course will be taught, and in particular the weight to be given to didactic and to practical teaching.

Behaviour modification comprises not only a body of knowledge but also a number of techniques and skills. Since these latter must be applied in practical situations it seems obvious that they should be taught, at least partly, by practical methods: students should have a chance to learn not only the theory but also the practice of the techniques. The underlying principle has been amply acknowledged; psychologists have often pointed out to other professionals that there is a difference between saying and doing, between 'telling what' and 'showing how' to do something. Advice on teaching new skills is readily available, and exhortations such as, 'Active learning is better than passive recognition', abound in the literature. And yet many of the early texts and descriptions of the training of both professional and lay people in behaviour modification techniques appear to have ignored practical skills training. It was, it seemed, enough to *tell* psychologists what to do rather than to show them and to give them practice. It is clear enough where this type of training can lead – all those involved in professional teaching will recognise the student who can pass written examinations while still being a one-person disaster in inter-personal work with patients. How to ensure that students acquire practical skills as well as the theory of behaviour modification has not been an easy problem to solve, and a variety of methods have been tried in the teaching of parents, nurses, teachers and others.

At an elementary level of training parents were 'instructed' in the treatment procedure (Williams, 1959) and then closely supervised in its application (MacKay, 1971). In another study parents were required to interact with a child while being watched by an experienced therapist, who then corrected their performance; this was supplemented by occasions when the therapist worked with the child while the parent watched and discussed with another therapist what was going on (Terdal & Buell, 1969). Video feedback of the student's own performance has been found a useful teaching technique (Bernal, 1969; Bricker *et al.*, 1972; Doleys *et al.*, 1976; Kiernan & Riddick, 1973). Behavioural rehearsal and role-playing have been used to teach teaching-parents and pre-delinquent boys (Phillips *et al.*, 1971), ward attendants, with trainees alternating the roles of therapist and child (Gardner, 1972; Watson *et al.*, 1971), and parents (Patterson *et al.*, 1973; Hirsch & Walder, 1969, cited by Berkowitz & Graziano, 1972). Role-playing has also been used to evaluate the effects of training. Kirigin *et al.* (1975) using pre- and post-training tests in five role-playing situations showed that parents who had undergone a five-day workshop made significantly greater gains than those who had had access only to written materials. Gardner (1973) also used role playing techniques to assess the skills acquired in training by ward attendants. He points to the advantages of using a trainee to act as the retarded child: that learning can be speeded up and complexities of training dealt with in one session which would normally take far longer to cover; that the staff under assessment are not subjected to the differences in behaviour of different residents but experience near-uniform behaviours; and that problem behaviours such as hyperactivity can be programmed at will in order to assess the competence of staff in dealing with such a problem.

The role-play method seemed to us to offer much of value to students learning behaviour modification techniques. Although it is widely used there is no detailed account in the literature of how to go about it. For those who may want to use role-playing in their teaching, what follows is a description of the method as we used it.

## WORKSHOPS

In our five-day course each day was divided into a morning and an afternoon session. Each session began with a one-hour lecture with videotape illustrations on one of the topics covered by Chapters 2-7 and 10-12 in the present book. From time to time it has been suggested that the lectures are unnecessary, and we have considered dispensing with them. Although we do not have experimental evidence either way, we have felt that it would be difficult for students to embark on practical training without having some prior knowledge of what they were supposed to do. The lectures also ensure that all students have in common at least a minimum fund of theoretical knowledge to draw on. Hence, on balance, we think the lectures useful and have continued to use them in our teaching. Each lecture was followed by a 1½-hour workshop focusing on the lecture material. The students were divided into workshop groups, 8 or 9 to a group, and each workshop was run by two tutors, one of whom acted as trainer and the other as 'stooge' – the 'retarded child'. The trainer explained the problems and learning difficulties, *a propos* of the particular workshop, of the 'retarded child', and gave a short demonstration of the appropriate techniques to be used, already discussed in the preceding lecture (e.g., prompting, modelling, etc.). The students then took it in turn to act as therapist to the 'child', attempting to put into practice the principles and techniques which had been described and demonstrated. The tutor asked for comments from the other students on the therapist's methods, and gave suggestions of his own. The stooge, although usually maintaining the part of a retarded and, often, mute child, would occasionally remark on the therapist's handling as seen from the receiving end.

For the students, attempting to use the techniques in a practical situation, as opposed to hearing them described or even watching them on videotape, offered an entirely different learning experience. All sorts of problems in the use of the techniques, both major and minor, emerged which had not been apparent until then. For example, in the workshop on reinforcement, students often found it difficult at first to deliver edible reinforcers quickly enough, or to have them readily to hand and yet not available for the stooge to grab. Many students had difficulty in giving clear directions, whether verbally or by gesture or physical prompting. Fading prompts was found to be a much more delicate and complicated task than it sounds. Even after they had been told that attention was a reinforcer students would find their attention unwittingly glued to the stooge's inappropriate behaviours. With practice, discussion, demonstration and more practice it was possible to overcome many of these difficulties and for the students to feel they had a clearer idea of how to undertake this kind of work with retarded subjects.

## ROLE OF THE STOOGE

The two tutors in any one group alternated roles as trainer and stooge and usually found a session as stooge a rest-cure compared with one as trainer. Nevertheless, the stooge also has an exacting part to play. It is essential that he should be familiar with a wide range of retarded children and with their various behaviours and responses. He must be constantly alert to the behaviours of the trainer-therapists and to how these would affect his own behaviour as a retarded child. A very real difficulty is knowing how far his own reactions as a normally intelligent person can be a guide to how the retarded child he is impersonating would react in a similar situation. For example, rough or feeble handling may be experienced similarly, but boredom with a task perhaps differently. Some stooges found it helpful to take as a model a particular retarded child whom they knew well, and to behave as they felt he would in similar circumstances. However, it was important that this should not be carried too far, and that the stooge should always be aware of the needs of the teaching situation. On one course a stooge became so engrossed in her role as a profoundly retarded passive child that she failed to react to the inappropriate behaviours of the trainer-therapists such as leaving reinforcers within reach. Another pitfall the stooge must avoid is playing for laughs. This applies particularly in workshops on decelerating undesirable behaviours, or in others where tantrums are scheduled. It is all too easy for the stooge to be carried away by the disinhibiting effects of diminished responsibility, especially as the audience usually enjoys the sight of a professional person stamping and screaming and throwing chairs. The stooge has to remember to use behaviours to enable the students to learn how to cope with them, not to feed his own ego.

On another course, another problem concerning the stooge became apparent. It is accepted that the stooge must be fully acquainted with retarded children; what now became obvious was that the stooge must also be very well acquainted with behaviour modification. This emerged during a course for parents, run by one tutor on her own, and based at a school. In order that the teachers at the school should have a part in the course they were asked to act as stooges in the workshops, and accepted with enthusiasm. However, in spite of careful briefing on the lines of the previous paragraph, they were not really successful as stooges because they did not know enough about behaviour modification to respond to appropriate techniques when these were used. For example, in a session on extinction a parent-therapist correctly withheld attention, but the teacher-stooge continued with the inappropriate behaviour far beyond what would have been reasonable, to the point where the tutor wondered whether to intervene. At long last, however, the stooge responded appropriately. This might be what would happen in a real-life situation with a real retarded child, but one of the advantages of working with a stooge is that action and learning are packed into a shorter time than is possible in real-life; by the time the stooge finally capitulated there was no time to go on to other aspects of the workshop. So, ideally, stooges should be at a fairly high level of sophistication. Where this is not possible, some intensive training of the stooges, not just written instructions and verbal discussion, might be helpful.

Being a stooge is a highly instructive process. One experiences for the first time the frustration of being inarticulate, the irritation of inappropriate handling, the ineffectiveness of unvarying reinforcers be they edible or social, and the compelling effectiveness of a varied schedule of reinforcement. This being so, the question arises as to whether each student should have the opportunity of doing a stint as stooge. Much depends on the time available. Students need to have had considerable experience of workshops – say half a dozen sessions – before they can be asked to change from trainee therapist to stooge; and they need a considerable time as stooge, at least one whole workshop each, to allow them to gain the maximum benefit from experiencing several different therapists. Other factors to be taken into account are the greater difficulty of programming students to carry out the role of stooge in a way that will give the most benefit to the other participants, and the resulting uncertainty of the participants as to whether the behaviours shown are really those that they are expected to be able to cope with. On the whole, we have not usually thought it feasible, on our short courses, to allow students to act as stooges, but have recommended they try to arrange for sessions as such when they return to their own places of work. On a longer course, experience as a stooge might be possible and valuable for the students.

Students have sometimes asked whether it would be possible for workshops to centre round a real child rather than a stooge. Apart from the ethical problems involved, we feel that this is not desirable because of the impossibility of programming the real child's behaviour. A stooge can be asked to be profoundly or mildly retarded, to learn slowly or quickly or, if necessary, to skip essential stages of learning, to stop a tantrum or to throw another straight away. What we lose in realism we more than make up for in flexibility. The course is a teaching device aimed at covering a broad spectrum of possible behaviours in a short time. We hope that the students will be able to use and try out their skills more realistically on real children when they return to their places of work.

### WORKSHOP PROBLEMS

For the tutors there are many problems in running a workshop. There is the question of how much the tutor should demonstrate the 'right' way to carry out the techniques. Since time on our course was limited, it seemed preferable that the students should use as much of it as possible in working with the stooge and gaining practical experience, but some students felt that they had had too little chance of seeing the techniques appropriately modelled. More time spent in modelling the techniques in person, or in repeated video demonstrations, might pay dividends.

Another problem concerned how long any one student should be allowed to go on working with the stooge. If the student's method of working was faulty, should the tutor interrupt the session and point out what was wrong, or allow the student to continue in order that his error might become apparent from the stooge's failure to make progress and the student be compelled to try different tactics? Ideally, the latter might have been the best way for the students to learn, but in practice, with all the constraints of time, it was not always possible. Instead, when a student-therapist persisted with a faulty technique, the tutor would usually stop him, and ask the other students whether they had any comments on how the session was going. Where necessary the tutor would steer these comments round to cover the point he wished to make to the student. Following the discussion the student would try again – hopefully, using a new approach, although sometimes students found it difficult to alter their habitual ways of behaving and might need to be stopped and corrected several times. Some students found it very difficult to show more than lukewarm enthusiasm in giving social reinforcement; others repeatedly failed to give reinforcement when it was appropriate or allowed long delays before delivery. When this happened they would be stopped again for more discussion and demonstration.

It was, however, very important not only to point out the student's mistakes and failures. Participating in a workshop is an alarming business, and some students found it extremely unpleasant to have to leave their seats and perform as trainee-therapists. If it is left to them, some participants will refuse to act as therapists, leaving this to a small number of braver volunteers.

In our workshops it was made clear to the participants that everyone was expected to take his turn as therapist and nobody would be allowed to act only as audience. The result of this was that, first, however nervous a student was of acting as therapist, he or she knew that all the other students were in the same position; second, perhaps partly because of this, the students were generally supportive of each other and their criticism of any one therapist's performance was tempered by an awareness that 'it's my turn next'; and lastly, because they were not allowed to avoid the alarming situation, the students may have found it less unpleasant than they had feared.

Nevertheless, almost all students, of whatever discipline, are nervous of having to come forward and take the part of therapist. It therefore behoves the tutors to make this as easy as possible for the students; to set each in turn a limited task which should be well within his capacity to accomplish given the teaching that has gone before; above all, to be generous with praise and sparing with criticism, concentrating on the reinforcement of the student's appropriate behaviours rather than on the punishment of his inappropriate ones. If they are to derive maximum benefit from the course, students should not only learn to use the techniques efficiently, but should also be encouraged to gain confidence in their own increasing skills.

Ideally, each student would have had the chance to work with the stooge on every aspect of every workshop, but in practice this was for us not possible. Indeed, in a 1½-hour workshop each student usually had only one or at most two sessions as trainer, although this could be stepped up in sessions that required more than one trainer at a time, as for instance when we worked on imitation, when a prompter as well as a trainer could be used. How long to go on working on a particular aspect of a workshop was another problem: it was tempting to continue with one aspect – for instance, prompting spoon feeding – until it had been thoroughly mastered, but this could only be done at the expense of other parts of the workshop. In fact we often found ourselves unable to complete the schedule for the workshops, in spite of much careful planning and timing. Nevertheless, we felt it necessary to allow ourselves some flexibility, so that if a particularly difficult problem arose it could receive special attention.

## PREPARATION OF WORKSHOPS

In order to ensure that as far as possible all students completing the course had had similar training experience, the workshops on any one particular topic followed an identical format in each of the workshop groups. Before the course opened, the content of the workshops was thoroughly discussed between the tutors after which the 'trainers' and 'stooges' guides were drawn up (see Appendix 1) and copies made for each group, mounted on cardboard for ease of handling. The two sets of guides were designed to be complementary; the trainer's guide gives the sequence of tasks to be worked through in the workshop, together with important points to be brought out and discussed; the stooge's guide also gives the sequence of tasks plus instructions as to how he is to behave – how 'bright' he is (this may vary from one task or session to another), when to throw a tantrum, when to show boredom with tasks or reinforcers and so on. Of course, the occasion for many of these behaviours depends partly on the trainee-therapist's method of working: we have sometimes been unable as stooges to display undesirable behaviours because the skilful handling of the trainee-therapist precluded them – in which case this too was explained and discussed.

The guides also contain a list of materials required for each workshop: materials to work with such as puzzles, posting boxes, threading beads; reinforcers including toys, edibles, drinks, and tokens; spoons, bowls, cups; paper, pencils and stop-watches. Each tutor kept the objects needed for all the workshops stored in a large box, while edibles, apart from sweets and packeted foods like crisps and peanuts, were collected afresh each day.

## CONCLUSIONS

Short courses in behaviour modification are popular, and those that are organised are well attended. Their organisation takes considerable planning, time and effort and may be difficult for those already fully committed in demanding jobs, but running such a course can also be rewarding to the tutors as they see the response of the students, their enthusiasm and increasing expertise. Students often discuss the relation of their new knowledge to their own background and experience, the problems and situations that they have encountered, and this, in raising new areas of application of the techniques, can be informative too for the tutors. Follow-up meetings, with students encouraged to report back – preferably with recorded data – on projects undertaken following the course, provide an opportunity for revision for the students and feedback for the tutors.

In spite of the problems attendant upon the running of practical workshops, we ourselves are convinced of their usefulness. Students too are enthusiastic about them, commenting that the workshops bring out and clarify questions that had not occurred to them before to ask; and that the students themselves feel a new confidence in embarking on using behaviour modification in real-life projects. In the ideal situation students would receive further teaching and supervision in these real-life projects. Where this is not possible, a short course may provide a starting point to learning for those wishing to use behaviour modification to help the severely retarded.

# APPENDIX 1: WORKSHOP GUIDES

Janet Carr and William Yule

Although many research reports describe 'workshop' approaches, few give any details of what is actually done in each session. Having arrived at a series of exercises which both we and our various students have found helpful, we present them here as guides for others who wish to carry out such practical training.

As presented, the workshop guides should be regarded as guides and not followed too rigidly. The workshop leader and the 'stooge' both need to be familiar with the aims of each workshop as well as with the background material in the rest of the book. The main purpose of each exercise is to illustrate a particular skill and to give trainees a feel for working in a situation where immediate, corrective, feedback is given. For this reason, the 'mentally handicapped child' will learn at a faster rate than is normally expected, so that many teaching points can be compressed into a short space of time.

We have presented the aims of each workshop followed by a list of exercises. The tutor's and stooge's guides are presented separately, and there is also a list of materials needed for all the exercises suggested for each workshop. Often we have listed more exercises than can be included in a workshop lasting one to one and a half hours, and tutors should select those exercises that are most relevant to the needs of their particular group. In our experience, exercises always take longer than planned for. It is therefore essential to plan ahead and decide on which principles and behavioural skills are to be rehearsed in each training session.

## WORKSHOP ON OBSERVATION AND RECORDING

### TUTOR'S GUIDE

**Aim**

To give participants practice in:

(1) defining target behaviours;
(2) choosing appropriate observational recording techniques;
(3) presenting the data in graph form.

Functional analysis should be discussed, although there may be insufficient time to carry out an exercise on it.

**Workshop**

(a) Participants are told that they will attempt continuous recording – to write down everything the stooge does.
Stooge performs for two minutes.
Ask participants what they recorded. Note gaps, discrepancies, discuss difficulties of continuous recording.

(b) Tell participants that they are to obtain baseline levels on 'use of plurals' and 'stereotypies'. No more detail or discussion at that point. Participants must select their own definitions, opt for recording method of their choice, etc. Stooge then performs for two minutes.

Discuss range of methods employed, and get some idea of variability between those who used the same method (i.e., frequency count). Make the point that agreement on total may mask unreliable recording of specific acts.

Get group to decide on more precise definitions of target behaviours. Decide on recording method (perhaps with half of group doing one and half another).

Stooge performs for two minutes. Write up results on blackboard and discuss.

(c) Short demonstration of block play by stooge.
Ask group to use duration recording and permanent product (no. of bricks built) to record constructive play. Stooge performs for two minutes. Discuss as before.

(d) Tell group they are to record on-task behaviour (drawing round stencil) using time-sampling or interval sampling. Stooge performs for two minutes. Discuss. If time, repeat using alternative recording method.

Reliability of observations should be computed;

$$\text{Reliability} = \frac{\text{No. of agreements}}{\text{No. of agreements + No. of disagreements}} \times 100$$

If behaviour infrequent, look at level of agreement for *occurrence* of behaviour only.
Emphasise point that high reliability does not necessarily mean high validity.
Discuss greater validity of momentary time sampling over interval

sampling (Murphy & Goodall, in press).
If desired, give participants practice in graphing, using pre-prepared data.

STOOGE'S GUIDE

(a) Look at picture book, naming pictures and using simple sentences and occasional plurals. Also show stereotyped repetitive movement – hair pulling, or face scratching – at a high rate (about 15 per min).

(b) – ditto –

(c) Play with blocks appropriately in short bursts, up to about 20 seconds at a time. At other times sit doing nothing constructive, fiddling about.

(d) Sit at table drawing round stencil for 10-15 seconds then get off seat, or rock, put pencil in mouth, look away, etc.; return to task for 10-15 seconds, and so on.

MATERIALS

Record sheets (for interval and time-sampling).
Graph paper.
Stop watches.
For stooge: picture book
blocks
pencil
stencil.

## WORKSHOP ON REINFORCEMENT

TUTOR'S GUIDE

**Aim**

To give participants practice in:

(1) identifying effective reinforcers for the individual;
(2) delivering reinforcement appropriately and promptly;
(3) pairing tangible with social reinforcers;
(4) being alert to the possibility of satiation;
(5) the use of fixed and variable schedules.

**Workshop**

*(a) Room preparation*

See that all obvious distractions are removed and that chairs and tables are suitably arranged.

*(b) Selection of reinforcer*

Have ready a variety of rewards; try social rewards as well as offering sweets, drinks, crisps, jumping and toys. Observe what the stooge shows interest in around the room or with jewellery, etc.

*(c) Train sitting on a chair to command*

Demonstrate correct administration of rewards following behaviour. Give clear instructions without excess chat and pair rewards with praise and social reinforcement. Gradually fade the rewards as the stooge sits more rapidly and stays for longer. Change rewards as stooge loses interest or becomes disruptive.

*(d) Train eye contact*

Stooge is now remaining seated but will not look at trainer. Use rewards to bring gaze towards face. Fade rewards away from face but reinstate if stooge loses interest. Can use ritualistic behaviour as reinforcer if no rewards appear effective.

*(e) Schedules of reinforcement*

Task: picture or letter matching.
Reinforcer: tokens (effective reinforcer for stooge).
Assume child used to task and to receiving tokens.

(a) Use FR 2 schedule;
(b) FR 4;
(c) VR 2 (see schedules p. 230);
(d) VR 4 (see schedules p. 230);
(e) If time, VI-10 (see schedules p.230).

STOOGE'S GUIDE

*(a) Beginning the training session – room preparation*

Stooge is very distractible and restless, wanders around the room, showing interest in some objects and ignoring others that are offered by the trainer. Continue until trainer removes distracting stimuli and room is relatively clear and uncluttered.

*(b) Selection of reinforcers*

At this stage stooge is unresponsive to social rewards.
Stooge responds rapidly to some objects or foods and ignores/rejects others. Pushes therapist away if approached, is unresponsive to smiles or praise.

*(c) Training of sitting behaviour – not involving prompting or fading*

Stooge is unresponsive to name or command to sit, but responds immediately but momentarily to any guidance to sit down. (Do not insist on physical prompts being faded at this stage.) With correct administration of edible rewards, sit for longer periods before getting up. Make the trainer change the reward by losing interest in the one that is offered.

*(d) Training eye contact*

Stooge is now seated and will remain on the chair, but doesn't look at trainer. Aim is to establish eye contact but not using physical prompts or fading. Stooge avoids eye contact but looks eagerly at the reward. After a few trials lose interest in the reward and fixate a new object, continuing until therapist changes rewards. At some stage lose interest in all rewards and only desire to sit and twiddle.

*(e) Training a simple task*

Child is able to do the task but is not particularly interested in it. Will co-operate if rewarded with tangible/edible reward. Stooge can match pictures or letters but is unwilling to do so. Will only work for a reward on each trial initially, but then can switch to more infrequent schedule.

**Schedules**

| | | | | | | | | | |
|---|---|---|---|---|---|---|---|---|---|
| VR 2 | 1 | 3 | 1 | 2 | 2 | 1 | 5 | 2 | 1 |
| | 1 | 2 | 3 | 1 | 2 | 3 | 1 | 1 | 4 |
| VR 4 | 4 | 2 | 7 | 3 | 1 | 8 | 6 | 6 | 2 |
| | 3 | 5 | 4 | 5 | 1 | 3 | 4 | 2 | 6 |
| VI 10″ | 5″ | 10″ | 6″ | 4″ | 15″ | 15″ | 8″ | 12″ | |
| | 5″ | 6″ | 12″ | 10″ | 22″ | 15″ | 5″ | 10″ | |

MATERIALS

*Reinforcers*: Smarties, crisps, peanuts, cheese, milk, orange juice, etc.
Toys – dolls, catherine wheel, cars, squeaky toy.
Tokens, watch, bracelet, or bead necklace.
Picture or letter matching task (make sure it is a *long* task).
Tray of some kind – for offering selection of back-up reinforcers in tasks.
Template for storing 4-6 tokens.

## WORKSHOP ON SHAPING, PROMPTING, FADING AND BACKWARD CHAINING

### TUTOR'S GUIDE

**Aim**

To give participants practice in:

(1) Defining the terminal behaviour, first response and subsequent responses to be reinforced;
(2) reinforcing successive approximations;
(3) using different kinds of prompts – the appropriate use and fading of physical, gestural and verbal prompts;
(4) breaking a task down into sufficiently small steps: fading prompts first on the last part of the task.

*(a) Shaping*

Stooge to learn to pick up ball and put it in the box.

(1) Watch stooge to see what behaviours already available for reinforcement.
(2) Reinforce when stooge first looks at, then touches, then picks up, etc. Puts into box, then box with large hole in lid, etc.
Stooge may be shaped to an irrelevant response.
*Discuss* what to do about this, and the disadvantages of shaping.

*(b) Prompting*

(1) Stooge to learn to put rings on stick, or over bendy wire.
Try different kinds of prompts – verbal and gestural prompts do not work at first, full physical prompts needed.
Gradually fade out physical prompts, move on to gestural

and verbal.

*Discuss* use of breaking task into small steps, and whether forward or backward chaining appropriate.

(2) Stooge to learn spoon feeding.

Stooge needs full prompts to move spoon to mouth and back to plate. Gradually reduce prompts, but go back to earlier stage if stooge doesn't learn. Use social reinforcement as well.

*Discuss* need to use favourite food, especially at first.

If time allows, for variation of task:

(3) Inset boards.

(4) Drinking.

Full prompts, and faded, as before. Need to prompt putting down cup even after lifting and drinking learned.

*(c) Backward Chaining*

STOOGE'S GUIDE

**(a) Shaping**

*Posting*

Look around, not knowing what to do, then look at ball. If reinforced, look again. Take a longer time in the beginning to learn what is expected of you. Then touch ball, pick it up, play with it, bang box with it, etc. 'Accidentally' knock box down with ball – if you are reinforced, continue knocking box down. Eventually learn to put ball in box.

**(b) Prompting**

*(1) Threading* – rings on stick and on bendy wire.

Do not respond to gestural and verbal prompts at first – you need physical prompting and reinforcement.

*(2) Spoon feeding*

Can hold spoon but not firmly: cannot scoop, lift spoon to mouth or return spoon to plate.

Learn lifting fairly quickly, but scooping more slowly. After taking mouthful, drop spoon if not prompted to return to the plate. If prompts faded too quickly, eat sloppily.

If time allows:

*(3) Inset boards*

*(4) Drinking* from cup.

Hold cup with both hands if prompted – if not, hold carelessly with one.
If cup too full, spill a bit.

**(c) Backward Chaining**

*Taking off jacket*

*Putting on jacket*

Learn fairly quickly, but show special difficulty of getting second hand in sleeve.

**General Note**

Look out for: steps broken down adequately; appropriate reinforcers, varied and given properly. Indicate by dropping level of performance, lack of interest, being mildly disruptive, etc.

MATERIALS

Cornflakes, milk (sugar), spoon, bowl.
Orange drink, cup, two-handled mug.
Ball
Box (with lids with graduated holes)
Rings on stick
Rings on bendy wire
Simple inset board
Loose jacket for stooge
Reinforcers as before.

## WORKSHOP ON IMITATION, GENERALISATION, DISCRIMINATION

TUTOR'S GUIDE

**Aim**

To give participants practice in:

(1) assessing the stooge's imitative ability;
(2) training imitation by the use of modelling, prompting, fading and reinforcement;
(3) teaching generalisation by extending teaching to new but similar situations;
(4) Teaching discrimination by reinforcing certain responses only.

**Workshop**

*Imitation*

(1) Find out if S can imitate by giving instruction, 'Do this', and modelling simple action. S can't.

(2) Train large movements:
   (a) touch box – 2 trainers: 1 model and reinf. dispenser, 1 prompter;
   (b) brick in cup;
   (c) mixture (a) and (b);
   (d) pat knees – stooge learns faster;
   (e) mix (a), (b) and (d).

(3) Sign language – Makaton (if model not clear, S shows confusion. T shows object and makes gesture):
   (a) cup (drink);
   (b) shoe, then cup and shoe;
   (c) biscuit, then all three.

(4) Imitate mouth movements (not expecting sounds) – ah, oo, ee. Some spontaneous sounds of S can be used. (S needs more prompts at the beginning. Reinforce all spontaneous sounds.)

*Generalisation* – stimulus/therapist

(1) Teach child (quite quickly with aid of prompts, etc.) to sit on command in particular chair. Introduce new chair or new trainer. Difficulties then occur. Child has to learn to respond to new stimulus or trainer. Gradually fade out original chair, until child sitting well in quite different chair and/or with different trainer.

(2) *Verbal labelling.* Child learns to give ball/car/doll. Then asked for different balls/cars/dolls. Needs re-training at first.

*Discrimination*

(1) *Of reinforcement for particular activity.* Teach child to do jigsaw. He flaps immediately before first piece put in. If reinforced by this flaps some pieces vigorously, not others. Students must not reinforce flapping plus placement but only reinforce for correct placement alone. If necessary, restrain flapping.

(2) *Of cues – colour matching task.* Have 2 rather similar coloured stimuli and objects to match them with (e.g., blue and green). Child fails even with prompting. If given clearly different colours, e.g., red and yellow, responds to prompts and reinforcers and matches correctly. Initial stimuli can then be gradually

reintroduced.

STOOGE'S GUIDE

Attention to reinforcers as before. They must be:
adequate (try grabbing, if incautiously available)
not satiating
given quickly.
If not, drop performance level and become disruptive.

(1) Imitation
Begin by being inattentive
This must be trained, but S learns quickly
(2) Large movements
Learn slowly at first, then more quickly
(3) Sign language – Makaton
If trainer model not clear, S shows confusion
(4) Imitate mouth movements
Sounds not expected, but S has some spontaneous sounds.

**Generalisation**

(1) Respond to prompts fairly quickly for first task of sitting in chair. However, if different chair or different trainer introduced – stooge becomes confused. Do not respond to instructor in new situation until the connection between first chair and second, or first therapist and second is demonstrated.
(2) *Object-name comprehension.* You will be taught to give trainer an object on response to request. Give me the ball/car/doll. Consequently, when different object of same class introduced do not respond correctly until given further training.

**Discrimination**

(1) *Of reinforcement for particular activity.* Taught to do jigsaw. Flap first piece vigorously before putting it in: when reinforced, flap many of the pieces. When flapping not reinforced, flap harder. When restrained and reinforced for placing only, leave off flapping.
(2) *Of cues – colour matching.* Show confusion over matching of similar colours – blue, green. Fail to learn. Succeed with more obviously different colours, and then with original ones.

MATERIALS

Cup, shoe, biscuit
2 chairs
Ball, cars, dolls
Jigsaw and inset puzzle
Colour matching apparatus for blue/green/yellow/red
Reinforcers.

## WORKSHOP ON DECREASING BEHAVIOURS

TRAINER'S GUIDE

**Aim**

Participants should have practice in the use of:

(1) time-out and its relation to positive reinforcement;
(2) extinction – identification of the reinforcers maintaining behaviour.
(3) restitution and over-correction;
(4) restraint;
(5) response cost.

**Workshop**

*(1)* *Time out.* Stooge to eat (e.g. dish of cornflakes with spoon). Stooge can use spoon but will finger feed (removal of dish), for various lengths of time e.g., 3 seconds, 20 seconds, 1 minute. Importance of not giving food back while misbehaving (banging spoon, etc.).

*(2)* *Extinction.* Problem behaviour, putting teaching material in mouth.

*Task: build tower box.* Aim to get stooge to complete task. Stooge will co-operate but will put pieces in mouth and look at trainer for response. Discuss methods of dealing with this. Emphasise complete withdrawal of attention for extinction (stooge will try to turn trainer's face round, etc.). Try out with several people so that stooge can become bored/inattentive (see below).

(3) *Restitution* (continues straight on from 2).
When stooge is on third or fourth attempt on the above task, he will become bored, inattentive and stroppy, and eventually sweep items off table on to floor. During restitution, discuss correct positioning of trainer so as to have full control of unwilling stooge. Mention over-correction.

(4) *Restraint.* Problem behaviour – hand-flicking, eye-poking – during task.
*Task*: putting rings on wire stick.
*Reinforcers*: Smarties or similar.
Aim to try to reduce flicking/poking which is interrupting on-task behaviour. Try emphatic, 'No', 'Hands down', removal of attention – stooge programmed not to respond to these. Try restraining (holding hands firmly down to stooge's side). Discuss duration of restraint, tightness of restraint, etc.

(5) *Reinforcement of other behaviour* (continues straight on from 4).

Task and problem as above. Try:

(a) reinforcement of on-task behaviour (stooge programmed to use one hand for task and other hand for flicking/poking);
(b) two-handed task – e.g., threading, playing a triangle.

(6) *Response cost.*

Problem behaviour – tantrums. Stooge on token programme which provides him with tokens for doing task without help.

*Task*: letter or picture matching.
*Rate*: one token for every three cards matched.
Stooge has already earned six tokens and earns four more, then tantrums (e.g., over difficult card).
*Discuss* possible costs (e.g., 10, 5, 2), how best to remove tokens, where best for stooge to wear his tokens (e.g., better on string round neck than in pocket).

(7) *General discussion.*

Any general points on uses and abuses of punishment or controversial issues, e.g., use of shock.

STOOGE'S GUIDE

*(1)* *Time-out.* Dish of (e.g.) cornflakes.

Start eating with spoon if prompted to; if not, start finger-feeding. If you do begin with spoon, finger-feed after a few mouthfuls (same or other hand). During time-out reach for food, bang spoon on table, etc.

*(2)* *Extinction.* Problem behaviour is putting teaching materials into your mouth; attention is your reinforcer.

*Task*: Trainer will try to get you to complete tower toy. Be co-operative but put a piece in your mouth and look for a reaction from trainer. If he attends or scolds, etc., stuff some more pieces in your mouth. If he does not attend (either at first or during extinction) pull his hand/shirt, turn his face round towards you, etc. Gradually stop misbehaving during extinction. When on your third/fourth go on the task, begin to get inattentive/bored (see below).

*(3)* *Restitution* (continues straight on from 2)

As you become more inattentive to the task, require more prompting to put in pieces correctly. Get stroppy when prompted and sweep items off the table onto the floor. During restitution be unco-operative, unless trainer positions himself right, and throw pieces if you are not well under control.

*(4)* *Restraint.* Problem behaviour: eye-poking or hand-flicking.
*Task*: putting rings on wire-stick.
*Reinforcer* being used: Smarties or similar.
Co-operate when not flicking/poking, do *not* respond to trainer saying your name, saying, 'No', 'Hands down'. When restraint tried, flick/poke less, but wriggle if restraint not tight enough.

*(5)* *Reinforcement of other behaviour* (continues straight on from 4).

Reinforcement will be given:

(a) for on-task behaviour – flick/poke with one hand and do task with other;
(b) two-handed task – e.g., threading. No flicking/poking when on task.

*(6)* *Response cost*. Problem behaviour: tantrums.

*Task*: Picture or letter matching.

You are on token programme and will earn one token for every three cards matched without prompting. You have already earned six tokens and you earn four more. Then show difficulty with the card you are matching and tantrum. During removal of tokens from you, resist if possible. (It might be easiest to be a verbal child and have a swearing tantrum.)

MATERIALS

Cornflakes, milk
Bowl, spoon
Tower toy (5-10 pieces)
Rings and wire stick
Letter or picture matching task
Threading task or triangle (or other two-handed task)
Tokens, token string
Stop watch or kitchen timer
Reinforcers

## WORKSHOP ON TOKEN PROGRAMMES

TUTOR'S GUIDE

**Aim**

To give participants practice in:

(1) teaching the stooge to accept a token and exchange it for the primary reinforcer: to delay exchange and store tokens;
(2) using tokens with groups;
(3) dealing with disruptive behaviours by adapting schedules, or fining;
(4) altering the schedules of token delivery;
(5) organising the exchange of tokens for back-up reinforcers.

**Workshop**

*(1) With non-speaking individual child*

*(a)* *Introduction to tokens*

*Task*: letter matching, or similar – stooge is familiar with task and is reinforced after every 2 letters done.

*Reinforcers*: edibles/drink.

Begin by showing that stooge will do task with primary reinforcers. Then introduce tokens, prompting stooge to hold the token if necessary and prompting him to exchange it for primary reinforcer.

*(b)* *Delayed exchange*

*Task* and *reinforcers* as above.

Lengthen time gradually – e.g., to 5 seconds, then 10 seconds, 20 seconds, etc. Prompt stooge to keep hold of token if necessary, fading prompts before increasing time again.

*(c)* *Storing tokens*

*Task* and *reinforcers* as above.

Begin by prompting stooge to place single token on table before exchanging it. Once stooge does this, require him to get 2 tokens before exchanging them. If necessary, prompt stooge to match second two letters so he can receive his second token and exchange with minimum delay.
Repeat procedure once stooge used to 2 tokens until he can store three and then four.
N.B. Be careful stooge still gets one back-up $S^{R+}$ for each token. May be useful to have tray with selection of reinforcers at this stage, so stooge can choose different items if he wishes. Also may be useful to have jig so stooge can see when he has enough tokens to exchange (even if can't count).

*Discuss*:

(1) Different reinforcement schedules (e.g., convenience of FI schedules with token programmes).

(2) Possibility of establishing tokens as secondary reinforcers before using them in a task (as is done on

most t.e. ward programmes).

(3) Need to explain programme, and discuss it with subject whose language is up to it.

*(2) Tokens with small group*

*(a) Deciding on schedules*

*Task:* Stooges to do task of making simple Christmas cards, involving folding paper, cutting out pictures, sticking picture onto card.

*Stooges*: Ask for 2 extra stooges from your group (to work with the 'professional' stooge). Tell the stooges that their job is to act like fairly untroublesome retarded adults, doing task quite quickly, accepting tokens. The 'professional' stooge will be very slow.

*Reinforcers*: Tokens, which all stooges are used to receiving. Start by using an FR schedule (e.g., continuous schedule if all your stooges are quite slow, FR 2 if faster, etc.). The pro stooge will be especially slow, will earn less tokens than the others and will pinch tokens from the others.

Discuss how to prevent stealing (e.g., different colour tokens).

Discuss basic problem (one slow stooge) and try an FI schedule instead. If time, also try individualised programme with low $S^{R+}$ criterion for slow stooge, gradually raising criterion (towards that of the other stooges) as pro stooge improves.

*(b) Response cost*

*Task, stooges, reinforcers* as above.

When supervisor not looking, stooge will pinch or kick other stooges. Try response cost. *Discuss* when to fine, whether to scold as well, and other possible methods (e.g., time-out). Discuss possibility of giving stooge special task to do to regain lost token, and try this out if time.

*(c) Token exchange (if time)*

*Task*: To exchange tokens earned by one stooge during day.

*Stooge*: One stooge only (professional stooge from above).

*Back-up reinforcers*: cigarettes, magazines, sweets, crayons, pens, writing paper, make-up, privilege cards, etc.

Exchange stooge's tokens, coping with misunderstandings over prices, stooge wanting more items than has tokens, what to do with left-over tokens.

STOOGE'S GUIDE

*(1) Non-speaking child, individual programme*

*(a) Introduction to tokens*

*Task*: Letter matching. You can do this (occasional mistakes) and are used to edible reinforcers on an FR 2 schedule.

*Training*: When given token instead of reinforcer don't know what it is for (drop it, eat it, etc.) You will be prompted to hand it back for your reinforcer, and prompts will be gradually faded. If fading too fast, drop token again, otherwise learn quickly.

*(b) Delayed exchange*

*Task*: as above.

*Training*: You will be taught to hold token longer once it is delivered. If time lengthened too fast, grab for reinforcers, lose interest in tokens. When time lengthened gradually, behave yourself but require prompts to hold token if you think necessary.

*(c) Storing tokens*

*Task*: as above.

*Training*: You will be taught to store up to four tokens before exchange – first two, then three, then four.

To begin with, if not prompted to put first token down on table, make it get in the way of doing the task. When trainer gets you to continue task after first token, look puzzled, try to hand over token, refuse to continue task again until given slight physical prompt to do so. If exchange after getting two tokens is slow, or if trainer tries to get you to store four tokens straight off, get cross. Also, grab at reinforcers if not given one reinforcer for *each* token.

(2) *Speaking adult, group programme*

(a) *Deciding on schedule*

*Task*: making Christmas cards – folding, cutting, sticking pictures. You can do task but are slow.

*Training*: You are much slower than the other two stooges (from the floor). During FR schedule you therefore earn less tokens than they do, steal some of their tokens and deny it if accused.

An FI schedule will then be tried, and you will earn as much as the others but won't learn to speed up – i.e., production rate still low. Other stooges may complain or trainer may notice this.

If time, an individualised system will be tried, with you on a lower FR than the other stooges. When your schedule is gradually stretched, speed up; if schedule stretched too fast don't speed up and steal tokens again.

(b) *Response cost*

*Task*: As above, but you start pinching and kicking the other stooges when supervisor not looking; look as if you enjoy their screams!

*Trainer*: You will be fined for aggression. Refuse to hand over token at first. Then go on strike for a bit. The possibility of offering you a special task to earn token back will be discussed and will be tried if time. If tried, start work again, after fining, more happily.

(c) *Token exchange (if time)*

*Task*: You will be exchanging your tokens at end of day's work.

*Training*: Try to confuse trainer by misunderstanding prices, wanting too many items, changing your mind, etc. If explanations clear, be satisfied; if not clear, continue objections.

Make sure you have one or two tokens left over at end and refuse any items of this price. If it is clearly put to you that you can bring them back tomorrow, agree; if not clear, argue.

MATERIALS

(1) Letter matching task, or similar (make sure it is a potentially long task, with lots of small responses to complete).
(2) Small sheets of paper for folding into cards (about 30 sheets).
(3) Scissors.
(4) Glue (or sticky-backed paper, see 5).
(5) Pictures for cutting up or sticky-backed coloured paper.
(6) Tokens – several colours, preferably 3 × 7.
(7) Back-up reinforcers: edibles, drinks, tray (for first part), selection of 'adult' reinforcers (for second part), e.g., cigarettes, magazines, etc.
Price list (for 'adult' reinforcers).
(8) 'Jig' for storing tokens.

## WORKSHOP ON LANGUAGE TRAINING

### TUTOR'S GUIDE

**Aim**

To give participants practice in:

(1) teaching comprehension, through reinforcement of appropriate responses to verbal commands;
(2) teaching expressive language by:
    (a) reinforcing imitation of sounds
    (b) reinforcing response to prompted nouns, verbs, adjectives, etc.
    (c) fading of verbal prompts.

**(a) Comprehension**

(i) Command training – stand up, sit down, come here, give me.
(ii) *Object discrimination.* One object on table. Instruct, 'Give me the. . .' Test generalisation with similar objects/pictures. Proceed to two-object display, then to more if necessary. Discuss which objects to start with, etc.
(iii) Go on to more complex words, verbs (running/jumping, etc.) or prepositions (in, on, etc.) Do verbs, etc., only if time allows – if not, proceed to (iv).
(iv) Using *signs* – request S to give you objects.

**(b) Expression**

(i) *Imitation.* Increase frequency of spontaneous sound made by S. Prompt new sound, 'Ah', using physical prompts. Fade prompts.
Go on to new sound (B). Then alternate sounds.

(ii) *Sound chaining.* Train two already acquired sounds together (K-Ah). Decrease interval between sounds until word approx. is reasonable. If time, proceed to another chain, e.g., ball/cup. Have *objects present.*

(iii) Increase imitation of simple words when objects are presented. (Brief demo. only.)

(iv) *Naming objects.* Ask, 'What is it?' Give immediate prompt. Fade prompts till S answering appropriately.
Go on to new object and then on to naming display of objects (2-3).

(v) *Verbs.* Pictures of actors. Ask, 'What are they doing?' and prompt answer – or use child's own actions. Omit (v) if time short – go on to (vi).

(vi) *Simple signs.* Prompt signs for simple objects – cup/car, etc. Ask S 'What is it?' Fade prompts.

STOOGE'S GUIDE

**(a) Comprehension**

(i) *Command training.* Physical prompts needed at first. Improve if prompts and reinforcers good. Do badly if inadequate prompts, no $R^+$, too rapid fading. When new activity introduced perseverate on original unless prompts adequate.

(ii) *Object selection.* Respond as above. Learn quickly if prompts etc., OK; do badly, perseverate on one item if not. Show confusion at first when new item introduced. Don't generalise to pictures or alternative objects unless these similar to original at first.

(iii) *Verbs/prepositions.* As above. Lots of prompting and $R^+$ needed at first. Make progress only if these faded at appropriate rate.

(iv) *Signing.* Give appropriate object *only* if association between object and sign has been appropriately demonstrated and prompts are adequate.

**(b) Expression**

(i) Make variety of spontaneous sounds – one or two being particularly frequent. Increase sounds in frequency if reinforced.
(ii) Imitate trainer's sound if this adequately prompted. Respond slowly at first. Imitation becomes more rapid if reinforcers given well. If new sound introduced perseverate on old sound unless well prompted.
(iii) Imitate separate sounds quickly. Reduce interval between sounds if reinforced appropriately.
(iv) *Naming objects.* Repeat prompt if this given clearly. Echo question if this not distinguishable from correct answer. Respond to reduction in prompts if this done slowly and $R^+$ is adequate.
(v) *Verbs.* As above.
(vi) *Signing.* Learn signs only if physical prompting adequate and association between sign and object is clear.

MATERIALS

Simple objects – car, ball, doll, sock, shoe, spoon, etc.
Variety of these and pictures, to teach and test generalisation.
Picture cards of actions – sitting, running, jumping, crying, etc. – for verbs.
Reinforcers.

## WORKSHOP ON TEACHING OTHERS

### TUTOR'S GUIDE

**Aim**

To give participants practice in:

(1) teaching an adult (parent, teacher or nurse) how to assess a behaviour they wish to modify in a child;
(2) teaching an adult how to implement a behavioural approach to teach a child a new skill, and reduce undesirable behaviour;
(3) discussing some of the specific issues of implementing programmes in home, school and hospital settings.

**Note: Running the Workshop.** Most of the time could be spent on scenarios with the parent. If there is not enough time to practice teacher/nurse scenarios allow some time to discuss school and hospital settings.

**Workshop**

*Home*

(1) *Interview mother* to elicit problems (description on stooge's guide).
Select problems to work on first. Discuss question of how many; acceleration in addition to deceleration target.

(2) Do *functional analysis* on language and temper tantrums. Get description and details on frequency, circumstances, how she deals with problems. What has she tried, is she consistent? Extent of disagreement between parents.

(3) Find out about *reinforcers.*

(4) Discuss *use* of reinforcement. Deal with M's queries, objections.

(5) *Language*
   (a) Work out plan for collecting baseline data (e.g., simple frequency count in brief play session).
   (b) Increase vocalisation in play. M to reinforce (social) C whenever vocalises; also to withhold certain toys and only give contingently on sound production. Model sound/word if necessary. Model and train M directly, get 'child' from group.
   (c) Suggest 5-10-min daily session on language. Shape specific sounds (e.g., b, oo, m) and words (book, car, shoe). Teach by modelling and direct training of M. (Need 'child' again.) Need to be explicit about use of reinforcement, prompts, selection of content, dealing with C's lack of interest.
   (d) Two weeks later. Discuss data already collected, problems about reinforcement and fading. (N.B. Prepare dummy data for discussion.)

(6) *Temper tantrums*
   (a) Collect multiple baseline data – meal-time; ½-hr free play, shops.
   (b) Discuss extinction and TO and select one treatment approach. Discuss M's doubts about whether she will implement programme; practical problems.
   (c) Suggest treat tantrums systematically at meal-times only first.
   (d) Go through 2 further weekly contacts discussing data on progress, problems.

*School*

(7) Same child at *school.* Interview teacher about problems. Get baseline data on tantrums, hitting children.

(8) TO treatment for tantrums. Discuss why prefer TO to extinction in group situation (because child likes attention from peers; disruptive) and problems of implementing.

(9) Hitting children – as for tantrums. Introduce treatment 2 weeks later.

(10) Develop positive social interaction – 10-min session. Use prompts to shape approaches incompatible with hitting. Grade situations to increase extent of contact between S and another child (e.g., sitting on each side of teacher to play with bricks, or next to each other working on same activity of pasting cut-outs). Introduce a third child. Discuss progress at 2-3 meetings.

*Ward*

(11) *Nurse* working on independent dressing.
Baseline, multiple baseline.
Training 2 garments – jumper, socks. Demonstrate.
Discuss progress and data over 3 weeks at weekly meetings.
Problems: time, N's motivation, conflicting demands, singling out one child.

(12) Discussion on problems in teaching, special problems in group setting, etc., if these have not been discussed in course of workshop.

STOOGE'S GUIDE

Stooge is *adult.* Get *child* from group when needed.

(1) Stooge is *mother* of 9-year-old-boy who has very limited language. His comprehension is better than his use of language, which is limited to some sounds and 2-3 words which he seldom uses. Other skills are better. Can spoon-feed himself, is partly toilet trained, cannot dress. Can occupy self for 5-10 mins with puzzles, books, in garden. Has lots of temper tantrums, generally when he can't get his own way, esp. at meal-times – is fussy about food; and in shops.
Mother is at end of her tether but very concerned, and wants to help child. Reacts by anticipating his every need/wish, and pacifying him and giving in when he has tantrums, esp. in public.

Offers choice of 2-3 meals.
Father – much as mother except that he reacts to child's temper tantrums impatiently, shouting at child, who then weeps. Two other younger children.
Only mother is seen for treatment.

(2) In interview, give tantrums, language, dressing as main problems. Choose to work on tantrums and language. Give some vague descriptions so that T must elicit behavioural descriptions.

(3) Reinforcers – chocolate, cuddling, toys – especially bus, etc.

(4) Reluctant to use contingent reinforcement but agree to try. (Unfair on other children; gives the reinforcers anyway.)

(5) Request clarification if T is unclear. Object if asks for complex data.
 (a) Give free access to reinforcers initially; learn to use contingently. Get cross when child is disobedient – learn to use TO.
 (b) Find it difficult to use prompts initially – improve. Try to work on too many words at once.
 (c) Produce data. Be dissatisfied with progress – too slow. Problem that C went off reinforcers used. Still giving full prompts.

(6) Temper tantrums
 (a) Request clear definition of what 'counts', e.g., ask if tantrum provoked by brother counts. Dubious re collective data in play time.
 (b) Unhappy about extinction because 'can't ignore him'. Reluctantly agree to try TO, but need it spelt out clearly. Fuss about C not getting his food.
 (c) Discuss data, problems – other children need attention too. Worried about eating cold food, or enough. But pleased with progress.

(7) Stooge as *teacher*. Same problem child. At school, he has tantrums when he is not getting attention. Hits other children when sitting/working near them. No other contact with children. Provide information about child. Collect simple baseline data.

(8) Raise objections/difficulties in implementing treatment, e.g., effect on other children, can't single out one child, disrupts routine.

(9) Agree to extend TO to hitting because working reasonably with tantrums.

(10) Make T explain details. Again raise difficulties like finding time, special treatment for one child.
Bring data (prepared sheet) and difficulties.

(11) Stooge as *nurse.* Describe child's dressing in general terms till asked for specific details. Be vague about some so that you need to find out in baseline observations.
Raise problems in carrying out programme: staff shortage one week, time, conflicting demands, special attention to one child, other nurses' attitudes; and specific to training – prompts, reinforcers, child distracted by others.

MATERIALS

Reinforcers: chocolate, toy bus, crayons and paper.
Toys: car, bus, book, shoe.
Data sheets: language training, tantrums.
Bowl, cornflakes, spoon and milk.
School data sheets – tantrums, hitting children.
Sock, jumper.

# APPENDIX 2: THE BEHAVIOUR MODIFICATION INFORMATION TEST

Janet Carr

## Introduction

Please read through the questions and answer them where you can. Usually the answer will consist of filling in a missing word or words. Please don't worry if you don't know all the answers. The course is intended to give you the answers and we shall be asking you to do the test again at the end of it. If you do know all the answers the course may be a waste of time for you.

If you are not sure of the answer, but have some idea, put down your guess.

## Test

1. Before we attempt to change a child's behaviour we must . . . . .it.
2. To know the level of a particular behaviour we must . . . . . . . . . . how often it occurs.
3. Noticing what happens is not enough; for permanency the observations must be. . . . . . . . . . . . . . . . . . . . . . . . . . . . . . . . . . . . . . .
4. A teacher wrote down how many times a child got out of his chair without permission during the morning. This is called . . . . . . . . . . . . . . . . recording.
5. A mother wrote down everything her child did during one hour. This is called . . . . . . . . . . . . . . recording.
6. A nurse observed how much time a child spent smiling during one afternoon. This is called . . . . . . . . . . . . . . recording.
7. A nurse watched a child eating his lunch. At the end of every 10 second interval she recorded whether the child had shown poor eating habits (used his fingers, spilt his drink etc.) during the 10 seconds. This is called . . . . . . . . . . . . . . . recording.
8. A student doing a project sought out a particular child every hour on the hour and noted whether his pants were wet at that moment. This is called. . . . . . . . . . . . . . . . . . . . . . . . . . . . . . . . . . (two words).
9. Two nurses simultaneously recorded a child's lunch time

behaviour as in 7 above. By comparing their records and seeing how far they agreed they could get a measure of the .......... of their observations.

10. A record of the occurrence of a behaviour before any attempt is made to change it is called a..........................
11. If this record shows the behaviour increasing it will not be appropriate as a starting point for your treatment where the behaviour is one you wish to ..........................
12. A reinforcer may be defined as any event which, when it follows a behaviour,............... the chance of that behaviour recurring.
13. How can we tell whether a certain consequence is really a reinforcer for a child's behaviour? .......................... ................................. (several words).
14. When building up a new behaviour the reinforcer should be given ....................................... (when?).
15. a. If a child has been accustomed to receiving reinforcement for a behaviour and the reinforcement is then stopped, the behaviour will............................. (one or more words).
    b. This process is known as..........................
16. ............... reinforcement works by giving the child something good,............... reinforcement by taking away something bad.
17. The best reinforcement schedule for establishing a new behaviour is ............................. (one or more words)
18. To maintain behaviour the best reinforcement schedule is......
19. In order to determine whether or not a particular reward or punishment is affecting behaviour we can................. these for a short time.
20. This procedure is known as a ............... technique.
21. Scolding is often used as a punishment. Could it ever be a positive reinforcer? YES/NO.
22. If a child cannot do a task, which is about at his level, we can help him to learn to do it by guiding him through the task. This is called ..........................
23. When we set out to teach a child a complicated task such as putting on his jumper it is best to begin by teaching him the ............... part of the task. This is called ............ ............... (two words).
24. In a programme to encourage a socially isolated child to interact with other children, the teacher started off by reinforcing her

when she looked at another child, and then when she approached another child, then when she touched the child, and finally when she played with him. This process is called . . . . . . . . . . . . . . . . . . .

25. If a child will urinate in a red potty but never in a blue potty then his toiletting behaviour is said to be under the . . . . . . . . . . . . . . . . . . . . . . . . . . . . . . . of the red potty.
26. When he has been taught to use both the red potty and the blue potty then we can say that some . . . . . . . . . . . . . . . . . . . . . . . . . . has occurred.
27. Sometimes a child will learn a task more quickly if he sees someone else carrying out and reinforced for doing this task. This procedure is known as . . . . . . . . . . . . . . . . . . . . . . . . . . . . . . . . .
28. There are three types of prompts . . . . . . . . . . . . . . . . . . . . . . . . . . . . . . . . . . . . . . . . . . . . and . . . . . . . . . . . . . . . . . . . . . . . . .
29. Nurse A said she would work on a child's concentration, Nurse B said she would work on a child's ability to persist with tasks. From this information only, which project has the better chance of success? Nurse A's/Nurse B's.
30. If you have used 15 minutes' time-out contingent on inappropriate behaviour for a child and decide to reduce the period to 5 minutes the behaviour will probably. . . . . . . . . . . . .
31. If you have used 5 minutes' time-out contingent on inappropriate behaviour for a child and increase the period to 15 minutes, the behaviour will probably . . . . . . . . . . . . . . . . . . . . . . . . . . . . . .
32. A boy earns tokens for appropriate behaviours during the day, exchanging them at the end of the day for reinforcers. You decide to fine him tokens for hitting other boys: this is called . . . . . . . . . . . . . . . . . . . . . . . . . . . . . . (two words).
33. Aversive stimuli are susceptible to scheduling effects. TRUE/FALSE.
34. If you put up with a child's inappropriate behaviour until you can stand it no longer you will teach him to. . . . . . . . . . . . . . . . . the behaviour.
35. When your main target is to decrease a problem behaviour you should wait until it has dropped considerably before you start reinforcing and shaping up another behaviour. TRUE/FALSE.
36. A child invariably misbehaves at meal-times and you therefore decide to remove his meal from him for 2 minutes contingent on each misbehaviour. This procedure is called . . . . . . . . . . . . . . . . . . . . . . . . . . . . . . . . . . . . . . . . . . . . . . . . . (two or more words).
37. Name 2 types of problem behaviour for which you would be

cautious about using extinction procedures . . . . . . . . . . . . . . . . . .
. . . . . . . . . . . . . . . . . . . . . . . . . . . . . . . . . . . . . . . . . . . . . . . .
. . . . . . . . . . . . . . . . . . . . . . . . . . . . . . . . . . . . . . . . . . . . . . . .

38. When you advise parents to use extinction procedures to treat their child's problem behaviour you should always warn them to expect. . . . . . . . . . . . . . . . . . . . . . . . . . . . . . . . . . . . . . . . . . . .
. . . . . . . . . . . . . . . . . . . . . . . . . . . . . . . . . . . . . . . . . . . . . . . .

39. To use the Premack principle means to use a . . . . . . . . . . . . . . . activity of the child as a reinforcer for a new behaviour you are teaching him.

40. A child whines: an adult gives the child a sweet: the child stops whining. This is an example of . . . . . . . . . . . . . . . reinforcement for the child and. . . . . . . . . . . . . . . reinforcement for the adult.

41. To carry out a functional analysis, especially of a behaviour problem, means to examine that behaviour in the context of its . . . . . . . . . . . . . . . and. . . . . . . . . . . . . . . . . . . . . . . . . . . . . . . . . .
We should also examine the behaviour itself in terms of its
. . . . . . . . . . . . . . . . . . . . . . . . . . . . . . . . . . . . . . . . . . . . . . . .
and. . . . . . . . . . . . . . . . . . . . . . . . . . . . . . . . . . . . . . . . . . . . . .
. . . . . . . . . . . . . . . . . . . . . . . . . . . . . . . . . . . . . . . (give 2).

**BMIT Scoring Criteria** (Total possible score: 51)

| Question No. | Right – score 1 | Half-right – score ½ | Wrong – score 0 |
|---|---|---|---|
| 1. | Observe: define: functionally analyse | Specify: assess: analyse: record | Measure: describe: study |
| 2. | Record: measure: count: monitor: tabulate | Observe: discover: determine: establish: assess | See: note: know: estimate: discuss. collate |
| 3. | Recorded: written down: charted | | Replicable: stable: systematic: consistent over time |
| 4. | Event | Frequency: rate: event occurrence | Action: item: baseline |
| 5. | Continuous | | Period: event: temporal: descriptive observation: category baseline: complete |
| 6. | Duration | | Temporal: affective baseline: time-on-task: incident |
| 7. | Interval | Time interval: time sampling | Time ratio: tabulated occurrence: space sampling |
| 8. | Momentary time sampling | Time sampling | Event sampling: sampling technique: time spacing: time response: toiletting programme |
| 9. | Reliability | Concordance: accuracy: correlation: agreement: consistency | Validity: percentage: average: mean |
| 10. | Baseline | Basal estimate: basal level: basal recording | Behaviour analysis: functional analysis: probe: definition |
| 11. | Increase: encourage: reinforce: accelerate: promote: strengthen | | Eliminate: extinguish: modify |
| 12. | Increases: strengthens | | Reinforces: changes: alters: increases or decreases |

| Question No. | Score 1 | Score ½ | Score 0 |
|---|---|---|---|
| 13. | Any answer stating: if it has the effect of increasing the behaviour, *or* a definition of extinction – i.e., if the reinforcer is discontinued and the behaviour decreases | Any answer stating: observe effect of reinforcer (without giving direction of change): use reversal design: demonstrate experimental control of the behaviour: remove it and see if the behaviour continues: if it alters the rate of the behaviour: observe its effect on the behaviour it follows | By withdrawing the reinforcer: whether the child's behaviour is contingent on it: if the desired behaviour is elicited by that reinforcer: by observing the child's reaction to different reinforcers to see which he likes: the child will show particular interest to the consequence: if the behaviour increases or decreases as desired |
| 14. | Immediately and continuously: continuously | Contingently: immediately | When the task is done: simultaneously: often |
| 15a. | Decline: decrease: go down: diminish: get less: extinguish: go up and then down | Go up at first: stop: cease: regress: fade out | Continue: increase |
| 15b. | Extinction | | Fading: return to baseline: extermination |
| 16a. | Positive | | Token: negative |
| 16b. | Negative | | Aversive: positive |
| 17. | Continuous: CRF: 100 per cent: if reinforcement is given after every response | | Primary reinforcement, e.g., edibles: repetition: fixed interval |
| 18. | Variable | Varied: intermittent: variable ratio: partial: V1 | Consistent: primary: positive |
| 19. | Discontinue: stop: suspend: withdraw: withhold: remove | Alter | Try: give: record: observe: decrease |
| 20. | Reversal: AB: ABA | ABAB: return to baseline: extinction | Probing: change of environment: fading of reinforcement: time out: recording: sampling |
| 21. | Yes | | No |

| Question No. | Score 1 | Score ½ | Score 0 |
|---|---|---|---|
| 22. | Prompting | | Modelling: shaping: structuring |
| 23a. | Last: final | Final or easiest | Simplest: common sense: easiest |
| 23b. | Backward chaining: reverse chaining | Chaining: backward training | |
| 24. | Shaping: successive approximation | Shaping and fading | Hierarchical: forward chaining: social reinforcement |
| 25. | Discriminative stimulus: stimulus control | Discriminate control | Specific contingency: behavioural control: conditioned stimulus: discrimination |
| 26. | Stimulus generalisation | Transfer: generalisation | Experimental control: transference: improvement: restructuring: toilet training |
| 27. | Modelling: vicarious learning: observational learning | Imitation: vicarious reinforcement: model: copying | Social facilitation |
| 28a.<br>b.<br>c. | Physical<br>Verbal<br>Gestural } any order 1 mark each | Imitative: demonstration: modelling: manual: signed: sign | Shaping: visual: full and partial |
| 29. | B | | A |
| 30. | Increase: deteriorate: get worse | | Decrease less rapidly: recur: continue: stay the same |
| 31. | Decrease: improve: get better. | | |
| 32. | Response cost | Token cost: punishment | Delayed reinforcement: displaced reinforcement: token economy: counter cost |
| 33. | True | | |
| 34. | Persist with: prolong: intensify: continue: maintain: lengthen: increase | Use: repeat | Produce: extinguish: moderate: manipulate with |

| Question No. | Score 1 | Score ½ | Score 0 |
|---|---|---|---|
| 35. | False | | |
| 36. | Time-out | Punishment | Response cost |
| 37a.<br>b. | Self-injurious: aggressive or dangerous to others (1 mark each)<br>*or*<br>self-administered reinforcement: e.g., masturbation, tongue-sucking etc., 1 mark.<br>Maximum: 2 marks | Any specific behaviour mentioned without a class-name (e.g., 'head banging'): preferred activities | Physical handicap: psychiatric disorder: approval-seeking |
| 38. | The behaviour to increase at first | The behaviour to increase: delayed response | Other changes in behaviour: a slow decrease in the behaviour: retaliation: spontaneous recovery: attention-seeking behaviours at first |
| 39. | Preferred: high probability: frequent: habitual | Usual: well-liked: favourite: desired: pleasurable | Pre-potent: alternative |
| 40a.<br>b. | Positive } 1 mark<br>Negative } each | | Contingent: and non-contingent |
| 41. | Antecedents $X_1$<br>Discriminative stimuli $X_1$<br>Stimulus conditions $X_1$<br>Controlling stimuli $X_1$<br>Environment $X_2$<br>Situation $X_2$<br>Consequences $X_3$<br>Reinforcers $X_3$<br>Intensity<br>Duration<br>Frequency<br>Score a maximum of 4. Those marked $X_1$ $X_2$ $X_3$ are alternatives | Causes $X_1$<br>Social setting $X_2$<br>Strength: severity<br>Distribution | Exact nature: social unacceptability: cognitive ability of the child: importance: effectiveness: its ability to prevent the child learning anything else |

| Question No. | Score 1 | Score ½ | Score 0 |
|---|---|---|---|
| | (score only one in each case)<br>For example, an answer giving: antecedents, environment, consequences and stimulus conditions: score = 3 | | |

# APPENDIX 3: QUESTIONNAIRE FOR COURSE PARTICIPANTS

Janet Carr

We would like to know how you felt about this course, and would be grateful if you would fill in these evaluation sheets.

We suggest you fill in Section I at the end of the course and Section II immediately after each of the lectures and workshops. Please give each item a rating from 0 (positive) to 3 (negative) by ringing the marker in the appropriate column (and any comments you have on the back of the page – these are especially welcome).

*Example.* Supposing Lecture 1 was thought fairly interesting, Lecture 2 boring. The ratings would be marked as follows:

| | Presentation | | | |
|---|---|---|---|---|
| | Boring | | Interesting | |
| | 3 | 2 | 1 | 0 |
| Lecture 1 | – | – | ⊖ | – |
| 2 | ⊖ | – | – | – |

Please remember to underline the identifying letter of your workshop

**Section I**

Balance between theoretical and practical aspects of the topic.

| Too much practical | | | About right | | | Too much theory |
|---|---|---|---|---|---|---|
| 3 | 2 | 1 | 0 | 1 | 2 | 3 |
| – | – | – | – | – | – | – |

Was the coverage of the topic adequate? YES/NO

If No: why not?

## Section IIa: Lectures

| Title | Content | | | | | | | Relevance to work in the area | | | | Presentation | | | | Time allowed for discussion | | | | | | |
|---|---|---|---|---|---|---|---|---|---|---|---|---|---|---|---|---|---|---|---|---|---|---|
| | Over familiar | | | Useful | | | Over specialised | Irrelevant | | | Relevant | Boring | | | Interesting | Too much | | | | | | Too little |
| | 3 | 2 | 1 | 0 | 1 | 2 | 3 | 3 | 2 | 1 | 0 | 3 | 2 | 1 | 0 | 3 | 2 | 1 | 0 | 1 | 2 | 3 |
| 1. Observation and recording | – | – | – | – | – | – | – | – | – | – | – | – | – | – | – | – | – | – | – | – | – | – |
| 2. Reinforcement | – | – | – | – | – | – | – | – | – | – | – | – | – | – | – | – | – | – | – | – | – | – |
| 3. Shaping, prompting and fading | – | – | – | – | – | – | – | – | – | – | – | – | – | – | – | – | – | – | – | – | – | – |
| 4. Imitation, generalisation and discrimination | – | – | – | – | – | – | – | – | – | – | – | – | – | – | – | – | – | – | – | – | – | – |
| 5. Language | – | – | – | – | – | – | – | – | – | – | – | – | – | – | – | – | – | – | – | – | – | – |
| 6. Decreasing undesirable behaviours | – | – | – | – | – | – | – | – | – | – | – | – | – | – | – | – | – | – | – | – | – | – |
| 7. Teaching others | – | – | – | – | – | – | – | – | – | – | – | – | – | – | – | – | – | – | – | – | – | – |
| 8. Using tokens | – | – | – | – | – | – | – | – | – | – | – | – | – | – | – | – | – | – | – | – | – | – |
| 9. Evaluating programmes | – | – | – | – | – | – | – | – | – | – | – | – | – | – | – | – | – | – | – | – | – | – |
| 10. Working in practical settings | – | – | – | – | – | – | – | – | – | – | – | – | – | – | – | – | – | – | – | – | – | – |

Other comments overleaf please

## Section IIb' Workshops

**Please underline your workshop letter A B C D E**

| Title | Was this a useful way of learning? | | | | | | | | Amount of content | | | | | | | Tutor's handling of workshops | | | | | | | | | | |
|---|---|---|---|---|---|---|---|---|---|---|---|---|---|---|---|---|---|---|---|---|---|---|---|---|---|---|
| | Little value | | | Useful | Stressful | | | Enjoyable | Too much | | | About right | | | Too little | Passive | | | About right | | | Authoritarian | Confusing | | | Clear |
| | 3 | 2 | 1 | 0 | 3 | 2 | 1 | 0 | 3 | 2 | 1 | 0 | 1 | 2 | 3 | 3 | 2 | 1 | 0 | 1 | 2 | 3 | 3 | 2 | 1 | 0 |
| 1. Observation and recording | – | – | – | – | – | – | – | – | – | – | – | – | – | – | – | – | – | – | – | – | – | – | – | – | – | – |
| 2. Reinforcement | – | – | – | – | – | – | – | – | – | – | – | – | – | – | – | – | – | – | – | – | – | – | – | – | – | – |
| 3. Shaping, prompting and fading | – | – | – | – | – | – | – | – | – | – | – | – | – | – | – | – | – | – | – | – | – | – | – | – | – | – |
| 4. Imitation, generalisation and discrimination | – | – | – | – | – | – | – | – | – | – | – | – | – | – | – | – | – | – | – | – | – | – | – | – | – | – |
| 5. Language | – | – | – | – | – | – | – | – | – | – | – | – | – | – | – | – | – | – | – | – | – | – | – | – | – | – |
| 6. Decreasing undesirable behaviour | – | – | – | – | – | – | – | – | – | – | – | – | – | – | – | – | – | – | – | – | – | – | – | – | – | – |
| 7. Teaching others | – | – | – | – | – | – | – | – | – | – | – | – | – | – | – | – | – | – | – | – | – | – | – | – | – | – |
| 8. Using tokens | – | – | – | – | – | – | – | – | – | – | – | – | – | – | – | – | – | – | – | – | – | – | – | – | – | – |

## REFERENCES

Abelew, P.H. (1972) Intermittent schedules of reinforcement applied to the conditioning treatment of enuresis. *Dissertation Abstracts International*, **33**, 2799B-800B

Abramson, E.E. & Wunderlich, R. (1972) Dental hygiene training for retardates: an application of behavioural techniques. *Ment. Retard.*, **10** (3), 6-8

Albin, J.B. (1977) Some variables influencing the maintenance of acquired self feeding behavior in profoundly retarded children. *Ment. Retard.*, **15** (5), 49-52

Alevizos, K.J. & Alevizos, P.N. (1975) Effects of verbalizing contingencies in time-out procedures. *J. Behav. Ther. Exper. Psychiat.*, **6**, 253-5

Aronwitz, R. & Conroy, C.W. (1969) Effectiveness of the automatic toothbrush for handicapped persons. *Am. J. Phys. Med.*, **48** (4), 193-205 (from abstract in *Mental Retardation Abstracts*, 1971, **8**, No. 576)

Ashkenazi, Z. (1975) The treatment of encopresis using a discriminative stimulus and positive reinforcement. *J. Behav. Ther. Exper. Psychiat.*, **6**, 155-7

Attwood, T. (1978) Priory Parents' Workshop. *Parents' Voice*, **28** (1), 12-15

Ayllon, T. & Azrin, N.H. (1968) *The Token Economy: A Motivational System for Therapy and Rehabilitation.* New York: Appleton-Century-Crofts

Azrin, N.H. & Armstrong, P.M. (1973) The 'mini-meal' – a rapid method for teaching eating skills to the profoundly retarded. *Ment. Retard.*, **11** (1), 9-13

Azrin, N.H. & Foxx, R.M. (1971) A rapid method of toilet training the institutionalized retarded. *J. Appl. Behav. Anal.*, **4**, 89-99

Azrin, N.H., Gottlieb, L., Hughart, L., Wesolowski, M.D. & Rahn, T. (1975) Eliminating self-injurious behavior by educative procedures. *Behav. Res. Ther.*, **13**, 101-11

Azrin, N.H. & Holz, W.C. (1966) Punishment. In: W.K. Honig (ed.) *Operant Behavior: Areas of Research and Application.* New York: Appleton-Century-Crofts

Azrin, N.H., Kaplan, S.J. & Foxx, R.M. (1973) Autism reversal:

eliminating stereotyped self-stimulation of retarded individuals. *Amer. J. Ment. Defic.*, **78**, 241-8

Azrin, N.H., Schaeffer, R.M. & Wesolowski, M.D. (1976) A rapid method of teaching profoundly retarded persons to dress by a reinforcement-guidance method. *Ment. Retard.*, **14** (6), 29-33

Azrin, N.H., Sneed, T.J. & Foxx, R.M. (1973) Dry-bed: A rapid method of eliminating bed-wetting (enuresis) of the retarded. *Behav. Res. & Ther.*, **11**, 427-34

Azrin, N.H., Sneed, T.J. & Foxx, R.M. (1974) Dry-bed training: Rapid elimination of childhood enuresis. *Behav. Res. & Ther.*, **12**, 147-56

Azrin, N.H. & Wesolowski, M.D. (1974) Theft reversal: An overcorrection procedure for eliminating stealing by retarded persons. *J. Appl. Behav. Anal.*, **7**, 577-81

Azrin, N.H. & Wesolowski, M.D. (1975) The use of positive practice to eliminate persistent floor sprawling by profoundly retarded persons. *J. Appl. Behav. Anal.*, Vol. 6, pp. 627-32

Bachman, J.A. (1972) Self-injurious behavior: a behavioral analysis. *J. Abnorm. Psychol.*, **80**, 211-25

Baer, D.M., Peterson, R.F. & Sherman, J.A. (1967) The development of imitation by reinforcing behavioral similarity to a model. *J. Exp. Anal. Behav.*, **10**, 405-16

Baer, D.M., Wolf, M.M. & Risley, T.R. (1968) Some current dimensions of applied behavior analysis. *J. Appl. Behav. Anal.*, **1**, 91-7

Baker, B.L., Brightman, A.J., Heifetz, L.J. & Murphy, D.M. (1976) *Steps to Independence: A Skills Training Series for Children with Special Needs.* Champaign, Illinois: Research Press

Baker, R., Hall, J.N. & Hutchinson, K. (1974) A token economy project with chronic schizophrenic patients. *Brit. J. Psychiat.*, **124**, 367-84

Baldwin, V.L., Fredericks, H.D.B. & Brodsky, G. (1973) *Isn't It Time He Outgrew This? or, A Training Program for Parents of Retarded Children.* Springfield, Illinois: Charles C. Thomas

Balson, P.N. (1973) Case study: encopresis: A case with symptom substitution. *Behav. Ther.*, **4**, 134-6

Bandura, A. (1969) *Principles of Behaviour Modification.* Holt, Rinehart & Winston

Barrett, B.H. (1969) Behavior modification in the home: parents adapt laboratory developed tactics to bowel-train a 5½-year-old. *Psychother. Theory Res. Prac.*, **6**, 172-6

Barton, E.S. (1975) Behaviour modification in the hospital school for the severely subnormal. In: C.C. Kiernan & F.P. Woodford (eds.) *Behaviour Modification with the Severely Retarded.* Elsevier North Holland: Associated Scientific Publishers

Barton, E.S., Guess, D., Garcia, E. & Baer, D.M. (1970) Improvement of retardates' meal-time behaviors by time-out procedures using multiple baseline techniques. *J. Appl. Behav. Anal.*, **3**, 77-84

Barton, E.S., Robertshaw, M.S., Barrett, H. & Winn, B. (1975) The introduction and development of behaviour modification in an ESN(S) school. *Behav. Mod.*, **8**, 20-38

Bates, P. & Wehman, P. (1977) Behavior management with the severely retarded: an empirical analysis of the research. *Ment. Retard.*, **15** (6), 9-12

Bath, K.E. & Smith, S.A. (1974) An effective token economy program for mentally retarded adults. *Ment. Retard.*, **12**, 41-4

Baumeister, A.A. (1967) Learning abilities of the mentally retarded. In: Baumeister, A.A. (ed.) *Mental Retardation: Appraisal, Education and Rehabilitation.* University of London Press

Bayley, M. (1973) *Mental Handicap and Community Care: A Study of Mentally Handicapped People in Sheffield*. London: Routledge and Kegan Paul

Bender, L. (1969) Secondary punishment and self-punitive avoidance behaviour in the rat. *J. Comp. Physiol. Psychol.*, **69**, 261

Berkowitz, B.P. & Graziano, A.M. (1972) Training parents as behaviour therapists: A review. *Behav. Res. & Ther.*, **10**, 297-317

Berkowitz, S., Sherry, P.J. & Davis, B. (1971) Teaching self-feeding skills to profound retardates using reinforcement and fading procedures. *Behav. Ther.*, **2**, 62-7

Bernal, M.E. (1969) Behavioral feedback in the modification of brat behaviors. *J. Nerv. Ment. Dis.*,**148**, 375-85

Bernal, M.E. and North, J.A. (1978) A survey of parent training manuals. *J. Appl. Behav. Anal.*, **11**, 533-44

Bernal, M.E., Williams, D.E., Miller, W.H. & Reagor, P.A. (1972) The use of videotape feedback and operant learning principles in training parents in management of deviant children. In: R.D. Rubin, H. Festerheim, J.D. Henderson and L.P. Ullman (eds.): *Advances in Behavior Therapy.* New York: Academic Press

Bidder, R.T., Bryant, G. & Gray, D.D. (1975) Benefits to Down's Syndrome children through training their mothers. *Arch. Dis. Childhood*, **50**, 383-6

Bijou, S.W. (1963) Theory and research in mental (developmental) retardation. *Psychol. Rec.*, **13**, 95-110

Birnbrauer, J.S. (1968) Generalization of punishment effects: A case study. *J. Appl. Behav. Anal.*, **1**, 201-11

Birnbrauer, J.S., Peterson, C.R. & Solnick, J.V. (1974) Design and interpretation of studies of single subjects. *Amer. J. Ment. Defic.*, **79**, 191-203

Birnbrauer, J.S., Wolf, M.M., Kidder, J.D. & Tague, C.E. (1965) Classroom behavior of retarded pupils with token reinforcement. *J. Exper. Child Psychol.*, **2**, 219-35

Blackman, D. (1974) *Operant Conditioning: An Experimental Analysis of Behaviour.* London: Methuen

Bloom, L. (1970) *Language Development: Form and Function in Emerging Grammars.* Cambridge, Mass.: MIT Press

Bloom, L. (1973) *One Word at a Time: The Use of Single Word Utterances Before Syntax.* The Hague: Mouton

Boe, R.B. (1977) Economical procedures for the reduction of aggression in a residential setting. *Ment. Retard.*, **15** (5), 25-8

Bonvillian, J.D. & Nelson, K.E. (1976) Sign language acquisition in a mute autistic boy. *J. Speech Hear. Dis.*, **41**, 339-47

Bowerman, M. (1973) Structural relationships in children's utterances: Syntactic or Semantic? In: T.E. Moore (ed.) *Cognitive Development and the Acquisition of Language.* New York: Academic Press

Bricker, D.D. (1972) Imitative sign training as a facilitator of word-object association with low-functioning children. *Am. J. Ment. Defic.*, **76**, 509-16

Bricker, W.A. & Bricker, D.D. (1970) A program of language training for the severely language handicapped child. *Excep. Child.*, **37**, 101-11

Bricker, W.A., Morgan, D.G. & Grabowski, J.G. (1972) Development and maintenance of a behaviour modification repertoire of cottage attendants through T.V. feedback. *Am. J. Ment. Defic.*, **77**, 128-36

Brierton, G., Garms, R. & Metzger, R. (1969) Practical problems encountered in an aide administered token reward cottage program. *Ment. Retard.*, **7**, 40-3

Brown, R. (1973) *A First Language: The Early Stages.* London: George Allen and Unwin

Brown, R. & Hanlon, C. (1970) Derivational complexity and order of acquisition in child speech. In: J.R. Hayes (ed.) *Cognition and the Development of Language.* New York: Wiley

Bry, P.M. (1969) The role of reinforcement in imitation by retardates. Unpublished doctoral dissertation. University of Missouri. Quoted by Gardner, W.I. (1971)

Bucher, B. & Lovaas, O.I. (1968) Use of aversive stimulation in behavior modification. In: M.R. Jones (ed.) *Miami Symposium on the Prediction of Behaviors: Aversive Stimulation.* Florida: University of Miami Press

Bundschuh, E.L., Curtis Williams, W., Hollingworth, J.D., Gooch, S. & Shirer, C. (1972) Teaching the retarded to swim. *Ment. Retard.*, **10** (3), 14-17

Burchard, J.D. & Barrera, F. (1972) Analysis of time-out and response cost in a programmed environment. *J. Appl. Behav. Anal.*, **5**, 271-82

Calhoun, K.S. and Matherne, P. (1975) The effects of varying schedules of time-out on the aggressive behaviors of a retarded girl. *J. Behav. Ther. Exper. Psychiat.*, **6**, 139

Callias, M. & Carr, J. (1975) Behaviour modification programmes in a community setting. In: C.C. Kiernan & F.P. Woodford (eds.) *Behaviour Modification with the Severely Retarded.* Elsevier-North Holland: Associated Scientific Publishers

Callias, M., Carr, J., Murphy, G., Tsoi, M. & Yule, W. Parent group training. In preparation

Callias, M. & Jenkins, J.A. Group training in behaviour modification: a pilot project with parents of severely retarded children. In preparation

Campbell, D.T. & Stanley, J.C. (1963) Experimental and quasi-experimental designs for research and teaching. In: N.L. Gage (ed.) *Handbook of Research on Teaching.* Chicago: Rand McNally

Campbell, H.J. (1972) Getting through to the handicapped child. *World Medicine*. 28 June, 17-20

Campbell, M.F. (1970) Neuromuscular uropathy. In: M.F. Campbell & H. Harrison (eds.) *Urology 2.* Philadelphia, P.A.: Saunders

Carr, J. (1975) *Young Children with Down's Syndrome.* Butterworth

Carr, J. (1980) *Helping Your Handicapped Child: A Step-by-step Guide to Everyday Problems.* Harmondsworth: Penguin Books

Carr, J. Progressive wakening: The treatment of bedwetting in a mentally handicapped boy. In preparation

Carr, J. & Yule, W. The evaluation of short courses in behaviour modification. In preparation

Carrol, J.B. (1964) *Language and Thought.* Englewood Cliffs, N.J.: Prentice Hall

Cazden, C. (1968) The acquisition of noun and verb inflections. *Child Dev.*, **39**, 433-48

Christensen, D.E. (1975) Effects of combining methylphenidate and a classroom token system in modifying hyperactive behavior. *Am. J. Ment. Defic.*, **80**, 266-76

Clark, H. & Clark, E.V. (1977) *Psychology and Language: An Introduction to Linguistics*. New York: Harcourt-Brace

Clark, H.B., Rowbury, T., Baer, A.M. & Baer, D.M. (1973) Time-out as a punishing stimulus in continuous and intermittent schedules. *J. Appl. Behav. Anal.*, **6**, 443-55

Clarke, A.D.B. & Cookson, M. (1962) Perceptual motor transfer in imbeciles: a second series of experiments. *Brit. J. Psychol.,* **53**, 321-30

Clarke-Stuart, K.A. (1973) Interactions between mothers and their young children: characteristics and consequences. *Monogr. Soc. Res. Child Dev.*, **38** (Nos. 6-7) Serial No. 153

Clements, C.B. & McKee, J.M. (1968) Programmed instruction for institutionalized offenders: contingency management and performance contracts. *Psychol. Rep.*, **22**, 957-64

Cook, C. & Adams, H.E. (1966) Modification of verbal behaviour in speech deficient children. *Behav. Res. Ther.*, **4**, 265-71

Corbett, J. (1975) Aversion for the treatment of self-injurious behaviour. *J. Ment. Defic. Res.*, **19**, 79-96

Craighead, W.E., Kazdin, A.E. & Mahoney, M.J. (eds.) (1976) *Behaviour Modification: Principles, Issues and Applications.* Boston: Houghton Mifflin

Cromer, R.F. (1974) The development of language and cognition: The cognition hypothesis. In: B.M. Foss (ed.) *New Perspectives in Child Development.* Harmondsworth: Penguin

Cromer, R.F. (1978) Normal language development: Recent progress. Paper presented at conference on 'Language Problems: Current Status'. Royal College of Psychiatrists, London

Crowley, C.P. & Armstrong, P.M. (1977) Positive practice, over-correction and behaviour rehearsal in the treatment of three cases of encopresis. *J. Behav. Ther. & Exp. Psychiat.*, **8**, 411-16

Cunningham, C.C. & Jeffree, D.M. (1971) *Working with Parents: Developing a Workshop Course for Parents of Young Mentally Handicapped Children.* NSMHC, N.W. Region

Cunningham, C.C. & Jeffree, D.M. (1975) The organisation and structure of workshops for parents of mentally handicapped children. *Bull. Br. Psychol. Soc.*, **28**, 405-11

Davids, A. & Berenson, J.K. (1977) Integration of a behavior modification program into a traditionally oriented residential

treatment center for children. *J. Aut. Child. Schiz.*, **1**, 269-85
Davidson, P.O. & Costello, C.G. (eds.) (1969) *N = 1: Experimental Studies of Single Cases.* New York: Van Nostrand
Deitz, S.M. (1977) An analysis of programming. DRL schedules in educational settings. *Behav. Res. Ther.*, **15**, 103-11
Deitz, S.M. & Repp, A.C. (1973) Decreasing classroom misbehavior through the use of DRL schedules of reinforcement. *J. Appl. Behav. Anal.*, **6**, 457-63
Deitz, S.M. & Repp, A.C. (1974) Differentially reinforcing low rates of misbehavior with normal elementary school children. *J. Appl. Behav. Anal.*, **7**, 622
Department of Health and Social Security (1971) *Better Services for the Mentally Handicapped.* London: HMSO
Department of Health and Social Security (1976) *Fit for the Future.* London: HMSO
De Villiers, J. & De Villiers, P. (1973) A cross-sectional study of the acquisition of grammatical morphemes in child speech. *J. Psycholing. Res.*, **2**, 267-78
De Villiers, J.G. & Naughton, J.M. (1974) Teaching a symbol language to autistic children. *J. Consult. Clin. Psychol.*, **42**, 111-7
Dixon, J. & Smith, P.S. (1976) The use of a pants alarm in daytime toilet training. *Brit. J. Ment. Subn.*, **42**, 20-5
Doernberg, N.L. (1972) Parents as teachers of their own retarded children. In: J. Wortis (ed.) *Mental Retardation: An Annual Review.* Vol. 4. New York: Grune & Stratton
Doleys, D.M. (1977) Behavioral treatments for nocturnal enuresis in children: A review of recent literature. *Psychol. Bull.*, **84** (1), 30-54
Doleys, D.M. & Arnold S. (1975) Treatment of childhood encopresis: Full cleanliness training. *Ment. Ret.*, **13**, 14-16
Doleys, D.M., Doster, J. & Cartelli, L.M. (1976) Parent training techniques: Effects of lecture-role playing followed by feedback and self recording. *J. Behav. Ther. & Exp. Psychiat.*, **7**, 359-62
Doleys, D.M. & Wells, K.L. (1975) Changes in functional bladder capacity and bedwetting during and after retention control training: A case study. *Behav. Ther.*, **6**, 685-8
Doty, D.W., McInnis, T. & Paul, G.L. (1974) Remediation of negative side effects of an on-going response-cost system with chronic mental patients. *J. Appl. Behav. Anal.*, **7**, 191-8
Duker, P. (1975) Behavioral control of self-biting in the Lesch-Nyan patient. *J. Ment. Defic. Res.*, **19**, 11-9

Edelman, R.I. (1971) Operant conditioning treatment of encopresis. *J. Behav. Ther. & Exp. Psychiat.*, **2**, 71-3

Edwards, K.A. (1974) Physical restraint as time-out in therapy. *Psychol. Rec.*, **24**, 393-7

Elardo, R., Bradley, R. & Caldwell, B.M. (1977) A longitudinal study of the relation of infants' home environments to language development at age three. *Child Dev.*, **48**, 595-603

Epstein, L.H., Doke, L.A., Sajwaj, T.E., Sorrell, S. & Rimmer, B. (1974) Generality of side-effects of overcorrection. *J. Appl. Behav. Anal.*, **7**, 385-90

Epstein, L.H. & McCoy, J.F. (1977) Bladder and bowel control in Hirschsprung's disease. *J. Behav. Ther. & Exp. Psychiat.*, **8**, 97-9

Ervin-Tripp, S. (1973) *Language Acquisition and Communicative Choice.* Stanford: Stanford Univ. Press

Evans, I.M. (1971) Theoretical and experimental aspects of the behaviour modification approach to autistic children. In: M. Rutter (ed.) *Infantile Autism: Concepts, Characteristics and Treatment.* London: Churchill Livingstone

Eysenck, H.J. (1963) Psychoanalysis – myth or science? In: S. Rachman (ed.) *Critical Essays on Psychoanalysis.* Oxford: Pergamon

Feldman, C. (1971) The effects of various types of adult responses in the syntactic acquisition of two to three year olds. Unpublished paper. Univ. Chicago, Mimeo

Fenn, G. (1976) Against verbal enrichment. In: P. Berry (ed.) *Language and Communication in the Mentally Handicapped.* London: Edward Arnold

Ferber, H., Keeley, S.M. & Shemberg, K.M. (1974) Training parents in behaviour modification: Outcome and problems encountered in a program after Patterson's work. *Behav. Ther.*, **5**, 415-9

Fernandez, J. (1978) Token economies and other token programmes in the United States. *Behav. Psychotherapy*, **6**, 56-69

Ferster, C.B. & Skinner, B.F. (1957) *Schedules of Reinforcement.* New York: Appleton-Century-Crofts

Fewtrell, W.D. (1973) A way of toilet training retarded children. *Apex*, **1**, 26-7

Fielding, D., Berg, I. & Bell, S. (1978) An observational study of postures and limb movements of children who wet by day and at night. *Dev. Med. & Child Neurol.*, **20**, 453-61

Fielding, L., Errickson, E. & Bettin, B. (1971) Modification of staff behavior: A note. *Behav. Ther.*, **2**, 550-3

Finley, W.W., Besserman, R.L., Bennet, L.F., Clapp, R.K. & Finley, R.M. (1973) The effects of intermittent and 'placebo' reinforcement on the effectiveness of the conditioning treatment for enuresis nocturna. *Behav. Res. & Ther.*, **11**, 289-97

Flavell, J.E. (1973) Reduction of stereotypies by reinforcement of toy play. *Ment. Ret.*, **11** (4), 21-3

Foxx, R.M. (1976) The use of overcorrection to eliminate the public disrobing (stripping) of retarded women. *Behav. Res. Ther.*, **14**, 53-61

Foxx, R.M. & Azrin, N.H. (1972) Restitution: A method of eliminating aggressive disruptive behaviour of retarded and brain damaged patients. *Behav. Res. Ther.*, **10**, 15-27

Foxx, R.M. & Azrin, N.H. (1973a) The elimination of autistic self-stimulatory behavior by overcorrection. *J. Appl. Behav. Anal.*, **6**, 1-14

Foxx, R.M. & Azrin, N.H. (1973b) Dry pants: A rapid method of toilet training children. *Behav. Res. Ther.*, **11**, 435-42

Foxx, R.M. & Azrin, N.H. (1973c) *Toilet Training the Retarded.* Champaign, Illinois: Research Press

Foxx, R.M. & Martin, E.D. (1975) Treatment of scavenging behaviour (coprophagy and pica) by overcorrection. *Behav. Res. Ther.*, **13**, 153-62

Frankel, F. (1976) Unravelling the effects of programme inconsistency: A reply to Gilbert. *Mental Retard.*, **13**, Oct., 8-9

Frankel, F. & Simmons, J.Q. (1976) Self-injurious behavior in schizophrenic and retarded children. *Amer. J. Ment. Defic.*, **80**, 512-22

Fraser, D. (1978) Critical variables in token economy systems: A review of the literature and a description of current research. *Behav. Psychother.*, **6**, 46-55

Freedle, R.O., Keeney, T.J. & Smith, N.D. (1970) Effects of mean depth and grammaticality on children's imitations of sentences. *J. Verb. Learn. Verb. Behav.*, **9**, 149-54

Freedman, P. & Carpenter, L. (1976) Semantic relations used by normal and language impaired children at Stage I. *J. Speech Hear. Res.*, **19**, 784-95

Freeman, S.W. & Thompson, C.L. (1973) Parent-child training for the MR. *Ment. Retard.*, **11** (4), 8-10

Galloway, C. & Galloway, K.C. (1970) Parent groups with a focus on precision behavior management. *IMRID Papers & Reports*, Vol. 7, No. 1, Nashville, Tennessee

Galvin, J.P. & Moyer, L.S. (1975) Facilitating extinction of infant crying by changing reinforcement schedules. *J. Behav. Ther Exper. Psychiat.*, **6**, 357-8

Gamlin, P.J. (1971) Sentence processing as a function of syntax, short-term memory capacity, the meaningfulness of stimulus and age. *Lang. Speech.*, **14**, 115-34

Garcia, E., Baer, D.M. & Firestone, I. (1971) The development of generalized imitation within topographically determined boundaries. *J. Appl. Behav. Anal.*, **4**, 101-12

Gardner, J.M. (1972) Selecting non-professionals for behavior modification programs. *Am. J. Ment. Defic.*, **76**, 680-5

Gardner, J.M. (1973) Training the trainers: A review of research on teaching behavior modification. In: R.D. Rubin, J.P. Brady & J.D. Henderson (eds.) *Advances in Behavior Therapy*, Vol. 4. London: Academic Press

Gardner, J.M. (Unpublished) Results of training in behavior modification on experienced and inexperienced institution attendants. Cited in Gardner, J.M. (1973)

Gardner, J.M., Brust, D. & Watson, L.S. (1970) A scale to measure skill in applying behaviour modification techniques to the mentally retarded. *Am. J. Ment. Defic.*, **74**, 633-6

Gardner, J.M. & Giampa, F.L. (1971) The attendant behavior check-list: A preliminary report. *Am. J. Ment. Defic.*,**75**, 617-22

Gardner, W.I. (1969) Use of punishment procedures with the severely retarded: A review. *Amer. J. Ment. Defic.*, **74**, 86-103

Gardner, W.I. (1971) *Behavior Modification in Mental Retardation.* Chicago: Aldine–Atherton

Gast, D.L. & Nelson, C.M. (1977a) Time-out in the classroom: Implications for special education. *Excep. Child.*, **43**, 461-3

Gast, D.L. & Nelson, C.M. (1977b) Legal and ethical considerations for the use of time out in special education settings. *J. Spec. Educ.*, **11**, 457-67

Gelfand, D.M. and Hartmann, D.P. (1975) *Child Behavior Analysis and Therapy.* New York: Pergamon

Georgiades, N.J. & Phillimore, L. (1975) The myth of the hero-innovator and alternative strategies for organizational change. In: C.C. Kiernan & E.P. Woodford (eds.) *Behaviour Modification with the Severely Retarded.* Elsevier-North Holland: Associated Scientific Publishers.

Gewirtz, J.L. & Baer, D.M. (1958) Deprivation and satiation of social reinforcers as drive conditions. *J. Abn. & Soc. Psychol.*, **57**, 165-72

Gilbert, G.D. (1975) Extinction procedures: Proceed with caution. *Mental Retard.*, **12**, Dec., 28-9

Giles, D.K. & Wolf, M.M. (1966) Toilet training institutionalized, severe retardates: An application of behaviour modification techniques. *Am. J. Ment. Defic.*, **70**, 766-80

Girardeau, F.L. & Spradlin, J.E. (1964) Token rewards in a cottage program. *Ment. Ret.*, **2**, 345-51

Glogower, F. & Sloop, E.W. (1976) Two strategies of group training of parents as effective behavior modifiers. *Behav. Ther.*, **7**, 177-84

Goldberg, J., Katz, S. & Yekutiel, E. (1973) The effects of token reinforcement on the productivity of moderately retarded clients in a sheltered workshop. *Brit. J. Ment. Subn.*, **19**, 80-4

Gould, J. (1977) Language development and non-verbal skills in severely mentally retarded children. *J. Ment. Defic. Rec.*, **20**, 129-45

Graham, N.C. & Gulliford, R.A. (1968) A psychological approach to the language deficiencies of educationally subnormal children. *Educ. Rev.*, **20**, 136-45

Greene, D. & Lepper, M.R. (1974) Effects of extrinsic rewards on children's subsequent intrinsic interest. *Child Dev.*, **45**, 1141-5

Gripp, R.F. & Magaro, P.A. (1974) The token economy program in the psychiatric hospital: A review and analysis. *Behav. Res. & Ther.*, **12**, 205-28

Guess, D. (1969) A functional analysis of receptive language and productive speech: Acquisition of the plural morpheme. *J. Appl. Behav. Anal.*, **2**, 55-64

Guess, D. & Baer, D.M. (1973) An analysis of individual differences in generalization between receptive and productive language in retarded children. *J. Appl. Behav. Anal.*, **6**, 311-29

Guess, D., Sailor, W. & Baer, D.M. (1974) To teach language to retarded children. In: R.L. Schiefelbush & L.L. Lloyd (eds.) *Language Perspectives – Acquisition, Retardation and Intervention.* London: Macmillan

Gunzburg, A. (1976) An operational philosophy of enrichment applied to the design of a children's family unit. *Brit. J. Ment. Subn.*, **22** (2), 112-7

Gunzburg, H.C. (1965) *Progress Assessment Charts.* London: National Society for Mentally Handicapped Children

Gunzburg, H.C. (1968) *Social Competence and Mental Handicap.* London: Bailliere Tindall

Hall, J. (1978) Ethics, procedures and contingency management. *Behav. Psychother.*, **6**, 70-5

Hall, R.V. (1971a) *Managing Behavior, Parts I, II and III.* Lawrence, Kansas: H & H Enterprises

Hall, R.V. (1971b) Training teachers in classroom use of contingency management. *Educ. Technol.*, **9**, 33-8

Hall, R.V., Cristler, C., Cranston, S.S. & Tucker, B. (1970) Teachers and parents as researchers using multiple baseline designs. *J. Appl. Behav. Anal.*, **3**, 247-55

Hallahan, D.P., Kauffman, J.M., Kneedler, R.D., Snell, M.E. & Richards, H.C. (1977) Being imitated by an adult and the subsequent imitative behaviour of retarded children. *Am. J. Ment. Defic.*, **81**, 556-60

Hanf, C. (1968) Modifying problem behaviors in mother-child interaction. Standardized laboratory situations. Paper presented at the meetings of the Association of Behavior Therapies, Olympia, Washington. Cited in Berkowitz & Graziano (1972)

Hart, B.M., Allen, K.E., Buell, J.S., Harris, F.R. & Wolf, M.M. (1964) Effects of social reinforcement on operant crying. *J. Exper. Child Psychol.*, **1**, 145-53

Hemsley, R., Cantwell, D., Howlin, P. & Rutter, M. The adult-child interaction schedule (In preparation)

Hemsley, D. (1978) Limitations of operant procedures in the modification of schizophrenic functioning: the possible relevance of studies of cognitive disturbance. *Behav. Anal. Modif.*, **2**, 165-73

Hemsley, R., Howlin, P., Berger, M., Hersov, L., Holbrook, D., Rutter, M. & Yule, W.C. (1978) Treating autistic children in a family context. In: M. Rutter & E. Schopler (eds.) *Autism: Reappraisal of Concepts and Treatment.* New York: Plenum

Henriksen, K. & Doughty, R. (1967) Decelerating undesired mealtime behavior in a group of profoundly retarded boys. *Amer. J. Ment. Defic.*, **72**, 40-4

Hersen, M. & Barlow, D.H. (1976) *Single-case Experimental Designs: Strategies for Studying Behavior Change.* Oxford: Pergamon

Hewett, F.M. (1965) Teaching speech to an autistic child through operant conditioning. *Amer. J. Orthopsychiat.*, **35**, 927-36

Hingtgen, J.N., Coulter, S.K. & Churchill, D.W. (1967) Intensive reinforcement of imitative behavior in mute autistic children. *Arch. Gen. Psychiat.*, **17**, 36-43

Hingtgen, J.N. & Trost, F.C. (1966) Shaping co-operative responses in early childhood schizophrenics: II. Reinforcement of mutual physical contact and vocal responses. In: R. Ulrich, T. Stachnik &

J. Mabry (eds.) *Control of Human Behavior.* Chicago: Scott Foresman

Hirsch, I. & Walder, L. (1969) Training mothers as reinforcement therapists for their own children. *Proceedings of the 77th Annual Convention of the American Psychological Association*, **4**, 561-2. Cited by O'Dell (1974)

Hobbs, S.A. & Forehand, R. (1975) Effects of differential release from time-out on children's deviant behavior. *J. Behav. Ther. Exper. Psychiat.*, **6**, 256-7

Hobbs, S.A. & Forehand, R. (1977) Important parameters in the use of time-out with children: A re-examination. *J. Behav. Ther. Exper. Psychiat.*, **8**, 365-70

Holland, C.J. (1970) An interview guide for behavioral counselling with parents. *Behav. Ther.*, **1**, 70-9

Holz, W.C., Azrin, N.H. & Ayllon, T. (1963) A comparison of several procedures for eliminating behavior. *J. Exper. Anal. Behav.*, **6**, 399-406

Horner, R.D. & Keilitz, I. (1975) Training mentally retarded adolescents to brush their teeth. *J. Appl. Behav. Anal.*, **8**, 301-9

Houston, J.C., Bradbury, R., Jelley, C., Adams, R.J., McGill, P., Sampson, M., Davies, J.H., de Castro, M., Lees, J., Bush, A., Harper, J. & Ager, A. (1979) The behavioural approach in mental handicap. *Bulletin, British Psychological Society*, **32**, 41

Howlin, P. (1976) How to help the parents and the children. Paper read at National Society for Autistic Children Conference on 'Early childhood autism and other problems affecting language and communication'. Churchill College, Cambridge

Howlin, P. (1978) Home treatment of infantile autism. Paper presented at conference on 'Language Problems: Current Status'. Royal College of Psychiatrists, London

Howlin, P., Cantwell, D., Marchant, R., Berger, M. & Rutter, M. (1973) Analyzing mother's speech to young autistic children: A methodological study. *J. Abnorm. Child Psychol.*, **1**, 317-39

Howlin, P., Marchant, R., Rutter, M., Berger, M., Hersov, L. & Yule, W. (1973) A home-based approach to the treatment of autistic children. *J. Aut. Child. Schiz.*, **3**, 308-36

Hughson, E.A. & Brown, R.I. (1975) A bus training programme for mentally retarded adults. *Br. J. Ment. Subn.*, **21** (2), 79-83

Hunt, J.G., Fitzhugh, L.C. & Fitzhugh, K.B. (1968) Teaching 'exit-ward patients appropriate personal appearance by using reinforcement techniques. *Am. J. Ment. Defic.*, **73**, 41-5

Hunt, J.G. & Zimmerman, J. (1969) Stimulating productivity in a simulated sheltered workshop setting. *Am. J. Ment. Defic.*, **74**, 43-9

Isaacs, W., Thomas, J. & Goldiamond, I. (1960) Applications of operant conditioning to reinstate verbal behavior in psychotics. *J. Speech Hear. Dis.*, **25**, 8-12

Iwata, B.H. & Bailey, J.S. (1974) Reward versus cost token systems: An analysis of the effects on students and teacher. *J. Appl. Behav. Anal.*, **7**, 567-76

Jackson, M.W. (1976) A course member's view. *Nursing Mirror*, 30 Sept.

Johnson, S.M. & Bolstad, O.D. (1973) Methodological issues in naturalistic observation: Some problems and solutions for field research. In: L.A. Hamerlynck, L.C. Handy & E.J. Mash (eds.) *Behavior Change: Methodology, Concepts and Practice*. Illinois: Research Press

Johnson, C.A. & Katz, R.C. (1973) Using parents as change agents for their children. *J. Child Psychol. & Psychiat.*, **14**, 181-200

Johnston, J.M. (1972) Punishment of human behavior. *Amer. Psychol.*, **27**, 1033-54

Joint Board of Clinical Nursing Studies (1974) *Outline Curriculum in Behaviour Modification in Mental Handicap for Registered Nurses.* Course No. 700. London: JBCNS

Jones, F.H., Simmons, J.Q. & Frankel, F.C. (1974) An extinction procedure for eliminating self-destructive behavior in a 9 year old autistic girl. *J. Aut. Child. Schiz.*, **4**, 241-50

Jones, R.R. (1973) Behavioral observation and frequency data: Problems in scoring, analyses and interpretation. In: L.A. Hamerlynck, L.C. Handy & E.J. Mash (eds.) *Behavior Change: Methodology, Concepts and Practice.* Illinois: Research Press

Jones, R.R. (1974) Design and analysis problems in program evaluation. In: P.O. Davidson, F.W. Clark & L.A. Hamerlynck (eds.) *Evaluation of Behavioral Programmes in Community, Residential and School Settings.* Illinois: Research Press

Jordan, R. & Saunders, C. (1975) Development of social behaviour. In: C.C. Kiernan & F.P. Woodford (eds.) *Behaviour Modification with the Severely Retarded.* IRMMH Study Group No. 8. Elsevier, Holland: Associated Scientific Publishers.

Kanfer, F.M. & Grimm, L.G. (1977) Behavioral analysis: Selecting target behaviors in the interview. *Behav. Mod.*, **1**, 7-28

Kanfer, F.M. & Saslow, G. (1969) Behavioral diagnosis. Chapter 12. In: C.M. Franks (ed.) *Behavior Therapy: Appraisal and Status.* New York: McGraw Hill

Kaufmann, J.M., Hallahan, D.P. & Ianna, S. (1977) Suppression of a retardate's tongue protrusion by contingent imitation: A case study. *Behav. Res. & Ther.*, **15**, 196-8

Kaufmann, J.M., Lafleur, N.K., Hallahan, D.P. & Chanes, C.M. (1975) Imitation as a consequence for children's behaviour. Two experimental case studies. *Beh. Ther.*, **6**, 535-42

Kaufman, K.F. & O'Leary, K.D. (1972) Reward, cost and self-evaluation procedures for disruptive adolescents in a psychiatric hospital school. *J. Appl. Behav. Anal.*, **5**, 293-309

Kazdin, A.E. (1975) *Behavior Modification in Applied Settings.* Illinois: Dorsey Press

Kazdin, A.E. (1977) *The Token Economy: A Review and Evaluation.* New York & London: Plenum Press

Kazdin, A.E. (1978) *History of Behavior Modification.* Baltimore: University Park Press

Kazdin, A.E. & Bootzin, R.R. (1972) The token economy: An evaluative review. *J. Appl. Behav. Anal.*, **5**, 343-72

Kazdin, A.E. & Craighead, W.E. (1973) Behavior modification in special education. In: L. Mann & D.A. Sabatino (eds.) *The First Review of Special Education*. Vol. 2. Philadelphia: Buttonwood Farms

Keith, K.D. & Lange, B.M. (1974) Maintenance of behavior change in an institution-wide training program. *Ment. Retard.*, **12** (2), 34-7

Keller, F.S. (1968) 'Good-bye teacher. . .' *J. Appl. Behav. Anal.*, **1**, 79-89

Kendall, P.C., Nay, W.R. & Jeffers, J. (1975) Time-out duration and contrast effects: A systematic evaluation of a successive treatment design. *Behav. Ther.*, **6**, 609-15

Kennedy, W.A. & Sloop, E.W. (1968) Methedrine as an adjunct to conditioning treatment of nocturnal enuresis in normal and institutionalized retarded subjects. *Psychol. Rep.*, **22**, 997-1000

Kerr, N., Myerson, L. & Michael, J. (1965) A procedure for shaping vocalisations in a mute child. In: L.P. Ullman and L. Krasner (eds.) *Case Studies in Behavior Modification.* New York: Holt, Rinehart and Winston

Kiernan, C.C. (1973) Functional analysis. In: P. Mittler (ed.) *Assessment for Learning in the Mentally Handicapped.* London: Churchill

Kiernan, C.G. (1974) Behaviour modification. In: A.M. Clarke &

A.D.B. Clarke (eds.) *Mental Deficiency: the Changing Outlook.* London: Methuen

Kiernan, C.C. (1977) Alternatives to speech: A review of research on manual and other forms of communication with the mentally handicapped and other non-communicating populations. *Brit. J. Ment. Subnorm.*, **23**, 6-28

Kiernan, C.C. & Riddick, B. (1973) A draft programme for training in operant techniques: practical units. Univ. of London Institute of Education. Thomas Coram Research Unit. Research Papers Nos. 1 & 2

Kiernan, C.C. & Saunders, C. (1972) Generalized imitation: Experiments with profoundly retarded children. Second European Conference on Behaviour Modification, Wexford, Ireland. Quoted by Kiernan, C.C. (1974)

Kiernan, C.C. & Woodford, F.P. (1975) Training and reorganisation for behaviour modification in hospital and community settings. Institute for Research into Mental and Multiple Handicap, Action Workshop No. 2. Summarized in *Brit. Ass. Behav. Psychother. Bull.*, **3**, 31-4

Kiernan, C.C. & Woodford, F.P. (1975) *Behaviour Modification with the Severely Retarded.* Amsterdam: Associated Scientific Publishers

Kiernan, C.C. & Wright, E.C. (1973) The F6 Project – a preliminary report. *Proc. Roy. Soc. Med.*, **66**, 1137-40

King, R.D., Raynes, N.V. & Tizard, J. (1971) *Patterns of Residential Care.* London: Routledge and Kegan Paul

Kirigin, K.A., Ayala, H.E., Braukmann, C.J., Brown, W.J., Minkin, N., Phillips, E.C., Fixsen, D.L. & Wolf, M. (1975) Training teaching parents: an evaluation of workshop training procedures. In: E. Ramp & B. Semb (eds.) *Behavior Analysis: Areas of Research and Application.* New Jersey: Prentice Hall

Koegel, R.L., Firestone, P.B., Kramme, K.W. & Dunlop, C. (1974) Increasing spontaneous play by suppressing self-stimulation in autistic children. *J. Appl. Behav. Anal.*, **7**, 521-8

Koegel, R.L., Glahn, T.J. & Nieminen, G.S. (1978) Generalization of parent training results. *J. Appl. Behav. Anal.*, **11**, 95-109

Koegel, R.L., Russo, D.C. & Rincover, A. (1977) Assessing and training teachers in the generalized use of behavior modification with autistic children. *J. Appl. Behav. Anal.*, **10**, 197-206

Kohlenberg, R.J. (1970) The punishment of persistent vomiting: A case study. *J. Appl. Behav. Anal.*, **3**, 241-5

Kushlick, A. (1966) A community service for the mentally subnormal.

*Soc. Psychiat.*, **1**, 73-82
Kushlick, A. (1975) Improving the services for the mentally handicapped. In: C.C. Kiernan & F.P. Woodford (eds.) *Behaviour Modification with the Severely Retarded.* Elsevier North-Holland: Associated Scientific Publishers

Lal, H. & Lindsley, O.R. (1968) Therapy of chronic constipation in a young child by re-arranging social contingencies. *Behav. Res. & Ther.*, **6**, 484-5
Lance, W.D. & Koch, A.C. (1973) Parents as teachers: Self help skills for young handicapped children. *Ment. Retard.*, **11** (3), 3-4
Larsen, L.A. & Bricker, W.A. (1968) *A Manual for Parents and Teachers of Severely and Moderately Retarded Children.* IMRID pop. Rep. V, No. 22: George Peabody College, Nashville, Tennessee
LaVigna, G.W. (1977) Communication training in mute autistic adolescents using the written word. *J. Aut. Child. Schiz.*, **7**, 135-49
Leff, R. (1974) Teaching the TMR to dial the telephone. *Ment. Ret.*, **12** (2), 12-3
Leitenberg, H. (1973) The use of single-case methodology in psychotherapy research. *J. Abnorm. Psychol.*, **82**, 87-101
Lenneberg, E.H., Nichols, I.A. & Rosenberger, E.F. (1964) Primitive stages of language development in mongolism. *Dis. Comm.*, **42**, 119-39
Lent, J.R., LeBlanc, J. & Spradlin, J.E. (1970) Designing a rehabilitative culture for moderately retarded adolescent girls. In: R. Ulrich, T. Stachnik & J. Mabry (eds.) *Control of Human Behavior.* Vol. 2. Illinois: Scott, Foresman
Leonard, L.B., Bolders, J. & Miller, J. (1976) An examination of the semantic relations reflected in the language of normal and language disordered children. *J. Speech Hear. Res.*, **19**, 357-70
Lepper, M.R., Greene, D. & Nisbett, R.E. (1973) Undermining children's intrinsic interest with extrinsic rewards: a test of the 'over-justification' hypothesis. *J. Pers. Soc. Psychol.*, **28**, 129-37
Levick, M., McArdle, M. & Carr, J. Multiple behaviour problems in a boy with Down's syndrome. In preparation
Lewis, M. (1951) *Infant Speech: A Study of the Beginnings of Language* (2nd edn.) London: Routledge and Kegan Paul
Lichstein, K.L. & Schreibman, L. (1976) Employing electric shock with autistic children: A review of the side effects. *J. Aut. Child. Schiz.*, **6**, 163-73
Lindsley, O.R. (1964) Direct measurement and prosthesis of retarded

behavior. *J. Educ.*, **147**, 62-81

Longin, N.S., Cone, J.D. & Longin, H.E. (1975) Teaching behavior modifiers: mothers' behavioral and attitudinal changes following general and specific training. *Ment. Retard.*, **13** (5), 42

Lovaas, O.I. (1966) A program for the establishment of speech in psychotic children. In: J.K. Wing (ed.) *Early Childhood Autism.* London: Pergamon

Lovaas, O.I. (1967) A behavior therapy approach to the treatment of childhood schizophrenia. In: J.P. Hill (ed.) *Minnesota Symposia on Child Psychology*. Vol. I. Univ. Minnesota Press

Lovaas, O.I. (1977) *The Autistic Child: Language Development through Behavior Modification.* New York: Wiley

Lovaas, O.I., Berberich, J.P., Perloff, B.F. & Schaeffer, B. (1966) Acquisition of imitative speech in schizophrenic children. *Science*, **151**, 705-7

Lovaas, O.I., Freitag, G., Kinder, M.I., Rubinstein, B.D., Schaeffer, B. & Simmons, J.Q. (1966) Establishment of social reinforcers in two schizophrenic children on the basis of food. *J. Exp. Child Psychol.*, **4**, 109-25

Lovaas, O.I., Schaeffer, B. & Simmons, J.Q. (1965) Experimental studies in childhood schizophrenia: Building social behaviors by use of electric shock. *J. Exp. Pers. Res.*, **1**, 99-109

Lovaas, O.I. & Simmons, J.Q. (1969) Manipulation of self-destruction in three retarded children. *J. Appl. Behav. Anal.*, **2**, 143-50

Love, J.M. & Parker-Robinson, C. (1972) Children's imitations of grammatical and ungrammatical sentences. *Child. Dev.*, **43**, 309-19

Lucero, W.J., Frieman, J., Spoering, K. & Fehrenbacher, J. (1976) Comparison of three procedures in reducing self-injurious behavior. *Amer. J. Ment. Def.*, **80**, 548-54

Lyle, J.G. (1960) The effects of an institution environment upon the verbal development of institutionalized children. II. Speech and Language. *J. Ment. Defic. Res.*, **4**, 1-13

McCarthy, D.S. (1954) Language development in children. In: L. Carmichael (ed.) *Manual of Child Psychology* (2nd edn.). New York: Wiley

McConahey, O.L. (1972) A token system for retarded women: Behavior modification, drug therapy and their combination. In: T. Thompson & J. Grabowski (eds.) *Behavior Modification of the Mentally Retarded.* New York: Oxford University Press

McConahey, O.L., Thompson, T. & Zimmerman, R.A. (1977) A token system for retarded women: Behavior modification, drug therapy and their combination. In: T. Thompson & J. Grabowski (eds.). *Behavior Modification of the Mentally Retarded.* New York: Oxford University Press

McCoull, G. (1969-71) Report on the Newcastle-upon-Tyne Regional Aetiological Survey, Mental Retardation, Prudhoe Hospital, Northumberland

McDonald, G., McCabe, P. & Mackle, B. (1976) Self-help skills in the profoundly subnormal. *Br. J. Ment. Subn.*,**22**, 105-11

MacDonough, T.S. & Forehand, R. (1973) Response contingent time-out: Important parameters in behavior modification with children. *J. Behav. Ther. & Exper. Psychiat.*, **4**, 231-6

McInnis. T., Himelstein, H.C., Doty, D.W. & Paul, G. (1974). Modification of sampling exposure procedures for increasing facilities utilization by chronic psychiatric patients. *J. Behav. Ther. & Exp. Psychiat.*, **5**, 119-27

Mackay, D. (1971) Behaviour modification of childhood psychiatric disorders using parents as therapists. *London Hospital Gazette, Clinical & Scientific Supplement.* May, III-XIV

McKeowen, D., Jr., Adams, H.E. & Forehand, R. (1975) Generalization to the classroom of principles of behavior modification taught to teachers. *Behav. Res. & Ther.*, **13**, 85-92

Mackowiak, M.C., Chvala, V.B., Masilotti, V.M. & Hermann, G.P. (1978) A developmental guide for the education of severely and profoundly handicapped individuals, Part I. *Br. J. Ment. Subn.*, **24**, 35-45

McLean, L.P. & McClean, J.E. (1974) A language training program for non-verbal autistic children. *J. Speech. Hear. Dis.*, **39**, 186-93

MacNamara, R. (1977) The complete behavior modifier: Confessions of an over-zealous operant conditioner. *Ment. Retard.*, **15** (1), 34-7

McNeill, D. (1966) Developmental psycholinguistics. In: F. Smith & G.A. Miller (eds.) *The Genesis of Language*. Cambridge, Mass.: MIT Press

McReynolds, L.V. (1972) Generalization during speech discrimination training. *Lang. Speech*, **15**, 385-92

Mager, R.F. & Pipe, R. (1970) *Analyzing Performance Problems, or 'You Really Oughta Wanna'.* California: Fearon

Mahoney, K., van Wagenen, R.K. & Meyerson, L. (1971) Toilet training of normal and retarded children. *J. Appl. Behav. Anal.*, **4**, 173-81

Mansdorf, I.J., Bucich, D.A. & Judd, L.C. (1977) Behavioral treatment strategies of institution ward staff. *Ment. Retard.*,**15** (5), 22-4

Marchant, R., Howlin, P., Yule, W. & Rutter, M. (1974) Graded change in the treatment of the behaviour of autistic children. *J. Child Psychol. Psychiat.*, **15**, 221-7

Marshall, N.R. & Hegrenes, J. (1972) The use of written language as a communication system for an autistic child. *J. Speech Hear.*, **37**, 258-61

Martin, G.L. Kehoe, B., Bird, E., Jensen, V. & Darbyshire, M. (1971) Operant conditioning in dressing behavior. *Ment. Retard.*, **9**, 24-31

Martin, L., McDonald, S. & Omichinski, M. (1971) An operant analysis of response interactions during meals with severely retarded girls. *Am. J. Ment. Def.*, **76**, 864-8

Mash, E.J. & Terdal, L. (1973) Modification of mother-child interactions: Playing with children. *Ment. Retard.*, **11** (5), 44-9

Maxwell, A.E. (1958) *Experimental Design in Psychology and the Medical Sciences.* London: Methuen

May, J.G., McAlister, J., Risley, T., Twardosz, S. & Cox, C.H. (1974) *Florida Guidelines for the Use of Behavioral Procedures in State Programmes for the Retarded.* Tallahassee, Florida: Florida Division of Retardation

Meadow, R. (1977) How to use buzzer alarms to cure bed-wetting. *Brit. Med. J.*, **2**, 1073-5

Measel, C.J. and Alfieri, P.A. (1976) Treatment of self-injurious behaviour by a combination of positive reinforcement for incompatible behaviour and overcorrection. *Amer. J. Ment. Def.*, **81**, 147-53

Menyuk, P. (1964) Comparison of grammar of children with functionally deviant and normal speech. *J. Speech Hear. Res.*, **7**, 109-21

Menyuk, P. (1969) *Sentences Children Use.* Research Monograph No. 52. Cambridge, Mass.: MIT Press

Menyuk, P. (1977) *Language and Motivation.* Cambridge, Mass;: MIT Press

Metz, J.R. (1965) Conditioning generalized imitation in autistic children. *J. Exper. Child. Psychol.*, **2**, 389-99

Miller, G.A. (1964) The psycholinguists. *Encounter*, 5, **23** (July), 29-37

Miller, J.F. & Yoder, D.E. (1972) On developing the content for a language training program. *Ment. Ret.*, **10**, 9-11

Miller, R.S. & Morris, W.N. (1974) The effects of being imitated on children's responses in a marble-dropping task. *Child Dev.*, **45**, 1103-7

Minge, M.R. & Ball, T.S. (1967) Teaching of self-help skills to profoundly retarded patients. *Amer. J. Ment. Defic.*, **71**, 864-8

Mira, M. (1970) Results of a behavior modification training program for parents and teachers. *Behav. Res. & Ther.*, **8**, 509-11

Mischel, W. (1968) *Personality and Assessment.* New York: Wiley

Mittler, P. (1970) *Personality and Assessment.* New York: Wiley

Mittler, P. (1970) The use of morphological rules by four year children: An item analysis of the auditory-vocal automatic subtest of the Illinois Test of Psycholinguistic Abilities. *Brit. J. Dis. Comm.*, **5**, 99-109

Monaco, T.M., Peach, W., Blanton, R.S. & Loomis, D. (1968) Pilot study: Self-care program for severely retarded girls. *Central Missouri Synthesis on Mental Retardation*, **1** (1), 8-20 (from abstract in *Mental Retardation Abstracts*, 1970, **7**, No. 2788)

Moore, P. & Carr, J. (1976) Behaviour modification programme (to teach dressing to a severely retarded adolescent). *Nursing Times*, 2 September, and *Communication*, **11** (2), 20-7

Morehead, D.M. (1974) The study of linguistically deficient children. In: S. Singh (ed.) *Measurement in Hearing, Speech and Language.* Baltimore: University Park Press

Morrison, D., Mejia, B. & Miller, M.A. (1968) Staff conflicts in the use of operant techniques with autistic children. *Am. J. Orthopsychiat.*, **38**, 647-52

Morse, W.J. (1966) Intermittent reinforcement. In: W.K. Honig (ed.) *Operant Behaviors: Areas of Research and Application.* New York: Appleton-Century-Crofts

Muellner, S.R. (1960) Development of urinary control in children. *J. Amer. Med. Assoc.*, **172**, 1256-61

Murphy, G.M. (1978) Overcorrection: A critique. *J. Ment. Defic. Res.*, **22**, 161-73

Murphy, G. & Goodall, E. Measurement error in direct observation: A comparison of common recording methods. *Behav. Res. & Ther.*, in press

Murphy, G.M. & McArdle, M. (1978) Behaviour modification with the retarded: A six-month training course for nurses. *Nursing Mirror*, 27 April, 31-4

Murphy, G., Steele, K., Gilligan, T., Yeow, J. & Spare, D. (1977) Teaching a picture language to a non-speaking retarded boy. *Behav. Res. Ther.*, **15**, 198-201

Musick, J.K. & Luckey, R.E. (1970) A token economy for moderately and severely retarded. *Ment. Retard.*, **8**, 35-6

Myers, J.J. & Deibert, A. (1971) Reduction of self-abusive behavior in a blind child by using a feeding response. *J. Behav. Ther. Exper. Psychiat.*, **2**, 141-4

Nay, W.R. (1975) A systematic comparison of instructional techniques for parents. *Behav. Ther.*, **6**, 14-21

Neale, D.H. (1963) Behavior therapy and encopresis in children. *Behav. Res. & Ther.*, **1**, 139-49

Nelson, G.L., Cone, J.D. & Hansen, C.R. (1975) Training correct utensil use in retarded children: Modelling *vs.* physical guidance. *Am. J. Ment. Defic.*, **80**, 114-22

Nelson, K. (1973) Structure and strategy in learning to talk. *Monogr. Soc. Res. Child Dev.*, **38**, Serial No. 149

Nelson, K., Corscaddon, G. & Bonvillian, J. (1973) Syntax acquisition: Impact of experimental variation in adult verbal interaction with the child. *Child. Dev.*, **44**, 497-504

Nelson, R.O. & Evans, I.M. (1968) The combination of learning principles and speech therapy techniques in the treatment of non-communicating children. *J. Child Psychiat.*, **9**, 111-24

Nelson, R.O., Lipinski, D.P. & Black, J.L. (1975) The effects of expectancy on the reactivity of self-recording. *Behav. Ther.*, **6**, 337-49

Newfield, M.V. & Schlanger, B.B. (1968) The acquisition of English morphology by normal and educable mentally retarded children. *J. Speech. Hear. Dis.*, **11**, 693-706

Ney, P.G., Palvesky, A.E. & Markeley, J. (1971) Relative effectiveness of operant conditioning and play therapy in childhood schizophrenia. *J. Aut. Child. Schiz.*, **1**, 337-49

Nirje, B. (1970) The normalization principle – implications and comment. *J. Ment. Subn.*, **16** (2), 62-70

Norrish, M.P. (1974) Training parents to teach their young retarded children self-help skills. M. Phil. dissertation. University of London

O'Brien, F. & Azrin, N.H. (1972) Developing proper mealtime behaviors of the institutionalized retarded. *J. Appl. Behav. Anal.*,**5**, 389-99

O'Brien, F., Bugle, C. & Azrin, N.H. (1972) Training and maintaining a retarded child's proper eating. *J. Appl. Behav. Anal.*, **5**, 67-72

O'Dell, S. (1974) Training parents in behavior modification: A review. *Psychol. Bull.*, **81**, 418-33

O'Dell, S., Blackwell, L.J., Larcen, S.W. & Hogan, J.L. (1977) Competency based training for severely behaviorally handicapped children and their families. *J. Aut. & Child. Schiz.*, 7, 231-42

O'Dell, S., Flynn, J. & Benlolo, L. (1977) A comparison of parent training techniques in child behavior modification. *J. Behav. Ther. & Exp. Psychiat.*, **8**, 261-8

Orlando, R. & Bijou, S.W. (1960) Single and multiple schedules of reinforcement in developmentally retarded children. *J. Exp. Anal. Behav.*, **3**, 339-48

Paget, R., Gorman, P. & Paget, G. (1972) *A Systematic Sign Language.* Mimeographed Manual, London

Paloutzian, R.F., Hasazi, J., Streifel, J. & Edgar, C.L. (1971) Promotion of positive social interaction in severely retarded young children. *Am. J. Ment. Defic.*, **75**, 519-24

Panyan, M.C. & Patterson, E.T. (1974) Teaching attendants the applied aspects of behavior modification. *Ment. Retard.*, **12** (5), 30-2

Paton, X. (1976) Personal communication

Patterson, G.R. (1973) Multiple evaluations of a parent training program. In: T. Thompson & W.S. Dockens (eds.) *Proceedings of the International Symposium on Behavior Modification.* New York: Appleton-Century-Crofts

Patterson, G.R. (1974) Interventions for boys with conduct problems: Multiple settings, treatments and criteria. *J. Consult. Clin. Psychol.*, **42**, 471-81

Patterson, G.R. & Brodsky, G. (1966) A behaviour modification programme for a child with multiple problem behaviours. *J. Child Psychol. & Psychiat.*, **7**, 277-95

Patterson, G.R., Cobb, J.A. & Ray, R.S. (1973) A social engineering technology for re-training the families of aggressive boys. In: H.E. Adams & I.P. Unikel (eds.) *Issues and Trends in Behavior Therapy*. Springfield, Illinois: Charles C. Thomas

Patterson, G.R. & Gullion, M.E. (1968) *Living with Children: New Methods for Parents and Teachers.* Champaign, Ill.: Research Press

Patterson, G.R., McNeal, S., Hawkins, N. & Phelps, R. (1967) Reprogramming the social environment. *J. Child Psychol. Psychiat.*, **8**, 181-95

Patterson, G.R., Ray, R.S., Shaw, D.A. & Cobb, J.A. (1969) A manual for coding of family interactions. Unpublished manuscript, Oregon Research Institute

Patterson, G.R. & Reid, J.B. (1973) Intervention for families of aggressive boys: A replication study. *Behav. Res. & Ther.*, **11**, 382-94

Peek, R.M. & McAllister, L.W. (1974) *Behavior Modification Guidelines.* State of Minnesota: Dept. of Public Welfare

Perkins, E.A., Taylor, P.D. & Capie, A.C.M. (1976) *Helping the Retarded: A Systematic Behavioural Approach.* Institute of Mental Subnormality, Kidderminster

Perske, R. & Marquiss, J. (1973) Learning to live in an apartment: Retarded adults from institutions and dedicated citizens. *Ment. Ret.*, **11** (5), 18-9

Phillips, E.L., Phillips, E.A., Fixsen, D.L. & Wolf, M.M. (1971) Achievement Place: Modification of the behaviors of predelinquent boys within a token economy. *J. Appl. Behav. Anal.*, **4**, 45-59

Powell, J., Martindale, B., Kulp, S., Martindale, A. & Bauman, R. (1977) Taking a closer look: Time sampling and measurement error. *J. Appl. Behav. Anal.*, **10**, 325-32

Premack, D. (1959) Towards empirical behaviour laws. 1. Positive reinforcement. *Psychol. Rev.*, **66**, 219-33

Raynes, N.V. (1977) How big is good? The case for cross-cutting ties. *Ment. Retard.*,**15** (4), 53-4

Redd, W.H. & Birnbrauer, J.S. (1969) Adults as discriminative stimuli for different reinforcement contingencies with retarded children. *J. Exp. Child. Psychol.*, **7**, 440-7

Reid, J.B. (1970) Reliability assessment of observation data: A possible methodological problem. *Child Dev.*, **41**, 1143-50

Repp, A.C., Deitz, S.M. & Speir, N.C. (1979) Reducing stereotypic responding of retarded persons by the differential reinforcement of other behavior. *Amer. J. Ment. Defic.*, **79**, 279-84

Reynell, J. (1969) *Reynell Developmental Language Scales.* Windsor: NFER

Rinn, R.C., Vernon, J.C. & Wise, M.J. (1975) Training parents of behaviorally-disordered children in groups: A three years' program evaluation. *Behav. Ther.*, **6**, 378-87

Risley, T.R. (1968a) Effects and side-effects of punishing the autistic behaviors of an autistic child. *J. Appl. Behav. Anal.*, **1**, 21-34

Risley, T.R. (1968b) Learning and lollipops. *Psychol. Today*

Risley, T.R. & Baer, D.M. (1973) Operant behavior modification: The deliberate development of behavior. In: B.M. Caldwell & H.N. Ricciuti (eds.) *Review of Child Development Research*, Vol. 3. Chicago: Univ. Chicago Press

Risley, T.R., Hart, B. & Doke, L. (1971) Operant language development: The outline of a therapeutic technology. In: R.L. Schiefelbusch (ed.)

*Language of the Mentally Retarded.* New York: University Park Press

Romanczyk, R.G. & Goren, E.R. (1975) Severe self-injurious behavior: The problem of clinical control. *J. Consult. Clin. Psychol.*, **43**, 730-9

Rose, S.D. (1974) Training parents in groups as behavior modifiers of their mentally retarded children. *J. Behav. Ther. Exp. Psychiat.*, **5**, 135-40

Rutter, M. (1978) Language training with autistic children: How does it work and what does it achieve? Paper presented at conference on 'Language Problems: Current Status'. Royal College of Psychiatrists, London

Rutter, M. & Bax, M. (1972) Normal language development. In: M. Rutter & J.A.M. Martin (eds.) *The Child with Delayed Speech.* Clinics in Developmental Medicine, No. 43. London: SIMP/ Heinemann

Sackett, G.P. (ed.) (1978) *Observing Behavior Volume 1: Theory and Applications in Mental Retardation.* Baltimore: University Park Press

Sailor, W., Guess, D., Rutherford, G. & Baer, D.M. (1968) Control of tantrum behavior by operant techniques during experimental verbal training. *J. Appl. Behav. Anal.*, **1**, 237-43

Sajwaj, T. (1973) Difficulties in the use of behavioral techniques by parents in changing child behavior: Guides to success. *J. Nerv. Ment. Dis.*, **156**, 395-403

Sajwaj, T. & Hedges, D. (1973) A note on the effect of saying grace on the behavior of an oppositional retarded boy. *J. Appl. Behav. Anal.*, **6**, 711-2

Sajwaj, T., Libet, J. & Agras, S. (1974) Lemon juice therapy: The control of life-threatening rumination in a six-month old infant. *J. Appl. Behav. Anal.*, **7**, 557-63

Sajwaj, T., Twardosz, S. & Burke, M. (1972) Side-effects of extinction procedures in a remedial pre-school. *J. Appl. Behav. Anal.*, **5**, 163-72

Salzberg, B. & Napolitan, J. (1974) Holding a retarded boy at a table for 2 minutes to reduce inappropriate object contact. *Amer. J. Ment. Defic.*, **78**, 748-51

Salzinger, K., Feldman, R.S., Cowan, J.E. & Salzinger, S. (1965) Operant conditioning of verbal behavior of two young speech deficient boys. In: L.P. Ullman & L. Krasner (eds.) *Case Studies in Behavior Modification.* New York: Holt, Rinehart, Winston

Salzinger, K., Feldman, R.S. & Portnoy, S. (1970) Training parents of brain-injured children in the use of operant conditioning techniques. *Behav. Ther.*, **1**, 4-32

Sapon, S.S. (1966) Shaping productive verbal behavior in a non-speaking child: A case report. *Monogr. Ser. Lang. Linguist.*, **19**, 155-75

Saunders, C.A., Jordan, R.R. & Kiernan, C.C. (1975) Parent-school collaboration. In: C.C. Kiernan & F.P. Woodford (eds.) *Behaviour Modification with the Severely Retarded.* Elsevier-North Holland: Associated Scientific Publishers

Schaffer, H.R. & Emerson, P.E. (1964) The development of social attachment in infancy. *Monogr. Soc. Res. Child Dev.*, **29**, Serial No. 94

Schlanger, B.B. & Gottsleben, R.H. (1957) Analysis of speech defects among the institutionalized mentally retarded. *J. Speech Dis.*, **22**, 98-103

Schoelkopf, A.M. & Orlando, R. (1965) Delayed *vs.* immediate reinforcement in simultaneous discrimination problems with mentally retarded children. *Psychol. Rec.*, **15**, 15-23

Scholes, J. (1969) The role of grammaticality in the imitation of word strings by children and adults. *J. Verb. Learn. Verb. Behav.*, **8**, 225-8

Schreibman, L. (1975) Effects of within-stimulus and extra-stimulus prompting on discrimination learning in autistic children. *J. Appl. Behav. Anal.*, **9**, 81-119

Seitz, S. & Hoekenga, R. (1974) Modeling as a training tool for retarded children and their parents. *Ment. Retard.*, **12** (2), 28-31

Sewell, E., McCoy, J.F. & Sewell, W.R. (1973) Modification of an antagonistic social behavior using positive reinforcement for other behavior. *Psychol. Rec.*, **23**, 499-504

Shapiro, M.B.(1957) Experimental method in the psychological description of the individual psychiatric patient. *Internal. J. Soc. Psychiat.*, **3**, 89-103

Shapiro, M.B. (1966) The single case in clinical-psychological research. *J. Gen. Psychol.*, **74**, 3-23

Shapiro, M.B. (1970) Intensive assessment of the single-case: An inductive-deductive approach. In: P. Mittler (ed.) *The Psychological Assessment of Mental and Physical Handicaps.* London: Methuen

Sherman, J.A. (1963) Reinstatement of verbal behavior in a psychotic by reinforcement methods. *J. Speech Hear. Dis.*, **28**, 398-401

Sherman, J.A. (1965) Use of reinforcement and imitation to reinstate verbal behavior in mute psychotics. *J. Abnorm. Psychol.*, **70**, 155-64

Shipley, E., Smith, C.S. & Gleitman, L. (1969) A study in the acquisition of language. *Language*, **45**, 322-42

Siegel, G.M., Lenski, J. & Broen, P. (1969) Suppression of normal speech disfluencies through response cost. *J. Appl. Behav. Anal.*, **2** 265-76

Skinner, B.F. (1957) *Verbal Behavior.* New York: Appleton-Century-Crofts

Sloane, H.N., Johnson, M.K. & Harris, F.R. (1968) Remedial procedures for teaching verbal behavior to speech deficient or defective young children. In: H.N. Sloane & B.D. MacAuley (eds.) *Operant Procedures in Remedial Speech and Language Training.* Boston: Houghton Mifflin

Slobin, D.I. (1970) Universals of grammatical development in children. In: G.B. Flores D'Arcais & J.W. Levett (eds.) *Advances in Psycholinguistics.* Amsterdam: North Holland Press

Slobin, D.I. (1973) Cognitive pre-requisites for the development of grammar. In: C.A. Ferguson & D.I. Slobin (eds.) *Studies of Child Language Development.* New York: Holt Rinehart Winston

Sloop, E.W. & Kennedy, W.A. (1973) Institutionalized retarded enuretics treated by a conditioning technique. *Am. J. Ment. Defic.*, **77**, 717-21

Smeets, P.M., Bouter, R.F. & Bouter, H.P. (1976) Teaching toothbrushing behaviour in severely retarded adults: A replication study. *Brit. J. Ment. Subn.*, **22** (1), 5-12

Smith, J. (1977) An evaluation of behavioural skills training. Unpublished M. Phil. thesis. University of London Institute of Psychiatry

Smith, P.S. (1979) A comparison of different methods of toilet training the mentally handicapped. *Behav. Res. & Ther.*, **17** (1), 33-43

Smith, P.S., Britton, P.T., Johnson, M., & Thomas, D.A. (1975) Problems involved in toilet training profoundly mentally handicapped adults. *Behav. Res. & Ther.*, **15**, 301-7

Smith, P.S. & Smith, L.J. (1977) Chronological age and social age as factors in intensive daytime toilet training of institutionalized mentally retarded individuals. *J. Behav. Ther. & Exp. Psychiat.*, **8**, 269-73

Smolev, S.R. (1972) Use of operant techniques for the modification of self-injurious behavior. *Amer. J. Ment. Defic.*, **76**, 295

Solnick, J.V., Rincover, A. & Peterson, C.R. (1977) Some determinants of the reinforcing and punishing effects of time out. *J. Appl. Behav. Anal.*, **10**, 415-24

Song, A.Y. & Gandhi, R. (1974) An analysis of behavior during the acquisition and maintenance phases of self-spoon feeding skills of profound retardates. *Ment. Retard.*, **12** (1), 25-8

Song, A.Y., O'Connell, R.D., Nelson, H.L. & Apfel, S. (1976) Cottage bound self-help skill teaching and intensive school training for the profoundly and severely retarded. *Br. J. Ment. Subn.*, **22** (2), 99-104

Speight, I.M. (1976) Course No. 700: Behaviour modification in mental handicap. *Nursing Mirror*. 30 September

Spradlin, J.E. & Girardeau, F.L. (1966) The behavior of moderately and severely retarded persons. In: N. Ellis (ed.) *International Review of Research in Mental Retardation*, Vol. 1. New York: Academic Press

Sprague, R. & Toppe, T. (1966) Relationship between activity level and delay of reinforcement in the retarded. *J. Exp. Child. Psychol.*, **3**, 390-7

Spreen, O. (1965) Language functions in mental retardation: A review. I. Language development, types of retardation and intelligence level. *Amer. J. Ment. Defic.*, **69**, 482-94

Stein, T.J. (1975) Some ethical considerations of short-term workshops in the principles and methods of behaviour modification. *J. Appl. Behav. Anal.*, **8**, 113-5

Stoffelmayr, B.E., Faulkener, G.R. & Mitchell, W.S. (1973) The rehabilitation of chronic hospitalised patients – a comparative study of operant conditioning methods and social therapy techniques. Final report to the Scottish Home and Health Dept. Quoted by Fraser, D. (1978)

Strichart, S.S. (1974) Effects of competence and nurturance on imitation of non-retarded peers by retarded adolescents. *Am. J. Ment. Defic.*, **78**, 665-73

Strichart, S.S. & Gottlieb, J. (1975) Imitation of retarded children by their non-retarded peers. *Am. J. Ment. Defic.*, **79**, 506-12

Sugaya, K. (1967) Survey of the enuresis problem in an institution for the mentally retarded with emphasis on the clinical psychological aspects. *Jap. J. Child Psychiat.*, **8**, 142-50

Taplin, P.S. & Reid, J.B. (1973) Effects of instructional set and experimenter influence on observer reliability. *Child Dev.*, **44**, 547-54

Tavormina, J.B. (1974) Basic models of parent counselling: A critical review. *Psychol. Bull.*, **81**, 827-35

Tavormina, J.B. (1975) Relative effectiveness of behavioral and reflective group counselling with parents of mentally retarded children. *J. Cons. & Clin. Psychol.*, **43** (1), 22-31

Tavormina, J.B., Hampson, R.B. & Luscomb, R.L. (1976) Participant evaluations of the effectiveness of their parent counselling groups. *Ment. Retard.*, **14** (6), 8-9

Taylor, P.D. & Turner, R.K. (1975) A clinical trial of continuous, intermittent and overlearning 'bell-and-pad' treatments for nocturnal enuresis. *Behav. Res. & Ther.*, **13**, 281-93

Terdal, L. & Buell, J. (1969) Parent education in managing retarded children with behavior deficits and inappropriate behaviors. *Ment. Retard.*, **7** (3), 10-13

Terrace, J.S. (1966) Stimulus control. In: W.K. Honig (ed.) *Operant Behavior: Areas of Research and Application.* New York: Appleton-Century-Crofts

Tharp, R.G. & Wetzel, R.J. (1969) *Behavior Modification in the Natural Environment*. New York: Academic Press

Thompson, T. & Grabowski, J. (eds.) (1972) *Behavior Modification of the Mentally Retarded.* New York: Oxford University Press

Tizard, B., Cooperman, O., Joseph, A. & Tizard, J. (1972) Environmental effects on language development: A study of young children in long stay residential nurseries. *Child Dev.*, **43**, 337-58

Tizard, J. (1975) Discussion of Thorpe (1975) Token economy systems. In: C.C. Kiernan & F.P. Woodford (eds.) *Behaviour Modification with the Severely Retarded.* Elsevier North-Holland: Associated Scientific Publishers

Tizard, J. & Grad, J.C. (1961) *The Mentally Handicapped and Their Families: A Social Survey.* London: Oxford University Press

Tognoli, J., Hamad, C. & Carpenter, T. (1978) Staff attitudes toward adult male residents' behavior as a function of two settings in an institution for mentally retarded people. *Ment. Retard.*, **16**, 142-6

Tomlinson, J.R. (1970) The treatment of bowel retention by operant procedures: A case study. *J. Behav. Ther. & Exp. Psychiat.*, **1**, 83-5

Toogood, R. (1977) Behaviour modification and mental handicap hospitals. *Apex*, **5** (2), 26-7

Topper, S.T. (1975) Gesture language for a severely retarded male. *Ment. Retard.*, **13**, 30-1

Treffry, D., Martin, G.L., Samels, J. & Watson, C. (1970) Operant conditioning of grooming behavior of severely retarded girls. *Ment. Retard.*, **8** (4), 29-33

Vukelich, R. & Hake, D.F. (1971) Reduction of dangerously aggressive behavior in a severely retarded resident through a combination of positive reinforcement procedures. *J. Appl. Behav. Anal.*, **4**, 215-25

Wahler, R.G. & Cormier, N.H. (1970) The ecological interview: A first step in out patient behavior therapy. *J. Behav. Ther. Exper. Psychiat.*, **1**, 279-89

Wahler, R.G. & Leske, G. (1973) Accurate and inaccurate observer summary reports: Reinforcement theory interpretation and investigation. *J. Nerv. Ment. Dis.*, **156**, 386-94

Wallace, J., Burger, D., Neal, H.C., Brero, M.V. & Davis, D.E. (1976) Aversive conditioning use in public facilities for the mentally retarded. *Ment. Retard.*, **12**, April, 17-18

Ward, J. (1975) Behaviour modification in special education. In: K. Wedell (ed.) *Orientations in Special Education.* London: John Wiley & Sons

Waters, J. (1970) Adapt dressing, clothes to child. *Ment. Ret. News*, **19** (3), 7 (from abstract in *Mental Retardation Abstracts*, 1971, **8**, No. 2043)

Watson, L.S. (1973) *Child Behavior Modification: A Manual for Teachers, Nurses and Parents.* New York: Pergamon

Watson, L.S., Gardner, J.M. & Sanders, C. (1971) Shaping and maintaining behavior modification skills in staff members in an MR institution: Columbus State Institute Behavior Modification Programme. *Ment. Retard.*, **9** (3), 39-42

Wehman, P. (1974) Maintaining oral hygiene skills in geriatric retarded women. *Ment. Retard.*, **12**, 20

Westling, D.L. & Murden, L. (1978) Self-help skills training: A review of operant studies. *J. Spec. Educ.*, **12**, 253-83

Wexler, D.B. (1973) Token and taboo: Behavior modification, token economics and the law. *Behaviorism*, **1**, 1-24

White, G.D., Nielson, G. & Johnson, S.M. (1972) Time-out duration and the suppression of deviant behavior in children. *J. Appl. Behav. Anal.*, **5**, 111-20

Whitman, T.L., Zakaras, M. & Chardos, J. (1971) Effects of reinforcement and guidance procedures on instruction-following behavior of severely retarded children. *J. Appl. Behav. Anal.*, **4**, 283-90

Whitney, L.R. & Barnard, K.E. (1966) Implications of operant learning theory for nursing care of the retarded child. *Ment. Retard.*, **4**, 26-31

Wickings, S., Jenkins, J., Carr, J. & Corbett, J. (1974) Modification of

behaviour using a shaping procedure. *Apex*, **2**, 6
Williams, C.D. (1959) The elimination of tantrum behavior by extinction procedures. *J. Abnorm. Soc. Psychol.*, **59**, 269
Williams, C. & Jackson, M.W. (1975) Nurse training in behaviour modification. In: C.C. Kiernan & F.P. Woodford (eds.) *Behaviour Modification with the Severely Retarded.* Study Group No. 8, IRMMH. Elsevier, North-Holland: Associated Scientific Publishers
Willoughby, R.H. (1969) The effects of time-out from positive reinforcement on the operant behavior of pre-school children. *J. Exper. Child Psychol.*, **7**, 299-313
Wiltz, N.A. (1969) Modification of behaviors through parent participation in a group technique. Ann Arbor, Mich.: University Microfilms Nos. 70-9482. Cited in O'Dell (1974)
Wing, L. (1971) Severely retarded children in a London area: Prevalence and provision of services. *Psychol. Med.*, **1**, 405-15
Wing, L. (1975a) *Autistic Children: A Guide for Parents.* Revised edition. London: Constable
Wing, L. (1975b) Practical counselling for families with severely retarded children living at home. *REAP*, **1**, 113-27
Winkler, R.C. (1971) The relevance of economic theory and technology of token reinforcement systems. *Behav. Res. & Ther.*, **9**, 81-8
Wolf, M.M. & Risley, T.R. (1971) Reinforcement: Applied research. In: R. Glaser (ed.) *The Nature of Reinforcement.* New York: Academic Press
Wolf, M., Risley, T. & Mees, H. (1964) Applications of operant conditioning procedures to the behavior problems of an autistic child. *Behav. Res. Ther.*, **1**, 305-12
Working Party on Behaviour Modification (1978) *Bulletin, British Psychological Society*, **31**, 368-9
Wright, D.F. & Bunch, G. (1977) Parental intervention in the treatment of chronic constipation. *J. Behav. Ther. & Exp. Psychiat.*, **2**, 93-5
Wunderlich, R.A. (1972) Programmed instruction: Teaching coinage to retarded children. *Ment. Retard.*, **10** (5), 21-3
Wyatt *v.* Stickney (1972) 344 Federal Supplement 373 and 387, Middle District, Northern Division, Alabama

Yates, A.J. (1970) *Behavior Therapy.* New York: Wiley
Young, G.C. & Morgan, R.T. (1972) Overlearning in the conditioning treatment of enuresis. *Behav. Res. & Ther.*, **10**, 147-51
Young, J.A. & Wincze, J.P. (1974) The effects of reinforcement of

compatible and incompatible alternative behaviors on self-injurious and related behaviors of a profoundly retarded female adult. *Behav. Ther.*, **6**, 614-623

Yule, W. (1975) Teaching psychological principles to non-psychologists: Training parents in child management. *J. Assoc. Educ. Psychol.*, **10** (3), 5-16

Yule, W. (1977) Behavioural approaches to treatment. In: M. Rutter & L. Hersov (eds.) *Child Psychiatry: Modern Approaches.* London: Blackwell Scientific Publications

Yule, W. & Berger, M. (1975) Communication, language and behavior modification. In: C.C. Kiernan & F.P. Woodford (eds.) *Behaviour Modification with the Severely Retarded.* Amsterdam: Associated Scientific Publishers

Yule, W., Berger, M. & Howlin, P. (1974) Language deficit and behaviour modification. In: N. O'Connor (ed.) *Language and Cognition in the Handicapped.* London: Churchill

Yule, W. & Hemsley, D. (1977) Single-case method in medical psychology. In: S. Rachman (ed.) *Contributions to Medical Psychology*, Vol. I. Oxford: Pergamon

Zeiler, M.D. & Jervey, S.S. (1968) Development of behavior: Self-feeding. *J. Consult. Clin. Psychol.*, **32**, 164-8

Zimmerman, J. & Baydan, N.T. (1963) Punishment of $S^{\Delta}$ responding of humans in conditional matching to sample by time-out. *J. Exper. Anal. Behav.*, **6**, 589-97

Zimmerman, J. & Ferster, C.B. (1963) Intermittent punishment of $S^{\Delta}$ responding in matching to sample. *J. Exper. Anal. Behav.*, **6**, 349-56

Zimmerman, J., Stuckey, T.E. Garlick, B.J. & Miller, M. (1969) Effects of token reinforcement on productivity in multiply handicapped clients in a sheltered workshop. *Rehab. Lit.*, **30**, 34-41

Zlutnick, S., Mayville, W.J. & Moffat, S. (1975) Modification of seizure disorders: The interruption of behavioral chains. *J. Appl. Behav. Anal.*, **8**, 1-12

# NOTES ON CONTRIBUTORS

Maria Callias, MA, MSc, is Lecturer in Psychology, University of London Institute of Psychiatry.

Janet Carr, BA, PhD, is Senior Research Officer, Thomas Coram Research Unit, University of London Institute of Education and former Lecturer in Psychology, University of London Institute of Psychiatry.

Chris Gathercole, BSc, DipClinPsychol, is Area Psychologist for Lancashire Area Health Authority.

Rosemary Hemsley, BSc, MSc, is Lecturer in Psychology, University of London Institute of Psychiatry.

Patricia Howlin, BA, MSc, PhD, is Lecturer in Psychology, University of London Institute of Psychiatry.

Glynis Murphy, BA, MSc, is Research Psychologist and former Lecturer in Psychology, University of London Institute of Psychiatry.

Mona Tsoi, BSocSci, MPhil, is Lecturer in Psychology, University of Hong Kong and former Lecturer in Psychology, University of London Institute of Psychiatry.

Barbara Wilson, BA, MPhil, is Senior Clinical Psychologist, Rivermead Rehabilitation Centre, Oxford, and former Lecturer in Psychology, University of London Institute of Psychiatry.

William Yule, MA, DipPsychol, PhD, is Senior Lecturer in Psychology and in Child and Adolescent Psychiatry, University of London Institute of Psychiatry.

# INDEX